Bob Harris, who col ❦ KT-380-359 n
this book, is current. n
Regional Newspapers. He has enjoyed a particular association with Liverpool over the years, becoming close
friends with Graeme Souness despite their conflicting
interests on the International scene!

GRAEME SOUNESS

No Half Measures

with Bob Harris

GRAFTON BOOKS
A Division of the Collins Publishing Group

LONDON GLASGOW
TORONTO SYDNEY AUCKLAND

Grafton Books
A Division of the Collins Publishing Group
8 Grafton Street, London W1X 3LA

This updated edition published by Grafton Books 1987

First published in Great Britain by
Willow Books, William Collins Sons & Co Ltd 1985

Copyright © Graeme Souness 1985, 1987

ISBN 0-586-07424-4

Printed and bound in Great Britain by
Collins, Glasgow

Set in Times

Contents

Foreword   7
Boy from the Red Stuff
by Alan Bleasdale

 1   No More Mr Nice Guy   11
 2   Spurs Runaway   19
 3   Beginnings   29
 4   A Wayward Lifestyle   39
 5   Charlton, Paisley and Fagan   47
 6   Meanest Man in Football   71
 7   Middlesbrough   89
 8   Chasing Pots at Liverpool   98
 9   European Challenge   116
10   The Treble   133
11   This is Anfield   161
12   Sometimes I wish I was English   177
13   Argentina Disaster   186
14   Jock Stein   199
15   Dalglish and Others   212
16   The Outer Fringe   225
17   The State of the Game   236
18   All Roads Lead to Rome   248
     Postscript   255

     Appendix: Career Record   264

To Elizabeth

Foreword

Liverpool. A hot summer's day. A film set. A crowded public house. Arc lights everywhere. Actors and extras and technicians by the sweating scores. A sauna with cameras. Scene 18, Episode 4 of *The Boys From The Black Stuff*. The scene where Yosser Hughes meets Graeme Souness. 'I could have been a footballer but I had a paper round . . .' Bernard Hill, playing Yosser Hughes, and six months away from reluctant but magnificent immortality on the television screens of the nation, was dressed in mad black, white-faced and worrying about how someone who had never acted before would cope with the pressure and the performance. It is easy to say that Graeme Souness was only playing Graeme Souness, but most actors I know will tell you that the hardest part to play is themselves. Secretly, everyone in the room that day was watching with curiosity, at angles, in lenses, through mirrors and out of the corners of their eyes, as Souness and that perfect gentleman Sammy Lee strolled into the room. And yes, of course, Souness seemed at ease, cracked jokes, signed autographs, knew his lines, and looked the part – but could he actually do it?

I don't think I have to tell you how well the scene went, but if you didn't see it, well, believe me. Graeme, through take after take, acted as though some years ago he must have had a very hard decision to make about whether to go to Tottenham Hotspurs as a young apprentice or to the Royal Academy of Dramatic Art as a promising actor. Every nuance and mood of the script brought exactly the right response. So much so that halfway through the day's filming, Bernard Hill came over to me and said, 'Bloody hell, I didn't expect this. I thought I'd have to look after him, but I've got to look after myself!' Graeme Souness has since said that he was terrified. If that's the truth, he's an even better actor than I have already given him credit for. In many ways I think that is indicative of the man. He isn't going to give a thing away, and he hasn't always had quite the credit he deserves. Some of our heroes are hollow men when we meet them. All that glitters is not gold. However, Graeme Souness grows in stature with every meeting, and with every story told about him by the people who really know him . . .

A 16-year-old apprentice professional at Liverpool Football Club: 'He's a proper captain. He's not just the captain of the first team, he's the captain of the club. Even if you're a nobody who cleans the boots and scrapes a game in the Youth Team, if he thinks you're getting picked on by someone, it doesn't matter who it is, "Charlie" will put them in their place if he thinks they deserve it. And I'll tell you one thing, he only has to do it once.'

A fellow first team player: 'He's the best, the very best, but you won't completely understand that until you play alongside him. You don't want admiration and commitment from your opponents, you want it from your own team, and that's what he's got from us. Everyone hates playing against Graeme Souness. He's a professional, and that's why some people don't like him – because they're not.'

Obviously, Graeme Souness has authority. He has so much authority he is occasionally reported to the authorities. Jealousy being what it is, he is the kind of man who can be disliked from a distance by the kind of people who usually become referees, television commentators, public hangmen, hangers-on, traffic wardens or fellow professionals with neither the courage nor the awareness ever to understand Graeme Souness.

John Roberts, writing in the *Daily Mail* recently about the hard men of football had the following perceptive comments to make: 'The most memorable sports picture of the week showed Graeme Souness, the Liverpool captain, carrying the injured 12-year-old Christopher Mitchell to safety after a wall had collapsed at Walsall. Souness undoubtedly is one of the hardest players in the game. Tommy Smith with a Rolls-Royce engine. Yet, seconds before an FA Cup tie at Blackburn a couple of years ago, Souness called to the tiny Rovers mascot, who was scurrying towards the touchline. He then passed the ball to him. The boy smiled shyly and set off again. Souness called a second time and delivered another pass. Win or lose, the boy's day was made.' It's also worth mentioning that when that wall collapsed at Walsall as Liverpool scored their second goal, the video recording of the game shows Graeme Souness hurtling deep and immediately into the crowd to rescue and reassure while all around him people were still celebrating the goal.

So. Where does this leave us? What will we remember about one of the great players of our time? Well, you must choose your own memories. Mine are vivid but varied. His staggering performance against Everton in the 1984 replay of the Milk Cup Final; the strutting two stags at bay conflict between Jimmy Case and Souness when he was still playing for Middlesbrough; his 60-yard sprint to pull away most of an Everton team determined to commit mass GBH on the same Jimmy Case when they both wore the red shirt together, (not forgetting a cheerful kick up the backside for the Everton skipper in passing!); that priceless gem of a 6-yard pass to Kenny

Dalglish against Bruges in the 1978 European Cup Final; and, of course, his articulate and charming presence in front of the cameras, albeit on *Match of the Day* or facing the maniacal Yosser Hughes.

Two memories above all, however, and both bearing the stamp of those seconds well spent with the Blackburn mascot. Some time after Graeme had completed his part in the series, Bernard Hill and I sat soberly in another pub in Liverpool and listened to this so-called 'hard man' Souness talk in the most passionate, genuine, lyrical and loving fashion about his children and his total commitment to his family. The thought struck me then that the only chance most midfield opponents could ever have against Graeme Souness would be if they asked him at kick-off how his kids were. It's nearly three years now since that conversation took place, but I haven't forgotten it. When Graeme asked me to contribute this foreword to his book and I knew that I wanted to show a man for all seasons, I asked him if he was going to concentrate purely on football or would he mention his private life. And very private man that he ultimately is, I could sense a reluctance to show the world too much of the heart that he rarely wears on his sleeve. He hesitated briefly, then smiled in memory and said, 'Well, above all, I really would like to mention my Mum'. The conversation was immediately changed, the sleeve gently wiped clean and the door marked 'private' was closed. But that, for me, is Graeme Souness.

ALAN BLEASDALE JUNE 1984

1

No More Mr Nice Guy

Being successful has always been more important to me than being popular. I long ago accepted that the name of Graeme Souness would top few popularity polls, regardless of whether the votes were cast by my fellow professionals or by the supporters. In that respect I suppose you could say that I have achieved my ambition for, thanks to Liverpool, I have a cupboard full of trophies and scarcely a friend on the terraces or in the dressing rooms.

Not that it bothers me. From the moment I decided that I wanted to be a professional footballer, I made up my mind that I was going to be a winner. First to prove myself as an individual and then, hopefully, as part of a successful team. I was so single-minded about it that I promptly left a very comfortable, very happy home in Edinburgh, turning down my local clubs, to seek my fortune South of the Border.

But, even in those formative days, I was a confident person, sure of myself and never feeling the need to have my ego massaged by other players or to be patted on the back by the coach or manager. In fact, come the end of a game it was a shower, change and out with my pals and that is more or less how it has been ever since.

Snobby? I don't think so. I would rather select my own friends than have them picked for me, but that probably applies to anyone in any job. When you are with a group of people for six days a week it doesn't always make sense to mix with them socially as well. Most of my best friends at the moment are outside the game: a brewery worker from the North East; a Scottish company director who works in the rag trade in Ireland; a Liverpool optician; a London journalist and an Edinburgh hairdresser. Sometimes it is good to be with people who want to talk about something other than soccer. It is nice to put the ball away now and again.

Let's be fair. I am hardly likely to make too many friends among my opponents. I admit that, now and again, I have trodden the thinnest of lines on the pitch. I challenge hard and play to win, but once the game is over, in most cases, it is forgotten. Then I will chat and be friendly in the players' tea room though it would be hypocritical to carry it further when, a couple of weeks later, you are going to be kicking lumps out of each other again. Don't get me wrong. I wouldn't say that I am aloof or distant from my fellow professionals. No one enjoys the dressing room banter more than me – that sometimes cruel, sarcastic football humour – which sharpens the mind so well for the job in hand. One of the highlights of the year while I was at Anfield was the night out with the lads for the Christmas party.

When I was an apprentice and then a young, somewhat unhappy professional at Spurs, my best friends were two players of the same age, Mick Dillon and Ray Clarke. In those lonely days with little money, living in digs and without a car, friends were important and I remember those two with great affection even though we were soon to go our separate ways with Ray going to Swindon, Holland, Newcastle, Brighton and Mansfield while Micky and I spent a summer in Canada before he went off to play for New York Cosmos and, eventually, settle in the United States.

Outside the game there was a young chap named Gary Ellingham whose father owned a greengrocers in Finchley, North London. I remember them well, not only because they made me welcome in their own home but because Gary's father John supplemented my meagre earnings by slipping me a few quid to help him load the lorry at the old Covent Garden. That was my first indication that playing football was preferable and a lot easier than working for your living!

Middlesbrough, my next port of call, provided another lesson through another friend. Never to count your chickens. My great friend at Ayresome Park was a brilliant player named Willie Maddren. He was my room-mate and as good a man as I have ever played with but he suffered a terrible knee injury which eventually forced him out of the game, robbing England of a very fine player. Good as Jackie Charlton and Bobby Murdoch were to me in those days, my other close friend in the North East was Phoebe Haigh. No, not a beauty queen or a model but the landlady at my digs and my second mother. In fact there were things I could tell her and talk to her about that I couldn't discuss with my own Mum.

I was lucky to have Willie as a room-mate while I was at Middlesbrough and I have been equally fortunate at Anfield where I have shared my time with my fellow Scot, Kenny Dalglish. They probably put us in together originally because I was one of the few who could understand Kenny's broad Glaswegian accent. Even then I spent a lot of time saying 'sorry?' But we got on well together and exchanged a great deal of chat in hotel rooms round the world while travelling with both Liverpool and Scotland.

It's a good thing we did get on so well for when you have shared as often as we have you really get to know the person, warts and all. You spend so much time together you end up sharing the other's personal life not only through confidences but even from overheard telephone calls. There can be little privacy in those circumstances. We may not be bosom buddies but we are certainly as close as you can get in that type of relationship.

Most definitely I am closer to Kenny than to some of the fans. And I am not talking about opposing teams' supporters but those at Liverpool and, particularly, those at Hampden Park, Scotland. Fortunately it came as no great shock. I learned very early on that I was not the sort of player who aroused the supporters' wild enthusiasm.

Although I never progressed beyond the substitutes' bench at Spurs, I had received so much publicity – good and bad – that my name tended to precede me. My first brush with opposition supporters was at Reading's Elm Park . . . and I was there only to watch the Spurs Reserves. Some yobs behind us were throwing missiles, coins and the like. I stood it until one hit me on the back of the head. That was pushing me too far and before anyone could stop me I was over the wall, up the steps and had one of them by the throat. What I didn't know was that there were two plain clothes policemen sitting right behind them but far from backing me they threatened to charge me if I persisted.

However, that was nothing compared with the stick I received from the Coventry City supporters when Spurs became involved in a marathon Youth Cup Final which took four matches to decide. I had a rare old battle with Dennis Mortimer, who went on to captain Aston Villa to European Cup success, and which culminated in my being booked during the second game and sent off in the third. I could still hear the abuse ringing in my ears as I cried in the dressing room for letting down my team-mates.

I suppose I am the kind of player spectators dislike. My style of play antagonizes them. Critics accuse me of being arrogant and mocking my opponents. I think it stems from the unfortunate way I run. I am not quick but run very stiffly with my head high in the air. I have never tried to develop a cocky style nor to copy anyone else. You have to be exceptional to suddenly start imitating someone else's game in the middle of a match or, for that matter, to make fun of an opponent. To be honest I don't think I am good enough to do either.

The animosity which is generated from the terraces goes over my head but it can be hard on the family when they sit in the stands and have to listen to the foul-mouthed abuse, whether it was my wife at Anfield or my family at international matches. It is not a reputation I have encouraged because, let's face it, it is not the sort of thing a father wants his children to read about.

I can, however, understand to some extent why the Liverpool supporters are not mad about me. It was emphasized when Bob Paisley made me captain, saying he wanted a bit of style, arrogance (that word again) and commenting that I had so much class I would probably toss up with a Gold American Express card. All very nice but how can the average punter on the terraces at Anfield relate to that? Half of them are out of work and on the dole, never mind having a gold credit card!

. There was also the fact that I took over the captaincy from a true Scouser, Phil Thompson. He was one of them, off the very terraces where they stood every week and everything Phil did they could identify with too. The same could be said of Emlyn Hughes before him because they could identify with a man so full of enthusiasm, so full of endeavour and so full of running. They could see he was ready to die for Liverpool. Phil Thompson and Emlyn Hughes both wore their emotion like a badge. I wanted Liverpool to win just as badly but I show it in a different way. It is not my style to dive in here and throw myself in there.

It hasn't helped to play for a club which has given its supporters so much success over the past few years. They are absolutely sated with it. Their support in the past was as legendary as the players they cheered. Ian St John told me that they used to frighten some opposing teams with the sheer volume of their noise while their humour was pure Jimmy Tarbuck. Today people go to Anfield and are amazed at how quiet they are. Now they are more likely to frighten their own team than their opponents because they have become so critical. They have seen so many good teams that they have been spoiled and if Liverpool don't score an early goal you can hear the 'oohs' and 'aahs'.

I suppose it is like coming home to pheasant and a good bottle of Burgundy every night of the week. On the eighth night you would say 'not that again', willing to settle for egg and chips and a cup of tea.

I can understand some of the antagonism and I can hope only that in future years they will look back and say maybe I was a better player than they gave me credit for and that the sides I played for could be compared favourably with those that went before.

Scotland is different again. No one from an English club ever has a good game up there. The English supporters have completely the wrong impression of their counterparts from north of the Border because they tend to judge them on that one day every couple of years when the Auld Enemy clash at Wembley. What they don't realize is that a great many of the Tartan Army save up for two years for that big day and nothing, not even the result, is going to spoil it for them. They come from all over England as well as Scotland, making a day of it and celebrating in traditional style before a ball is even kicked. They wouldn't let the Sassanachs say a word against us.

But up at Hampden Park, it is a different story. I have walked out of that ground with Phil Neal and Phil Thompson and been insulted and spat at while the two English boys have been praised. If you play for an English club you have to face up to the fact that this largely Glaswegian crowd simply do not like the Anglos. In fact they find it hard to like anyone who doesn't play for the club they support. They even used to have a go at Denis Law and Billy Bremner. It will be interesting, to say the least, to see how much that changes now I am a fully fledged Scot once more.

If you believed everything you heard up there then none of us from south of the Border have ever had a good game for Scotland; they are always saying Kenny Dalglish and I never play for our country the way we play for our clubs. That I can't accept. I have played with Kenny some 40 or more times for Scotland and you can count his bad games on the fingers of one hand and still have a couple left over to raise in the air at the bigoted idiots who cannot see further than their own noses. The top and bottom of it is that we have not been successful.

The Scots' supporters are so critical that I have even been jeered during the warm-up to an international while the Scottish journalists have had the nerve to ask if I am patriotic and if I really want to play for my country. There was a time when it made me angry – but not any more. It doesn't end with the supporters and journalists either. That outstanding manager Alex Ferguson told his Aberdeen players not to mix with us. I can imagine only that it was because he didn't want us to tell them what we were earning.

No, I am resigned to the fact that I am not going to be anyone's player of the season on either side of the Border but as long as I keep on helping my teams to win trophies then I won't lose too much sleep. If it all ended next week I would be able to look back on the cups and medals and feel that I had done my job regardless of what anyone thought of me. But I suspect that there are a few who would have rather had me in their side than playing against them.

2

Spurs Runaway

There is a gap in my trophy cabinet and I am still waiting for Spurs to keep their promise to fill the space. The prize was special for it was my first in professional football – the much coveted FA Youth Cup. What is more I felt that I had more than earned my plaque in a marathon four-game final against Coventry City.

I had scored the only goal in the first leg of the final at White Hart Lane; in the second I was booked for a clash with Dennis Mortimer; I was sent off for the first time in my life during a 2-2 draw in a play-off at Coventry; and then scored the only goal to win the Cup for Spurs at White Hart Lane. The rest of the boys all received their awards but, apart from being banned for 21 days and fined £10, the Football Association decreed in its wisdom that this naughty 17-year-old should also be denied the keepsake to remind him of his early success.

I wasn't letting on that the goal I scored to win the Cup was more than enough to be worth locking away in the memory bank and that the humiliation of being sent off at Coventry was far worse than any ban or fine they could come up with. Even my old boss Bill Nicholson thought so and he went so far as to go on record with this comment: 'It is a cruel decision, although I know it is within the rules of the competition. Souness suffered enough when, on the night he scored the winning goal, the rest of the team received plaques and he did not. We felt it was an injustice at the time, and that is why my directors wrote to the FA and asked if they would reconsider the case. Now that they have turned it down, I have no doubt the board will consider making a special presentation themselves.'

Although Bill Nicholson and his board of directors seemed to forget about it, neither Dennis Mortimer nor I did. It would make a good story to say that we started a vendetta from that day onwards but it simply wouldn't be true and we often have a chuckle about it. I wasn't rugged, I wasn't hard, in fact I thought that I was a bit of a player. Headstrong? Yes. Dirty? No way.

My reward for leading that talented young side to the big one was a princely £12. Divided by the four games it took to win it, that was £3 a game! How times have changed. But if you think I am waiting for an apology from White Hart Lane you couldn't be further from the truth. It should be the other way around for I owe that famous North London club more than one excuse for the way I behaved while I was with them.

For a kid who never kicked a ball for Spurs in a League match I received an awful lot of publicity, probably more than the honest, run-of-the-mill, one-club player has in his whole career. My name was in the papers even before I went south and speculation in Scotland was rife as to which club I would join.

My school in Edinburgh allowed me to leave ten minutes early every Tuesday and Thursday so that I could catch the train to Glasgow to coach with Celtic while their great rivals Rangers, the team I loosely supported in those days, were also keen, as were my home town clubs Hearts and Hibs. South of the Border there were Spurs, Nottingham Forest, Wolves, Burnley and West Bromwich Albion. There was all sorts of stupid talk about inducements and presents to my Mum and Dad but, in those days, money was not a consideration. Just one of the English clubs offered to top anything anyone else offered, and I didn't fancy them anyway, while I could have earned more by staying at home in Scotland.

I was ambitious and of all the English clubs bidding for me, Spurs were the biggest with such star names as Jimmy Greaves, Dave Mackay and Pat Jennings. It was the sort of stage I thought would befit a talent as great as mine. If I needed further convincing I had it when scout Charlie Faulkner turned up at our council house door dressed in an immaculate three-piece suit and sporting the sort of black cigarette holder I had only ever seen on television. He was an honest man, was Charlie Faulkner. He offered me nothing, not one brass farthing and he warned me that joining a club like Spurs was the beginning and not the end, and that a place in the team was still a long, long way off.

I wish only that I had listened. I went south absolutely full of myself and I liked it even more when the famous Spurs' manager, Bill Nicholson, not one of the world's great public relations men, started to compare me to the already legendary Dave Mackay. I suppose it was natural that people should do so as we were both born in Edinburgh, both went to Carrickvale School, both were hard-tackling midfield players and both won Scottish schoolboy honours.

At 16 Nicholson said of me: 'Souness is very skilful but, of course, is young and has a lot to learn yet. Still, there is every possibility he will come through to senior football in the near future.' I believed him totally and even more so a year later when he was quoted in a national newspaper as saying, 'I really think this boy will be another Mackay. For his age he has wonderful control. In one match two opponents came at him. He went one way, then the other. He didn't touch the ball but he beat both men and was off, through the gap. He has scored quite a few goals for our Youth team this season and with him, 17-year-old Steve Perryman and a third youngster coming through, I think we have something to look forward to.'

How right he was about Steve Perryman, one of the best servants a club could ever hope for, and how wrong he was about Graeme Souness. There must have been many a day that he wished that Spurs had not watched me play for Scotland Boys against England Boys at White Hart Lane back in March 1968. I will hold up my hands and say here and now that I was more trouble to Spurs than I was worth.

When I decided to seek my fortune in England my Mum and Dad said they would leave the decision to me so that if things went wrong I could blame only myself. It must have been hard for them as together with my brothers Gordon and Billy, we were a happy family. I am sure that if my son Fraser wanted to leave home at 15 years of age, and knowing what I know now, I would do all in my power to dissuade him.

During the next couple of years Mum and Dad must have wished I was the girl they had hoped to follow Gordon and Billy, eight and four years my senior respectively. Some opponents have probably felt the same.

However, I wasn't to know that when I became an apprentice at Spurs and I was convinced that there were great things to come when Dave Mackay, the great man himself, came across during a training session, put his arm round me and said in front of the other young lads that us Carrickvale Old Boys should stick together. It was special because Mackay was the name put forward by the boss as a glowing example of professionalism in the same way that Kenny Dalglish is held in such high esteem today.

I could use the excuse that all of this helped to put pressure on an impressionable youngster – but it simply would not be true. I loved every minute of it and it served to convince me only that I should be in the side instead of the likes of Alan Mullery and Martin Peters. It makes me cringe to think about it now. There were the usual people on the fringe of the club who confirmed my thoughts, telling me I should be playing. It only made me worse. I would watch the superstars like Mackay, Greaves and Cliff Jones on the pre-season training runs being given free pints of ice-cold milk by starry-eyed milkmen while we toiled away in the sun. How I wanted to be a member of that privileged crowd.

The closest I came was through my fellow Scot, Alan Gilzean. What a great player he was and what a superbly relaxed attitude he had to the game. He would thumb his nose at the world and get on with his own thing. He always maintained that the game was essentially concerned with players and not with coaches. He used to tell me that you could either play or you couldn't and all the coaching in the world could not change that. He used to make a great play of the fact that we were both Scots, saying in a voice loud enough for everyone to hear, that we Jocks had to support each other. He used to wind the English players up and he could get away with it because he had such great skill himself.

Martin Chivers also went out of his way to be friendly when he didn't need to be. He was an outstanding, world-class player for a year but he still found time to spend with a snotty-nosed kid like me. Looking back now it was a big thing to do. He took me out on a couple of Saturday nights and even invited me back to his house. He was a strange man who often seemed to live in a world of his own. Chivers was larger than life, but then there were a few household names at White Hart Lane in those days: Jennings; Mullery; Peters; Kinnear; Beal; England; Gilzean; Mackay. The fact that I thought I should have been one of them now seems faintly ridiculous.

Certainly we had a smashing youth side but, somehow, things just did not develop the way they should have done. But then that seems to happen with a great many successful youth sides. I would not fault youth team coach Pat Welton who went as far as his position would allow, nor could the finger be pointed at abrasive coach Eddie Baily. He could see what was wrong with me and, indeed, he made it clear that he loathed my attitude. But he would not help. His philosophy, like that of Jack Charlton later, was that you did it yourself or you got out. He was constantly on my back. I can understand why now and, in fact, I would probably do the same myself in his position and, in the end, I reckon that it was down to me to put things right. But not before I made a great many more mistakes.

In those early days I was highly motivated by Pat Welton but, gradually, I began to think it was too easy and that I knew it all. I was always quarrelling with Eddie Baily. Both of us are fairly argumentative but, then, I was hardly in any position to question his opinions on the game. It says a lot for Eddie that he can laugh about it now. A bust-up was inevitable. I thought I should be in the side and on three separate occasions went to demand of Bill Nicholson that he either pick me or let me go. As far as I was concerned I was simply not progressing as quickly as I considered I should be.

I had been home to Edinburgh for the close season and when I returned my dissatisfaction was at its peak and Bill Nicholson was utterly convinced that I had been approached by a Scottish club and that made him dig in his heels more than ever. I had been tapped but not by a football club. During that summer I had become romantically involved with a pretty, dark-haired civil servant named Julie Ingram and this, plus my lack of advancement, decided me I wanted out. I pleaded my case, saying I was homesick, fed up and any other reason which came to mind (never letting on about the girlfriend) but Bill was adamant and in the end I packed my bags and left.

I had run away once before with no money, no ticket, nothing. Fortunately, I had poured my heart out to a sympathetic stranger who bought my ticket, accepting my word of honour that I would send the money on and which, of course, I did. On that occasion I was back so quickly nothing was said. This time it was plastered across the newspapers and the club had little alternative but to suspend me. Spurs did everything they could to persuade me to return and finally they banned me for two weeks and promised the ban would be extended every fortnight until the end of my contract, effectively putting me out of the game for two years until my contract expired.

Suddenly the whole thing got out of control. I was painted as the poor, hard-done-by youngster, desperate to return to the bosom of his family while the club were the heavy-handed villains who were saying that I should play for them or no one.

It reached the stage where Scottish Member of Parliament, Tam Dalyell, made it his business and questions were asked in the House of Commons after he had written to Robert Carr, then the Secretary of State for Employment and Productivity, demanding an investigation. Tam, member for West Lothian, wrote: 'I am most concerned in the principles involved in the Souness case. I have no authority to act on behalf of the family, who are not my constituents. The issue that concerns me is: Should an employer, be he the boss of a great corporation, a small greengrocer, or the Tottenham Hotspur Football Club, acting through an Employers' Association, in this case the English Football League, have the right to deprive a minor of following his chosen profession, simply because he wants to go home, or on account of some evidently non-criminal offence? I would be grateful if your ministry would examine the whole position arising out of the Souness case.'

The former Spurs captain, Danny Blanchflower, in his capacity as a writer for the *Sunday Express*, came to see me at my parents' home and wrote a sympathetic piece. It was a memorable visit for me and it ended with the Irishman giving me a coaching lesson in the front room of our council house. There we were playing football between the sofa and the chairs and to this day I have followed some of the shrewd advice he passed on to me all that time ago. It has worked quite well for me over the years.

The question at the time was when I was going to be able to put it into practice! The nearest I came to a game of football was watching Hearts and Hibs from the terraces and, for a while, it looked as though I was going to have to get a job. A friend of mine was working in the removals business and he suggested I could earn a few quid to help me out by assisting him. Little did my friend, Gerry Ritchie, realize just how much he did for me on my one day as a removal man. Our first task, would you believe it, was to carry a piano up three flights of stairs and as the novice I was the one at the back. That, apart from helping load and unload a fruit lorry, was my only day's work outside football and it quickly proved to me what people said about hard work and football was very true.

As it turned out, it was not much later when Spurs travelled north to play Dunfermline at East End in a Texaco Cup tie and Bill Nicholson wrote to Mum and Dad asking them to take me to the game to discuss the matter further. What Bill did not know was that I had already decided to give in and return to London. Tam Dalyell had indicated that there was little else that he could do, while Cliff Lloyd, secretary of the Professional Footballers' Association, advised me to go back. Mum and Dad had also added their weight to the argument and by the time we arrived at East End it was all over bar the shouting. Who the hell wants to move pianos anyway? It had been a long seven weeks. Even so the meeting with Bill Nicholson was still acutely embarassing for he was never the best of communicators.

Looking back I felt that the club's attitude was never the same to me after my walk-out. I progressed no further than the substitutes' bench and only once, in a UEFA Cup tie in Iceland, did I make it onto the pitch for the first team.

I had put on weight while I had been at home in Scotland and I had to buckle down to some serious graft but even then I failed to realize that the club would not have taken so much trouble if they hadn't thought so highly of me. I was still impatient and I still couldn't be told. God, I must have been pretty horrible to have around. There I was, stuck in the second team again, unable to make the jump from the reserves to the first team. As usual, my attitude was the problem and I didn't try hard enough to put matters right.

I needed to be brought back down to earth and it did not happen at Spurs. Perhaps if someone had taken me by the scruff of the neck and given me a good talking-to it might have been different and I might have carved myself out a career at White Hart Lane. The problem was that I never really knew where I was going. No one ever took the trouble to take me to one side and tell me whether I had played well or badly and in your late teens, whatever work you do, you need that basic guidance and encouragement.

The end came unexpectedly. I had gone home to Edinburgh – this time with full approval – for a few days around Christmas and I was in a local sports shop when my brother Billy telephoned saying that Spurs wanted me to get in touch as soon as possible. Bill Nicholson promptly told me that Middlesbrough had made an offer which Spurs were willing to accept and that if I was interested I should go down and watch them play Fulham the next day. I didn't even know where Middlesbrough was!

Harold Shepherdson met me off the train and I was quite impressed with what I saw as Boro beat the Londoners. I knew that Spurs had not released me out of kindness and, just as I would now, I decided then and there that I wouldn't stay where I was not wanted. Spurs obviously thought that I had gone as far as I could with them and, after just one subs' appearance, all I wanted to do was play for someone else and prove them wrong.

I was angry at not making it with Spurs especially as they had, at that time, a very ordinary team. How ironic that I should pass them on the way down to the Second Division while I was on my way up to the First. We drew 1-1 at White Hart Lane and I then scored twice in the return at Ayresome Park to help them on their way. I felt momentarily smug, but later rather sad because they were, and still are, a great club.

3
Beginnings

It wasn't Spurs who turned me into a bad boy. I was a right bloody tearaway when I was a nipper in Edinburgh. The English tend to think of Glasgow as the roughest area of Scotland with Edinburgh, Festival and all, the cultural centre, Athens of the North and all that.

Well, like any city, it has its good, its bad and its ordinary areas. I would often have a chuckle to myself when the tough little nut from the Scotty Road in Liverpool had a dig at me in the Anfield car park because of my current car, my wife's fur coat or the latest rumour about my salary.

I have news for him and his ilk. I could have probably given him and his mates a head start. Fight! I had to fight to survive at my schools. For the first twelve years of my life I lived in a prefab. It was clean, it was smart and it was happy. There was no social stigma in that although, I must admit, it was a far cry from my last few houses.

While we lived in our prefab I muddled through my primary schooldays at Broomhouse which is still, I understand, the roughest in Edinburgh. I was always scrapping when I wasn't playing football and it was a good job for me that I learned to use my fists and feet because I needed them even more when I went on to Carrickvale School. I arrived at my new school as my brother Billy left. He was able to warn me of what was in store for me. Unfortunately, because the choice of school depended on where you lived, all my mates went to another school, leaving me with my reputation to defend.

Having played for Edinburgh Schools and having

appeared in the local papers once or twice, I was a prime target for the big boys. It was a question of fighting to survive. I survived. Obviously any talent I had for playing football had already begun to show itself in the early days. I had inherited a natural interest in the game from my father James, a left-winger, and my two older brothers.

Dad was a great encouragement and, in fact, I played my first Cup Final on the left wing for my primary school. Brother Billy was in goal and as he is four years older than me I suppose I was only seven or eight and considerably younger than the rest of the kids on the pitch. But I had learned to look after myself and their size did not bother me. We won and, from that moment, I developed a taste for success. A taste I never lost. The setting must have suited me because, in all modesty, I was outstanding. The bigger the stage the more I like it. It has always been that way.

Mind you, I was lucky to last the pace. We took some awful risks in those days. Billy could have died when he cut an artery in his wrist playing hide and seek while I was fortunate to only break an arm when I fell off the school roof. My mate Norm, from next door, was even luckier when I accidentally hit him with a pickaxe, although there was nothing accidental about the way the field across the road kept going up in flames. We must have been slightly less popular with that local farmer than we were with the local golfers. We lived near the short third hole where the decent players could drop the ball straight on the green from the tee. The only problem was that quite often when they got there the balls would be nowhere to be seen, mainly because they were safe in our pockets ready to sell back to the golfers at a cut-price over the next day or two.

If we sound young monsters you should have seen the

other lot from Glasgow. There is not too much that has frightened me, the odd hiccup in an aeroplane, the time the wall collapsed at Walsall in a Milk Cup semi-final, but the day I was most scared of all was at a bus stop in Glasgow. I had been training with Celtic at Parkhead and was waiting with a mate for a late bus home when we were attacked by a couple of hooligans. It wouldn't have been so bad but for the fact that one of our assailants was wielding a sword. Over the years people have accused me of not being quick. But, you should have seen me then; Allan Wells would have been proud.

Undoubtedly I would have been in a considerable amount of trouble but for my football. Because I was pretty good at kicking a ball I got away with murder and not just those odd ten minutes they allowed me to take off and go training with Celtic. I just about scraped through my lessons with the minimum of effort. Twice I was hauled before the Headmaster and each time my backside was spared simply because I could play football. Ex-pupil Dave Mackay was more than just a legend at Carrickvale. They had a couple of his mementoes and the Head would show them to me and tell me that I could follow along the same path if I worked hard enough. So I had Dave Mackay held up as a hero from a very early age!

Sport was clearly a fair old dodge. Apart from captaining the school football team I was also skipper of the basketball squad. I even tried rugby once but someone stood on my ear (who said they were too big to miss?) and I was not too keen on cricket because the ball was too damned hard. It may also surprise some to know that, in those days, I wasn't remotely interested in girls. Well, hardly.

By this time we had moved from our prefab to a new estate, or scheme as we called it, and with my Dad working as a glazier, and brothers Gordon and Billy each now earning a wage, we were reasonably well off. It was a proud day when we had the first television in the street. For once I was the most popular boy around. Watching Cowboys and Indians in our front room made a change from watching Cowboys and Indians in the local cinema on Saturday morning, especially as we were all reaching the stage where we were playing organized football on both Saturday morning and Saturday afternoon.

I thought nothing of playing for my school after breakfast, rushing home for a plate of my Mum's brilliant macaroni, and then tearing straight out again to play for the local boys' club. Although, perhaps, it did have an effect because, suddenly and for no apparent reason, I began to lose interest in the game. It could have been because my school did not have a particularly good team. I was a bad, bad loser even in those days and I even used to cheat against my brother Billy when I played him at Monopoly. It could all have slipped away then and there but for my mother Elizabeth – bless her.

My mother had a remarkable talent for always knowing when something was wrong. She would call me into the kitchen, sit me down and get me to tell her all about it. Not only that, she would always know when I was lying and, eventually, she would get the truth out of me. I remember quite vividly her telling me how important it was to start concentrating on my football again and that I was not as good as I should be.

She was, of course, right. But why anyone bothered with me I don't know. I still go hot under the collar when I think of how, as a 10-year-old, I lined up with my team for a photograph a couple of days after winning a cup. I was the captain but, instead of sitting in the middle of the front row with the trophy, I had to stand at the back. The photograph of my long, sulky face serves to remind me of what a brat I was.

But anyway, my Mum made me buckle down and work at my game again. I played for Tynecastle Boys Club, trained with my local team Hearts and then jumped at the chance of training with the mighty Celtic. The honours gradually began to come my way. I played for Edinburgh Secondary Schools and, despite missing a penalty in the semi-final against a Glasgow team which we lost 2-1, the selectors thought enough of me to pick me for the Scotland Schools team.

There is an odd coincidence in that my first football trip south was to Liverpool where Edinburgh Schools were supposed to play a Merseyside representative side at Goodison Park. However, it rained and rained and rained until, eventually, they were forced to call off the game. A friend and I killed time by going to Anfield where we were shown around the ground by two men dressed in long white coats. I swear to this day that those two backroom boys were Bob Paisley and Joe Fagan. They might like to deny it but I have it on good authority that, at around that time, they used to show visiting kids the sights.

I couldn't have been terribly impressed because I was much more taken with Goodison. Not that I fancied either Merseyside club in those days as, up in Scotland, the only two English clubs which counted were Manchester United and Spurs. By another coincidence my next representative game was for Scotland against the English Schools team at White Hart Lane. It was here, I am told, that Dave Mackay spotted me while watching the game from the touchline and recommended me to Bill Nicholson. I must confess that I didn't see him!

After beating England we went on to win against Wales in Cardiff and things were really looking up with a game in Northern Ireland and another in England to follow. However, that was before I blew it again. It happened at a get-together when the schoolmaster in charge told me to wear a number ten shirt for a practice match. I retorted that I wore number four for the team and so would wear number four in training only. He told me not to be so bloody daft and to put on the bib I was told. I dug my heels in, said no again and he, quite rightly, said I was to wear it or get dressed and go home.

Incredibly I got dressed, went home and missed those next two games. I was too stupid to even offer an apology. If some of the English clubs that were after me had bothered to check my credentials they would have run a mile. Still, it was a time of learning, even if sometimes I learned the wrong lessons. At least something must have been seeping through that thick skull of mine for me to last the pace.

Football was opening all sorts of doors and I scarcely realized it. There was the trial for West Bromwich Albion at, of all places, Whitley Bay just outside Newcastle. It was freezing cold and I recall them giving us short-sleeved shirts even though it was snowing, but my great memory of that trip was my first-ever taste of a prawn cocktail! My success at soccer also made me popular with the girls as well as the boys and when it became the done thing to get a girlfriend I was lucky to be able to have a kiss and a cuddle behind the bicycle sheds with pretty Sylvia Porteous and hold hands with her in the rough on the local golf course. The permissive society may have arrived on the Kings Road and at Stamford Bridge but it hadn't quite reached us.

One of my pals invited me to join him and his parents for a holiday at Butlins Camp in Ayr where I entered the swimming gala and won first prize – a free holiday back at the same camp. Mum and Dad had to pay their own way to go with me – clever prize that – and this time I won the Body Beautiful contest. Eat your heart out Cyrille Regis!

However, my head was not turned by these giddy heights and football dominated my young life more and more. Although I visited Hearts and Hibs now and again, it was playing that interested me rather than watching and, every spare minute, I would drag Billy out of the house to play in goal against me. When he wasn't available I would spend hour after hour kicking a ball against a wall. Because I watched so little football I wasn't terribly influenced by any one player, not even by my brother Gordon who played for Hearts for a couple of years. I suppose I should have found a hero when England won the World Cup in 1966 but, because it was England and not Scotland, it didn't inspire me.

Not that I didn't respect other players. I had tremendous admiration for Denis Law, Slim Jim Baxter and for the tigerish tackling of Billy Bremner. Most of all, however, I liked Pelé. I loved his style, his skill, his elegance, his charisma, in fact everything about him. But he was a one-off, the best there has ever been or ever will be. You couldn't copy his game, it would be an insult even to try, which is probably one of the reasons why I have always been my own man. Nor did I learn my football from coaching. I learned more from tapping a ball against a brick wall and getting used to its unexpected bounces than I ever did from a schoolmaster who had passed his FA coaching badge.

I learned how to be tough by having to defend myself at school and I believe that this goes a long way towards being a good player. I can see now some of the knowing nudges and winks as people read this, but though I was often in trouble off the field, I was rarely in trouble on it. I was never sent off as a schoolboy basically because I could impose myself on my opponents and they would back off. My fighting stopped one morning when I woke up and could still feel the pain from the day before. After that all my aggression was channelled through soccer.

I played with some good players in my schooldays. Some made it and some did not. But I will not accept the old cliché that so-and-so would have been a good player but for the women, the drink or bad luck. Injury and illness can be the only legitimate excuses because a great player will always come through. The lessons were there right in front of my nose. Kenny Watson was a year ahead of me at Broomhouse Primary School, a big lad with plenty of ability but, like me, he was a rebel and wouldn't be told. I eventually learned to accept discipline but he didn't and, after a year or two at Rangers, he drifted out of the game.

Then there was Eric Carruthers who was in the Edinburgh Schools team at the same time as me. He went to Derby and thought he had made it big when he came on as a sub in a televised game against Manchester United. He immediately thought he could run before he could walk, fell in with experienced professionals like Charlie George and Francis Lee and discovered that it took more than one game to gain the necessary experience to come through the rigours of football life. Our school team wasn't very good but we had just enough players to make a great little six-a-side team and of them Ian MacDonald was forced out of the Rangers' team with a knee injury while David Graham and Derek Henderson had both interested senior clubs before drifting out of the game.

What delights me is that so many of the players I played with at Scottish junior level went on to make it in the professional game. Players like John and Ally Robertson are still good mates of mine. I always find it strange that more Scottish youngsters seem to come through than their English counterparts. Certainly it was true of my generation.

On the face of it, with the degree of talent and the sheer weight of numbers, the English should murder us every time at the various below-senior levels. From my personal experience I would say this is due to overcoaching. My attitude towards youngsters would be to let them get out there and play. Until 16 or 17 the only way to learn is by match practice. I accept that you can probably teach defence-minded people to defend but how would you teach Glenn Hoddle to hit a 40-yard pass or Kenny Dalglish to become a defender or Ian Rush to score goals? You can encourage and advise but you can't teach a midfield player how to be creative or a striker how to score goals.

It is the same with physical fitness. Lads up to the age of 17 are naturally fit and full of energy. The last thing they need is shuttles and assault courses, far better that they are given a ball to play with. As a kid I went out for a couple of hours a day, five days a week whatever the weather. That was how I learned to get the feel of the ball, what it might do and, most important of all, how to make it do what I wanted it to do.

A quick mind can often be more useful than how fast you can run across the grass. If you are sharp-witted you can destroy people. I'm not the fastest man in football but then neither was Bobby Moore, Jim Baxter nor Franz Beckenbauer. Again it is not something you can coach, but it is something that you can learn.

I received some criticism from England manager Bobby Robson over some comments I made about the FA's school of excellence. It may surprise a few to discover that I think it is a good thing – but providing that the youngsters are going to be overseen by footballers only and not schoolteachers. Let the teachers teach their subjects in school and leave football to the footballers, goodness knows there are enough of my profession out-of-work who would love a chance to pass on their knowledge and skills. In my experience schoolteachers who try to coach are frustrated footballers. I learned nothing from them, though I readily admit I was not the best of pupils.

I was fortunate to go to Spurs as my finishing school, which must be the best place in the world to learn about the game. I may have appeared to have understood nothing while I was there but, somewhere along the line, something must have stuck and for that I will always remain grateful.

4

A Wayward Lifestyle

Spurs may have been my finishing school for football but I had to go to Canada to find out a little about the other side of life. Tottenham were approached by the Montreal Olympic FC Committee to send a couple of youngsters out to the North American Soccer League and, as luck would have it, my mate Mick Dillon and I were chosen. It could have been three months in the wilderness but, boy, did we have ourselves a time out there in that cosmopolitan city. In the first month I put on a stone in weight, hardly surprising considering that we would wake up at three or four in the morning and go out for a beefburger.

After being stuck in the Spurs Reserves this was the big time. Having flown us out there we immediately joined the side, big fish in a very little pond. Apart from the experienced West Ham defender Clive Charles, the rest of this motley crew comprised: a Bermudan goalkeeper; an Arab who doubled as a waiter in the close season; a Mafia boss's nephew; a brilliant Italian defender; a sprinkling of unknown Canadian and English players and, of course, Mick and me.

It was real Mickey Mouse football. The lad with the Mafia connections didn't even have to go through the normal passport routines, his uncle was so powerful, and he used to turn up for training and matches in a big black limousine, complete with tinted windows. Everyone was too scared to tell him he couldn't play, The Italian, Luigi Mascallito, was completely the opposite. He was tremendous and was brought into the side to appease the city's large Italian community. They loved him but they were not too keen on the rest of us when things were going badly.

I was rapidly beginning to learn that I was not the spectators' kind of player. Fortunately those in the game could see something more than the fans. Luigi tried to arrange it for me to play in Italy while another guy came and tapped me to go and play in Mexico. I will never forget the day he came to watch me. We played at Dallas and, would you believe it, I got myself sent off. I must have been the original JR but it didn't seem to bother the Mexican and he asked me whether I wanted to go and play for one of Mexico's top clubs. I priced myself out of the market by asking for £10,000 in the hand.

The money I was earning went straight to my head. Neither Mike nor I saved a penny of it. Every dollar burned a hole in my pocket until it was spent . . . on booze, birds or burgers. There was little or no discipline and I took the opportunity to do everything I could not do at home. We usually drew the line the night before a game but for the rest of the time it was one big round of parties. Even the manager would join us for a few beers after a game. It was my first experience of *la dolce vita* and I was going to make the most of it. We had hotel rooms instead of digs and there were groupies who were only too keen to share their time with a celebrity, even a small-time one like me.

I must confess that, as a fit, healthy 19-year old, I did not need too many hot water bottles nor did I have to make my own cup of tea in the morning very often.

Our one-bedroomed flat in Montreal was like the 'House of the Rising Sun'. Before long, Mike and I were sharing the bedroom and three other lads were sleeping in the lounge. There were people coming and going all the time. The block of apartments was smart enough to have its own swimming pool and it was usually a good place to while away the hours and recover from the latest hangover. But even that rebounded. One day we found ourselves sharing the pool with a rather stylish young lady who was almost wearing a bikini and she naturally caused some interest and rivalry among us young lads. It transpired that the lease on her flat had run out and she was enjoying a last dip before setting off in search of new accommodation. Needless to say she never got further than our rooms and, in a twinkling of an eye, there were six of us in a one-bedroom flat. There was certainly no room for modesty – in fact there was not much room for anything at all!

The football in Canada was not very different as it was totally chaotic. I will never forget the day that Aberdeen played us in a friendly – some friendly! Luigi, darling of the crowd, was sent off and the crowd went crazy. The Latin temperament came to the fore and we were forced to run for cover as the Italians threw everything they could find onto the pitch. Apart from the usual coins and cushions there was even a dustbin lid and, what will always remain in my memory, enough shoes to fill a cobbler's shop. Needless to say, the game was abandoned but I had to smile at the thought of all those people walking home barefoot.

Come the last game and all our new friends were desperate to bid us farewell. The only problem was that we were due to fly back to London straight after the final whistle. Simple solution. We had the party before the game. It was then the craze in North America to smoke marijuana and a lot of our acquaintances used to indulge. They were always urging me to give it a try, saying that it was less harmful than the booze I was drinking. Anything for a peaceful life. I shared a joint with them, went out, played and scored a rare goal with my head. On reflection it was a bloody stupid thing to do but it serves to show how easy it would have been to slip into that kind of habit.

I dread to think how I would have finished up if I had stayed in Canada for longer than three months but, at the end of September, we both returned to Spurs and just as quickly as we had become minor celebrities, we were back to being second-class citizens playing second-team football.

There were to be two more occasions when I came close to going overboard in search of a good time and could have gone off the rails. The next time was at Middlesbrough. I was fairly sensible when I first moved to Ayresome Park until the end of the first season when Eric Carruthers and I decided to take the car and drive to Greece via the South of France and Yugoslavia. We tried our best to drink those countries dry on the way through and by the time we arrived on that lovely British-influenced island of Corfu in the Ionian Sea we were frantically wiring home for more money.

For the first time in my life I had a few quid in the bank and I was doing my damndest to spend it in the longest bar crawl you can imagine. We tried the lot. We drank beer for breakfast, whisky for lunch and rough brandy after dinner to follow the even rougher local wine. Brains were switched off and left behind for almost two months as we blazed a trail from Greece across to Spain and the pubs of Lloret on the Costa Brava.

The nearest we came to keeping fit was dancing in the discos until dawn. We were up all night and usually up to mischief. There were nubile, bronzed young girls from all over Europe and our main aim in life was to flout the then very strict Spanish laws and get them up to our rooms.

One night I was triumphant when, before the night

porter could realize, I grabbed the key and whisked a gorgeous blue-eyed, blonde-haired Norwegian girl up to my room without any trouble at all. Poor Eric, who was just behind me, failed miserably and spent the night with his new friend in the back of the car. It was real oneupmanship and I was laughing so much about it the next day that I drove the car straight into a wall. It was a wonder we both survived without a scratch.

No one, least of all the girls we met, could believe we had been on holiday for so long without getting a tan so we decided one day that we would get up at 10 A.M. and do what all the other tourists were doing. We awoke at 10 A.M. all right but the only trouble was that it was a day later. We had been playing so hard that we had slept around the clock. In the end we left in a hurry after a Cockney pal of ours had to defend his honour and became involved in a punch-up. It threatened to go further and it acted like a cold shower. We were back to our hotel, packed and off.

The holiday had taken its toll and I returned to Teesside overweight, out of condition and in no mental state to play serious football. It was fortunate for my future career that the manager who had signed me, Stan Anderson, was replaced by hard man Jack Charlton.

I will never forget that first team meeting. I sat there with my stomach bulging over my shorts and trying to avoid the scrutiny of the new manager whose eyes were firmly fixed on me as he told us that there was no way he was coming to Middlesbrough to be a loser. He went on to tell us how it was first at Leeds when he arrived as a nothing player with a nothing team. Middlesbrough, he said, was exactly the same and he went on to tell us how success brought fame and fortune to those who were ready to give their all. He then pulled me to one side and really spelled it out. The essence of it was to get on or get out but those who know Jack will be able to imagine exactly how he phrased it. That, I suppose, was the second time I came to blowing it because of my lifestyle. The temptations are there for any footballer who wants to succumb, particularly for those who find themselves on the end of a big money transfer. Suddenly this healthy, fit, young athlete has money in his pocket and plenty of attention. There is always someone ready to buy the next drink and, more often than not, a girl whose main ambition is to make sure you don't miss your mother. As a kid you usually live in digs where there is someone to keep an eye on you but when I moved from Middlesbrough to Liverpool I was given a room in the Holiday Inn. This was the start of the third period in my life during which I very nearly managed to wreck my own career.

After my marvellous digs with Phoebe in Middlesbrough it was completely the wrong thing for me. Everyone was too nice to me from the Inn Keeper, Jack Ferguson, a fellow Scot and one of the best-known hoteliers around, down to the chambermaids.

I lived there for nine months and it was then I earned the nickname of Champagne Charlie. My drinks bill for the first two weeks, marked down as lemonade and orange juice, was £200 and club secretary Peter Robinson quickly informed me that I was to pay my own corner. If I had really drunk that much lemonade I would have gone off pop.

The routine was quickly established. I would train at Melwood, go back for lunch and a few beers, get involved in a session at the cocktail bar, sleep between 4 and 7 P.M. and then crawl back down for dinner. If that became a little too boring there was always a club open somewhere, where they were only too happy to have a Liverpool player gracing their bar or the dancefloor.

If Kenny Dalglish had not been staying in the hotel as well I would have gone completely crazy. He was in the room opposite mine and would always make his point with a joke, saying that I could bring in his breakfast on the way back to my room. Ironically I was still performing well on the pitch. If I hadn't, I would have been on my way. As it was, Liverpool didn't like the bar bill and they liked even less the tales of my high life that filtered back to Anfield. I am certain that if they could have transferred me at the time they would have done so.

All sorts of rumours were floating around the dressing room and the newspapers. David Johnston told me that Liverpool were about to swap me for Peter Barnes, then at Manchester City, while the papers were predicting that I would be sold to the ambitious Belgian club, Anderlecht.

Girls were another distraction and as a single boy there was nothing wrong with that. The problem is that Liverpool is like a village and by the next day's training everyone in the dressing room knew who you had been out with the night before. I tried to escape by nipping down to London and either catching the early train back or flying home in time for training. But it quickly became obvious that was just pushing things too far. The papers loved it when I was seen a couple of times with Miss World, Mary Stavin, and they tried to build it into a big romance. Sorry to spoil a good story but, as they say in Hollywood, we were just good friends and it never went beyond dinner for two at the Holiday Inn.

The helter-skelter life could have continued but, just as I had at Middlesbrough, I saw the signs in time and put things right. Footballers often get themselves into that sort of situation and, in the end, they must get themselves out. A football club has a certain responsibility but it cannot be expected to keep an eye on each one of its players night and day. As Eddie Baily and Jack Charlton used to say, it is up to the individual whether he wants to make it or not.

At one time it was even thought fashionable for star players to be seen in well-known night spots and featured in the gossip pages of the popular newspapers, especially when you played for one of the Manchester or London clubs. In those days the supporters did not mind reading about the money the players earned or the money they spent. As a result there were footballers with far bigger names, far greater notoriety, far more talent than me who fell by the wayside. Everyone who knows about football is aware of who they are and I refuse to make myself a vehicle for them to earn a few pounds by becoming involved in a slanging match.

Drink, as I know personally, is an easy excuse to make. Pressures? What pressures? There is no stress in being near the top, it is all part of what you are aiming for. If you have the character you will come through. Walk about drunk and you cannot enjoy the very thing you have worked so hard for – success.

There are no prizes in this game for being able to drink more than anyone else or knowing more nightclubs. There are plenty who will buy you a drink on your way up and ignore you on the way down. My desire for success was always greater than any urge to be the most popular fellow at the bar and the only things I have retained from my wilder days are a taste for vintage champagne and the nickname Charlie.

5

Charlton, Paisley and Fagan

I have come to the conclusion that nice men do not make the best football managers and though there is no perfect blueprint for the ideal boss it seems that a hard, if not mean, streak is crucial. You speak as you find and I found both Jack Charlton and Bob Paisley were major influences on my career and while Jack is instantly recognized as a tough character on and off the field Bob Paisley is everyone's genial uncle – or was he? But that is jumping ahead. I have been fortunate to play my football under some very different people with very different ideas.

The first was Bill Nicholson, one of the biggest names in the game and one of the most successful managers of modern times. It is a pity I never got to know him better, but one substitute appearance in a game in Iceland is scarcely a basis on which to develop a complete character breakdown. When I went to White Hart Lane I was only a kid and I didn't have a lot to do with him. His prime concern was the first team and, as I have already explained, I was never that involved. My earliest memory of the mighty man was shortly before I signed for Spurs when the club invited me and my Dad down to Tottenham to watch them play Manchester City.

He couldn't have been any more impressed with me than I was with Spurs that day, as when they were given the run around by Franny Lee and his Manchester City team-mates, Nic looked me up and down and obviously thought that there was not quite enough of me because he commented on my size and then, rather pointedly, asked me how big my brothers were. He welcomed his new apprentices in a warm and generally friendly manner and then left us to the care of Pat Welton and Eddie Baily, until I began demanding to see him about my future. To his credit he never refused and his door was always open.

Those meetings could not have given him any great pleasure for, while he struggled to communicate, I was not easy to talk to and refused to see any further than my own point of view. I hardly went in to discuss the weather or to compliment him on his latest signing and it was either to tell him I should be in his first team, that I wanted to move or that I was going to run home. He never once blew his top even though he had every right to put this precocious little know-all firmly in his place. Maybe that would have put me right but even when I threatened to go home, he simply said: 'Go then.'

I mentioned earlier that Spurs was my finishing school and a great place for learning the game. Do not, however, go away with the idea that White Hart Lane was some kind of Soccer University; you learned from what you saw and what I saw was an awful lot of high-quality players. That was what Bill Nicholson was good at. He was an outstanding judge of a footballer and also possessed a thorough knowledge of tactics.

It was the quality of the players who surrounded me at White Hart Lane that proved to be the biggest influence and motivator in those formative years. I became aware of the rewards, the benefits and the lifestyle that could be gained though they were distant prizes for a kid on the groundstaff, even one who had landed the cushy number of cleaning the brass and emptying the bins instead of sweeping the dressing rooms and cleaning the boots.

Not that Bill Nicholson seemed to think that the current crop of players were particularly wonderful because he

constantly harped back to the likes of Danny Blanchflower, John White and, inevitably, Dave Mackay. It was
Mackay who he really loved and how that man would be
held up as an example, not only to me but also to the
senior players, the big money earners, the internationals.
Maybe it was just Nicholson's way of winding them up
and getting them working because he was always even-
tempered and rarely went berserk.

Any flare-up would be brief and to the point. I thought
he was fairly strict until an incident shortly before I left. I
had been on the substitutes' bench a couple of times and,
therefore, involved in team talks. One day Martin Chivers
walked in halfway through the meeting and, without
saying a word, just sat on the treatment table with one
foot on the bed and the other dangling on the floor.
Eddie Baily shook his head in despair but Bill Nicholson
just glared and said nothing. Now, to a young man, it
was not the greatest of examples. For all I know Martin
received a severe dressing-down later on but I was not to
know. As far as I was concerned Martin Chivers had got
away with it because he was a superstar.

I have bumped into Bill Nicholson a couple of times
since I left Spurs all those years ago and he is unfailingly
charming, saying how pleased he was that it had all
worked out so well for me and that he was always sure it
would because I was a good player. Certainly there are
no hard feelings but if he really believed all of that he
would not have let me go – would he?

I was more than ready to leave by the time I finally
moved to Middlesbrough and the day I travelled down
from Edinburgh to the club I had already made up my
mind I was going to sign even if the manager was the
devil himself. Jack Charlton was to come later and,
instead, Harold Shepherdson introduced me to the then

Boro boss, Stan Anderson, softly spoken, mild and altogether far too nice to be a manager.

I don't think I got him the sack but he was around at Ayresome Park for only a couple of months after I arrived and, right from the start, I had the feeling that he knew that time had run out and that he was on his way. I am not even sure how much he had to do with buying me for I later discovered that two of my Spurs colleagues, Martin Peters and Cyril Knowles, had been praising my abilities to Shepherdson on England trips.

Soon after I joined we lost to Plymouth in the Cup and everyone knew that it was the last nail in the coffin, even before seeing Stan with his head buried in his hands. After that he was pretty resigned to the fact as he continued to get flak from every direction, while his right-hand man, Big Ian MacFarlane, did all the shouting and all the coaching. Stan Anderson was a gentleman in the wrong job but a similar sort to Ken Brown who worked miracles at Norwich so, perhaps, there is room after all, but not a lot. I should have been concerned that the man who signed me was about to leave but, at that age, I wasn't. All I worried about was planning the holiday in Greece and how I was going to spend the money which was burning a hole in my back pocket. I should have kept it there since that would have stopped me running headlong into a collision with the man who was to influence my career more than any other before or since.

There have been one or two forwards scattered around the world who have had cause to remember the bone-crunching tackles of Jack Charlton and I should think they were very similar to my first meeting with him though mine was without the physical pain. On reflection I was lucky to get away with that. If looks could kill I would have been part of the Ayresome Park subsoil now. I got the distinct impression that he was not at all keen on the sunken, black-rimmed eyes and even less happy about the Michelin tyre I was carrying around my waist.

To be frank, I did not know very much about him other than what I had seen of him on television playing for Leeds and England. That alone should have been ample warning and maybe it would have saved me the humiliation of that first slating. It was painfully obvious that I hadn't looked after myself and he let me know he knew! He told me that he had heard I could play but wanted proof of it before he would stake his reputation on mine. He had climbed on my back and there he stayed throughout pre-season training as he licked me into shape and got my weight down. Not that I had convinced him. We went to Scotland for warm-up games and I was not in the team. We then had a friendly at York and he gave me my chance at left back, our problem position at the time. Clearly I was not going to be the one to solve it, for Middlesbrough started the season without me.

My Dad still has this cutting from that first season at Middlesbrough which quotes Jack as saying, 'I had a big problem with Graeme when I took over. His trouble, I think, was that he had never played for the first team at Tottenham and wasn't a regular player at Middlesbrough; in short he had never been given responsibility. He was grossly over-weight when he reported for pre-season training, and I had to leave him out of the side for a while. I had to get it through to him that if he did not screw the nut, he'd be a bum for the rest of his life.'

Jack continued: 'I worked him terribly hard, as a punishment more than anything else, and all credit to the lad, he really knuckled down to it. Since then, I can honestly say, he's not given one moment's trouble.'

The first comments were spot on even if the last few words were stretching the imagination a little. But I did work hard and Jack rewarded me by beginning the season without me. In fact, I had to sit out the first two games against Portsmouth and Fulham and got my chance in the third only when Brian Turner had his nose smashed. I came on in a central midfield position and Willie Maddren dropped back into his favourite central defensive position and there we both stayed.

Jack, having laid down the law, stood back and waited to see what would happen. Like everyone else at the club, when Big Jack roared the players jumped. We were genuinely scared of him, the way he spoke, the way he acted and he quickly showed that his bite was every bit as bad as his bark. It was quite obvious from the start that he wasn't too fond of Eric McMordie and he soon went, as did anyone else whom Jack did not fancy. There was no messing about with him and he never needed to repeat himself.

He liked to pull a tracksuit on and get out there with Ian MacFarlane but he cut an incongruous figure. He used to cadge cigarettes off the old age pensioners who came to watch training and would stand about with a fag in one hand and a cup of tea in the other. To say he was unconventional would be an understatement. He has made news recently with his controversial views, not to mention a television series on blood sports. What his critics would have been interested to know was that when he was at Middlesbrough he used to get tracksuited apprentices to beat for him up on the Moors. I have been on a shoot with him, although I must confess that I would find it difficult to tackle anything much bigger than a pheasant and I certainly could not kill a deer. Each to their own, I say, and though I don't like fox hunting I recognize it is a part of English tradition, just like angling and cricket.

Once Jack had got a winning side established at Ayresome Park we scarcely saw him from match to match. He would leave trainer Jimmy Greenhalgh to keep things ticking over while he took his fishing rods and guns up to Scotland. Mind you, when things went wrong he was back larger than life and with a temper to match. I remember us once having to duck for cover at half-time, when we were not performing to his exacting standards, as he hurled a crate of lemonade across the dressing room. Fortunately it was usually just verbal abuse that he threw around. There was only one way and that was Jack's way. He had a sharp tongue and more than once I was on the wrong end of it. He used to find it particularly funny, for some reason, to see me using shampoo and conditioner on my hair in the bath after training or after a game. He would stand watching me and then take great pride in telling me how he had never used a drop of shampoo. If I had had a bit more courage in those days I would have told him that was why his hair always looked such a bloody mess. But you didn't take liberties with Jack. He did not take part too often in practice matches with us, probably because he didn't want to put too many of us out of action for the following Saturday, but he couldn't resist joining in one day when the television cameras were there to film Freddie Starr working out with us. It was all very gentle until John Craggs tripped Jack up and then there was hell to pay as he set off in pursuit of the unfortunate John who ran for his life.

If Jack didn't like something he would throw down a challenge but there was never anyone ready to take him on. Terry Cooper told us he was quite a handful at Elland Road as well. There was only one occasion when I came close to testing his reputation and that was on the coach on the way back from a drawn game at Wimbledon. Spirits were pretty high and there was a lot of childish flicking of paper backwards and forwards with Jimmy Greenhalgh, the coach, being the main target. Jimmy obviously thought I was the culprit and as his temper suddenly got the better of him, he stormed up the bus, picked up my bag and tossed it down to the other end. I leapt to my feet and threatened to punch him. Big Jack, quite rightly defending his staff, raised himself to his full height and in his best John Wayne voice told me that I would have to hit him first. I retorted that he and his henchman should get their facts right before they started hurling accusations and bags around the team bus and that I would be happy to take on both of them. That was the closest we came to blows and, from what I have heard since, I was rather fortunate he didn't take me at my word.

Jack is a hard, uncompromising man and he still kicks as hard as ever in charity matches and friendlies when some young whippersnapper tries to take advantage of those old legs of his. Neither has his tongue lost any of its sting and on the rare occasions he plays with brother Bobby he has a go at him as well. The strange thing is that during the whole time I worked under Jack I never once recall seeing Bobby at the ground. If there is any criticism to be levelled against Jack it is that he was a little too careful with his money. At Middlesbrough we were just a couple of players short of being a very good team indeed but Jack would not go out and buy them. He watched every penny, whether it was his own or that of the club he worked for.

It is strange that Jack took both Middlesbrough and Sheffield Wednesday so far without going all the way. I often had the feeling that he would always be happier with a struggling club, a challenge, rather than going to a big successful club and taking over someone else's squad of players. But one thing is certain and that is whatever club Jack Charlton becomes involved with, by the time he leaves they will be on an even keel and friends with their bank manager, which is more than what 90 per cent of clubs could say these days. Two players may have made Boro into a great team but they might have also put them into serious financial trouble and that was not Jack Charlton's style at all. I have a lot of time for him and his methods. He was a man to whom I could respond. He had done the job for Leeds and had gone to the very top by winning the World Cup with England at Wembley in 1966. He recognized my problems from the moment he took over and not only improved my whole attitude but also pulled me off the scrap heap and turned me into a professional.

Only one thing mattered to Jack in football and that was winning. He was one of the school who knew that there were no prizes for coming second and he was perfectly willing to bend the rules to ensure his success. He took me to one side before a game against Luton Town and told me that the only danger to us was through a midfield player named Peter Anderson and that under no circumstances was I to allow him to run the game. I took the point, made early contact and it was us who controlled the middle of the Park that day. It was not the only time I did a close marking job for Jack. The only time that I saw that piece of granite forced to compromise was when Stuart Boam said that he would sign a new contract for the club only if he were made captain. Jack gave in at the expense of my mate Willie Maddren. I never saw another weakness in Jack and neither Boam, nor anyone else, was ever able to exploit him again. There was a lad named Malcolm Smith who tried to while we were on tour in New Zealand one close season. He sat on the bench pleading to be put on, saying he could do better than the players out there. Jack stood this for some time before apparently relenting and sending the boy on. He gave the unfortunate kid about ten minutes and then, to his utter humiliation and obvious distress, he was pulled off and Jack substituted himself. It was a tough lesson and showed just how hard Jack Charlton was.

Jack Charlton took me and not only gave me my chance but also provided me with First Division football and turned me into an international player. It is hardly surprising he was such a dominant factor in my life. In contrast my next manager, John Neal, was a very gentle person indeed. Jack had always said that he would stay with Boro for only a short period and, sure enough, after five years he packed it in. We were all suitably shocked and went off on a tour of Australia with Harold Shepherdson. The first we knew we had a new manager was when John turned up in Melbourne. He introduced himself to us in a hotel lounge and told us to carry on as we were and that he would do nothing except observe. I was negotiating a new contract at the time and poor John Neal walked straight into what must have been for him a very embarrassing row. While we were in Adelaide I had agreed with a local club to play eight games for them when our tour was over for a nice little sum. Our last port of call was Sydney and while we were there the chairman, Charles Amer, wanted to use the money I was being paid by the local club as a lever in my new contract with Boro and he told me if I didn't sign I couldn't stay on in Australia. I felt that he was being more than a little unethical and I called his bluff. I got what I wanted, signed and stayed on down under.

When I returned to London there was a message for me to get in touch with the club. I flew to Teesside only to find that I had to report for pre-season training at the Welsh camp where John Neal used to take Wrexham. I picked up some fresh gear, jumped straight into coach John Coddington's car and drove to join the lads ignoring the jet lag. John Neal appreciated the gesture and from then on we had a good working relationship. He was an honest, quiet man and, I must say, I was staggered when he made the headlines in the national newspapers some while ago. I never thought I would see his name off the back pages.

I played under him for some six months and in that short time I was impressed by what a good motivator he was. He used to pat me on the back and tell me I was a great player. At the time it boosted my confidence greatly though I doubted his sincerity when he elected Tony McAndrew as skipper ahead of me.

John was a mild-mannered man, completely different from Jack Charlton. While Jack's word was absolute in the dressing room, John used to allow us to voice our opinions and to make suggestions. He tried hard to make me stay at Middlesbrough but I was ambitious for more than Boro could offer me and when Liverpool came in with a £352,000 bid I knew what I wanted for Christmas. I realized I had gone as far as I could with my club and I was frightened lest the big chance should pass me by. The club turned me down that time. However, John Neal knew that I could not stay and be happy and early in January I was told to make my way to the Queens Hotel in Leeds. I did not know who I was supposed to meet, Tony Book from Manchester City, maybe Jimmy Armfield from the local club, they gave me no clue at all. In fact, it was all I could do to see anyone as the call had awoken me to a hangover after a testimonial dinner. When I saw Liverpool Chairman, John Smith, General Secretary, Peter Robinson, and manager, Bob Paisley, sitting with the Boro officials in a private room finishing their lunch my head suddenly became as clear as a bell. This is what I had hoped for but didn't dare think about.

Of course I knew of Liverpool's interest in me because

it had been plastered across the papers day after day. They had already spent the £500,000 they had received from transferring Kevin Keegan to Hamburg on Kenny Dalglish and reserve goalkeeper Steve Ogrizovic. I was aware that they often plunged into the market towards the end of the tax year to spend money which would otherwise go to the Chancellor of the Exchequer and if they found someone else my chance to join the best club side in Europe would be lost, maybe for ever.

I have to own up to the fact that I worked desperately hard to make sure that the move would come off. I deliberately went around upsetting everyone, flaunting the situation and making myself so generally disliked that when John Neal and Charles Amer met with the Liverpool officials they agreed to the reputed £352,000 in doubly quick time. Just like when I joined Middlesbrough I had made up my mind that I would join Liverpool whatever they offered if they came in and my personal terms did not take very long to sort out. All the time we were talking my eyes kept straying to the well-known features of Bob Paisley. But he sat there and said absolutely nothing, letting the chairmen do all the talking, occasionally nodding or smiling. All that remained was to pass the medical and when we got to the steps of the hotel I turned to Bob and said that it would be just my luck to fail. At least that brought a response and a little chuckle for, as I was to find out, Bob prided himself on his ability to spot injuries and illness before the player even knew he had them. I had no preconceived ideas of what this outstanding manager was like, other than the genial, fatherly image which came over on his rare television appearances. I had, however, heard the tales of players signing for Liverpool and being kept in the reserves for a season while they learned the Liverpool

Way. Fortunately, that did not happen to me because the Reds had suffered a couple of below par performances.

I made an immediate début at West Bromwich Albion and earned rave reviews even though I was a little short on training and definitely not match fit. The important thing was that we won with a David Johnson goal after eight minutes. But if I was hoping for praise from my new boss I had another think coming. He confined himself to telling the assembled pressmen at the Hawthorns: 'Graeme settled in well.' I was to learn that praise from Bob Paisley was rather like a snowstorm in the Sahara. He may have been regarded as a fatherly figure by the supporters but, let me tell you, he ruled at Anfield with a rod of iron. You could tell when he was about by the changed atmosphere in the dressing rooms and training ground. He was a commanding man and there were few who dared mess around with him. If we looked as though we were becoming a little complacent or if we were not performing up to standard Bob would say, 'If you have all had enough of winning, come and see me and I will sell the lot of you and buy 11 new players.' Another time he warned: 'I am only a modest Geordie – but get me cornered and I am a mean bastard.' But it would be wrong to give the impression that we all walked around in fear and trepidation. He always kept a velvet glove on.

Bob had the attitude that if he didn't see it or hear about it, it was all right and quite often he gave a fair impression of those three wise monkeys, allowing us our heads as long as it did not affect what was going on during matches. Bob also used to have his leg pulled about his broad accent and his Geordie phrases, particularly by Terry McDermott who teased him about this continually. Terry seemed to get away with it – or did he? Maybe Bob got his own back when he sold Terry to Newcastle a little prematurely! Because I had spent so much time in the

North East I had no trouble in understanding the team talks but some of the new boys were baffled for months at expressions such as 'on that other one', 'jag down there', or most often, 'doings this' and 'doings that'. It was a whole new vocabulary and it earned him the dressing room nickname of 'Douggie Doings'. His team talks were littered with half-finished sentences and he would dart from one subject to another like a grass-hopper. But once you understood his ways you quickly realized that here was a football genius. I have never known anyone who could read a game better while there was no one who could equal his knowledge of players or his ability to spot an injury.

English managers have often been accused of not being able to use substitution to its full advantage. Bob Paisley was the best manager there was. I mentioned Jack Charlton sending on a sub and then bringing him off to teach him a lesson – well Bob did it to win a European Cup tie. It was backs-against-the-wall stuff playing against the West German Champions and European Cup favour-ites Bayern Munich in the Olympic Stadium. We had drawn at Anfield only and looked to be ready for the big chop when we lost Kenny Dalglish with a leg injury after just a few minutes. Bob Paisley was always in his element during those 'us against them' situations; Europe excited him and this time he surprised everyone, including us, by sending on our black winger Howard Gayle, the only one among the 16-strong squad whom the Germans knew nothing about. The long and short of it was that Howie ran them ragged and he took such a battering from the Germans as they sought to stop him, that Paisley pulled him off before the end to save him being carried off or, more likely, sent off for retaliating. By then Ray Kennedy had sneaked in to score the vital away goal which put us through to the final.

He loved that game, did Bob. He didn't get on particularly well with foreigners because he did not trust them, often with due cause, where football was concerned. I recall him throwing a fit in Poland when the lads ordered tea before our game against Widzew Lodz. He sent it back, telling us to remember where we were and asking us why we thought the club had gone to so much trouble to bring gallons of bottled water. The mistrust may have stemmed from his experiences in the War. He didn't talk about it often but we knew from others that he was something of a hero. One day, in Israel, he relaxed after dinner and told us the story of how a convoy of 20-odd vehicles had driven right into a German camp in the middle of the desert during a sandstorm. His was the only truck to escape and that, plus a few other stories, would probably explain why he was so quietly but obviously chuffed by that win against Bayern and other successes in Europe.

I can honestly say that, even when I was cavorting around Liverpool playing Jack the Lad before I settled down, we never had words or problems. This, however, was by no means the norm. Alan Kennedy and Craig Johnston used to get into awful trouble because they were a little slow to learn the Liverpool Way and even captain Phil Thompson used to come in for criticism. One day, at half-time during a dodgy performance at Villa Park, Bob asked Tommo if maybe the captaincy was not a bit too much for him. Phil, a proud Liverpudlian who treasured his captaincy, gave a very abrupt reply. Bob did not like that one bit and flew back at him. It was a rare sight and, a few days later, I was leaning against a goalpost helping to collect balls at shooting practice session when he asked me how I would feel about the captaincy. I knew that that was what I wanted and I told him that if it was offered I would take it and, sure enough, at the next match at Swansea I was captain. It was a great thrill and a great honour even though it ended any pretence of friendship between Phil Thompson and me. He took it as a personal affront and it was a long, long time before he would even say hello to me.

Not that I cared. My relationship with Bob Paisley was good and was being helped by the fact that we used the same garage every morning. He, of course, had been going there for years to have a cup of tea before training and pick out his horses for the day. The garage was just round the corner from where I lived and I used to pop in to look at the morning papers. Gradually, as we came to know each other, it developed into habit for us to sit and chew the fat about everything. He trusted me enough to use me as a sounding board and he would confide all sorts of things.

The prime reason for these visits, however, was a free session with the horse racing sections of the papers. Not that he was mean, for anyone who provides for his family as he does cannot be tight. He was certainly keen on the horses and I have even known him come in at half-time – when things were going well – and tell the boys which horse won the 3.30 at Catterick.

Mind you, if things were going badly he would tear a strip off everyone, telling us exactly where we were going wrong and what to do about it. Not that it happened much at Liverpool, we lost precious few while he was manager, so much so that he had to practise his verbals on us when we won. Even if we scored four he would tell us what a bad side the opposition were and how was it that we hadn't scored double figures against them? He would moan and grumble about how well the other teams were doing and generally bring us down to earth. The only time he would relent and hand round a bit of praise and a few laurel wreaths was when we had actually won a trophy. Next morning it would be back to basics and start all over again.

It may all sound a little strange to the outsider but this was Bob's way. This is what he believed in. He admitted that much to me when he retired. We were having a few lagers in Bangkok on our close season tour when he pulled me to one side and we had a real heart to heart. He even bought me a drink and explained that players had to keep their feet firmly on the floor and he was not at all bothered when I told him that the lads thought he was a miserable old so-and-so. That was the way he wanted it.

Bob did not lack a sense of humour. You had only to step into his office at Anfield with his clock which went backwards and the funny poster underneath it to realize that. Not that they distracted players from discussions about contracts for those never took place in there, but always upstairs in the secretary's office. Bob did not want to know, if he could help it; his interest was in football and not office work. His appearance was deceptive. He favoured a flat cap out-of-doors while he would always wear carpet slippers indoors; this was not done to enhance his amiable image but purely for comfort because of an injured ankle, damaged during his playing days.

He was very quick witted, often too sharp for those around him, and though he never put on an act, he had a poker player's face and was a great psychologist. A classic example of that was when we played Aberdeen in a European Cup tie and they had a talented young player who could have given us trouble. Bob went out of his way to say just how good the lad was and that he was worth at least £2 million. The word obviously got back to the boy, exactly as Bob had intended, for he spent the entire 90 minutes running with the ball to show how good he was. He was no problem to us doing that and Bob, in his own clever way, summed him up exactly.

Not that Bob would have any truck with the modern theoreticians or, rather, their phraseology. He would say that getting in round the back was what burglars did and that only electricians should talk about positives and negatives. He never used terms like that and didn't expect us to either. He did, however, like us to express an opinion or two. There was never any question of influencing matters such as team selection but the open discussion would now and again bring about a minor alteration though we generally found that everyone in the club was thinking along roughly the same lines.

If I owed a great deal to Jack Charlton for putting me back on the straight and narrow, I owed much to Bob Paisley for helping me to smooth off those rough edges. By making me captain he gave me a greater sense of responsibility and that not only made me a better player but also a better person. He demanded a certain code of conduct from me and I hope that he would agree that I adhered to it.

Bob was a great man and a great manager. He was a deep thinker on the game and a footballing 'intellectual'. Had he been more articulate he would have been hailed as one of the greatest thinkers and managers on the game.

My lasting memory of Bob will always be after winning the European Cup in Paris, with him sitting back with a cigar, a glass of whisky and wearing those old-fashioned slippers of his. Completely relaxed and apparently not at all excited. I had a lump in my throat when he stepped down from the Liverpool management even though we had known for a long time in advance that it was going to happen but, at least, we knew that he would not be far away and that the famous Liverpool continuity would be preserved. There would be no wasted time by trying to prove ourselves to a completely new manager.

Although there were no voices of dissent in the dressing room, I had one nagging doubt thanks to a brush I had had with Joe Fagan before he took over the reins and it had been serious enough for me to write out a transfer request! Fortunately the story never reached the newspapers as it would surely have made back page headlines and had it gone that far it could have soured the relationship between Joe and me for good. The circumstances arose due to one of those odd twists of fate; I was out of the team because of injury and Bob Paisley was sidelined by illness at exactly the same time. My back was bad enough for me to miss ten games and the team had more than proved that no one was indispensable by winning nine games and drawing one.

However, I was having my best-ever season and when I felt ready to return I went into the bootroom at Anfield and told Bob and the backroom staff, adding that I fully understood how difficult it would be to change a winning combination. Their unanimous response was that they wanted me back as quickly as possible and I was to miss the next game to ensure that I would be fully fit for the important visit to Tottenham the following week.

I was delighted, especially as I always hated the prospect of missing a game against my old club Spurs. I told all the lads that I would be back and I recall Terry McDermott cursing me about it and saying his neck would be on the chopping block as per normal. Nothing was said to alter the arrangement until moments after I had stepped out of my usual pre-match hot bath. Kenny Dalglish, my room-mate, had taken over in the bathroom when there was a knock at the door.

It was Joe Fagan and the moment I saw him I instinctively knew what he wanted and my blood began to boil.

Sure enough, he told me that they had decided I shouldn't play. I was so mad that I told Joe Fagan exactly what he could do with his team, the club and, for that matter, Tottenham's new stand. I added that if the manager were unable to tell me himself then I would not be a substitute either. I immediately sat down and carefully wrote out my transfer request and then telephoned my wife, Danny, to tell her what I had done.

I felt I could not possibly go into lunch with the rest of the team because I had lost face before them having told them that Bob Paisley and Joe Fagan had selected me to play against Spurs. Instead I went straight to the bar in the hotel and sank four very large gin and tonics on an empty stomach. I would have flown home to Liverpool then and there but there was a flight to Speke at 6 P.M. which gave me time to see Bob Paisley when he arrived after attending a morning funeral in Liverpool.

It was his first game back after his illness and it was a wonder he did not have a relapse when I immediately buttonholed him at the hotel in Swiss Cottage, to tell him that I had a transfer demand in my pocket and also why I had written it. He was stunned and explained that somewhere along the line there had been a misunderstanding and, in view of the team's success during my absence, I was to sit on the bench and be reintroduced into the side at half-time.

Bob made it abundantly clear that, illness or not, he was the manager, he was running the show and he would decide who would do what, where and when. The rest of the team must have sniggered to themselves to see me sitting on the bench, slightly the worse for wear after the shortest of naps on top of those afternoon G and Ts. It could have still proved to be very nasty but, that night, things could not have worked out better.

By half-time we were two goals down and on the end

of a roasting. My appearance after the break could not have been more apposite and when we drew 2-2 it was, according to the papers, all down to my return and Bob Paisley's brilliant tactical substitution. But I kept that transfer request in my pocket for another 24 hours and though I eventually tore it up the incident has remained in my memory.

If Joe Fagan remembered it then he never used it against me and his appointment as Bob's replacement was as logical, expected and welcome to me as it was to the rest of the team. There was an awful lot of speculation in the media before Joe's promotion became official. The fact that everyone knew that Bob was going only fuelled the situation as we waited outside ground after ground while the First Division clubs honoured a popular manager and the press nosed around for his successor.

Ronnie Moran and Roy Evans were constantly mentioned as likely candidates but they were hardly practicable suggestions as they both looked on Joe as a father figure and to have leapfrogged over him would have been as embarrassing for them as it would have been for him. Among the old boys tipped to succeed were John Toshak and Ian St John. Tosh was most of the uninformed's first choice because, at the time, he was enjoying phenomenal success with Swansea and was regularly featured on the front covers of the Sunday colour supplements. But we had heard through the grapevine that he had already turned down the number two spot behind Bob some time before and then the Board seemed to cool in its attitude towards him following a rather bizarre incident.

It came soon after the death of Bill Shankly when we played Swansea, with all their Liverpool connections, at Anfield. As we stood for a minute's silence Tosh peeled off his tracksuit top to reveal a Liverpool shirt underneath. The players thought it weird at the time and whether the Board thought it was going too far we shall never know but certainly things were never the same again.

The transfer of power, in the end, was as smooth as you would expect. The atmosphere was very relaxed as Joe had been the one involved in the day-to-day affairs of training while Bob spent his time on the phone in his other little office. Joe had also acted as a buffer on occasions, taking the sting out of situations before player-manager confrontations. He handled things so well that he should have been in the diplomatic service. He has a lovely way about him and is a very charming man.

In football matters he is shrewd but his strongest asset is the way he can handle people. He rarely loses his head and can make his point, usually without raising his voice. He and Bob had been so close for so many years that we hardly noticed the difference. We were using the same hotels, the same training methods and things ticked along very much the same. Joe's approach is similar and, if anything, he made the game even simpler than Bob.

If Joe had a weakness it is that he is another of these nice men and you always fear that someone may take advantage of the situation to undermine his authority. Not that I had much success in trying to persuade him that he smoked far too much. One of the hardest things for him when he took over was divorcing himself from the day-to-day banter and humour of the dressing room. He liked to be one of the chaps. Some of us, however, knew that underneath that jovial exterior was a slow burning fuse. We had collided with it in the dressing room in Belgium after losing to Anderlecht in the Super Cup. He got in before Bob and gave us such a slating that not a word was said in response. We had been sloppy and, to him, that was unforgivable.

It happened to a lesser degree in training when he

thought someone was trying to be clever or failing to concentrate on what he was saying. He rarely criticized an individual direct but would generalize, relying on the fact that the offender would catch the drift and realize the message was for him. He once spotted Alan Kennedy daydreaming during one of these discourses. He stopped and spelled it out to our full-back that the whole exercise had been for his benefit and that he was the only one not listening. It was the proverbial ton of bricks and we all felt for Alan that day.

Despite his promotion, Joe remained one of the boot-room boys and did not think twice about helping Ronnie and Roy carry the skips. He was once, from all accounts, a good professional himself, and he never forgot what it was like to be a player. The youngsters might have thought they had learned all the moves, but Joe went through all that same ducking and diving himself and always knew the score.

On the face of it his appointment was short term because of his age, but do not forget that Bob Paisley was originally supposed to be a temporary stop gap between the legendary Shankly and the new man – look how long he stayed and what he achieved! Joe was a fit man but the nightmare of the Heysel Stadium and the European Cup Final between Liverpool and Juventus seemed to knock all the stuffing out of him.

In fact he announced his retirement before that final and there was all the usual speculation over his replacement with the obvious names of Roy and Ronnie being touted. Phil Neal was another contender, but I was not in the least bit surprised when my old room mate and international colleague Kenny Dalglish was appointed. There were some raised eyebrows around the League but clearly the Board were thinking along the same lines when they offered Kenny a new four-year contract at the age of 33!

The critics said that to follow Bill Shankly was imposs-ible but Bob Paisley did even better. Then Joe came along and, at 63, topped them all by winning the League, Milk Cup and European Cup on his first attempt. It left Kenny an awful lot to live up to, but what did he do? – he went and won the double of FA Cup and League Championship not only managing but playing and scoring goals as well . . . if anyone told me he was painting the stands as well I would believe them – but only after seeing his contract.

6

Meanest Man in Football

There are plenty of people in football who have my number but I could barely believe my eyes when I read in the *Sun* newspaper that I was: 'the nastiest most ruthless man in soccer'. I shouldn't have been surprised because I had already been tipped by the *Sun's* chief soccer writer, Frank Clough, of what was coming but what really amazed me was that it was Frank Worthington who was saying it. Having read the blurb in the previous day's paper I was up bright and early to go round to Bob Rawcliffe's Wheatsheaf Garage where I had my daily cuppa and read through the papers.

The white on black headline blared out: 'I accuse Souness' and his ghost-written piece began by saying, 'If I had to nominate the hardest, most ruthless player I have come up against in 15 years of top-class football, I would give the dubious award to Liverpool captain Graeme Souness. Don Revie's bunch of assassins at Leeds were bad enough but there is a streak in Souness that puts him top of the list. He isn't just hard – there is definitely a nasty side to him.' He went on to say, 'One minute he is one of the best players around, the next that ruthless streak comes out,' and then added later, 'but the players know who not to tangle with, and you don't intimidate Souness.'

Well, to tell you the truth, we howled with laughter about the piece and I was still chortling when I walked into Anfield and the expected barrage of abuse. 'Quite right', was the comment that greeted me as I walked into the dressing room, 'Good lad that Frank Worthington', and 'I always knew that Frank Worthington was a good judge of a player', were some of the typical reactions from the lads. The funny thing is that while this was happening in Liverpool, down on the south coast at Southampton big Frank was walking into his own wall of sarcasm as, according to Mick Mills, not one of them had guessed correctly who he was going to name as the so-called most ruthless man in soccer.

But, again I ask, why Frank? I can honestly say that I cannot remember ever kicking the man with malicious intent in any of the many games I played against him. Was it because I called him a 'baldy bastard' when we drew with them at Anfield that season or maybe it was the memory of a strange night when our paths crossed in a London nightclub.

We had just beaten Manchester United in the Milk Cup Final at Wembley and after the game the whole team were invited to Stringfellows. But I needed to unwind away from the game and made my way across the city to Tramps with my wife Danny and her brother Mark. Who should we bump into almost as soon as we crossed the threshold but big Frank Worthington sitting with Phil Black, a well-known Manchester menswear retailer. I knew and liked both of them and went over to pay my respects but soon gave up a rather one-sided conversation that consisted of him mumbling into his drink and me nodding my head. I didn't see him again until it was time to leave and then, would you believe it, he tried to pinch my taxi. Fortunately, the doorman intercepted him over some other matter. However, the incident was hardly enough to justify calling me the most ruthless man in football! If I had known how he felt he could have had the damned taxi. I was heartened by the support I received with Kenny Dalglish responding in the *Sun* in the most derisory terms while Saint's manager

Lawrie McMenemy took the time and trouble to write a letter to our manager Joe Fagan disassociating himself from Frank's comments. He said in it that the views expressed were Frank's and no one else's at the Dell.

I would like to know how much Frank was paid for those views. When Frank Clough telephoned me before the article went into print he said he was authorized to offer me £500 for the right to reply. I told him I was not interested but a Liverpool solicitor I know, Rex Makin, was dealing with the national press at the time as he was handling the Merseyside sextuplets case and he mentioned to the Northern Editor of the paper that the item was almost certainly libellous.

They told him that, rather than let it go to court, they would pay me to reply. '£500,' I had said, 'I would think about it for £5,000!' To my amazement they came back and said that would be fine. That was a different matter all together and this time I had no hesitation in accepting. I suppose I could be accused of taking the 20 pieces of silver but five grand for a 20-minute chat was what I call good business and I wouldn't complain with one of those every week. It would not surprise me to hear from Frank that I got more for the reply than he received for the original article.

The incident does give rise to the question of whether I am a dirty player. Obviously quite a few people think so as I discovered when I was reading the newspapers before our local derby Milk Cup Final against Everton. I stopped after the first two reports when I read how my old boss Jack Charlton had said: 'He has a nasty streak', while Manchester United manager Ron Atkinson suggested: 'Some say he is evil'.

Even some of my own mates have implied I might not be an angel and the Liverpool chaps fell about when David 'Doc' Johnson turned round in a practice match and said in a very loud voice, 'Have you got a licence to go about kicking people in training?' There was no answer to that. No, I can't argue with the fact that there are people in the game and a lot on the terraces who think of me as a hatchet man. But I am not an arch villain and I take grave offence at the suggestions that I am. I go in hard and fair and I like to think that I am a good player and a good passer of the ball and not just a hard marker like Norman Hunter, but more like Dave Mackay. Others have classed me with the Italian Romeo Benetti. That I don't mind because he was a class player who could win the ball and use it.

There is even evidence in black and white that I am not the killer I am supposed to be. It is my complete disciplinary record lodged with the Football Association, charting every domestic booking, sending-off and misdemeanor since I turned professional with Spurs. I was sent off as a 16-year-old in the Youth Cup Final in April 1970 for the tussle with Dennis Mortimer and then again in October 1973 for throwing a punch at Stan Ternent.

During one 31-month period at Liverpool I was cautioned three times only, twice in one season and once in the next, and the latter was for dissent against Notts County! I am such a bad boy that when Frank wrote his piece about me I checked my record and discovered that, at that time, I had not been booked against Southampton in my entire career. And as for all his other clubs, I had never had my name taken against Huddersfield or Leicester while I had been booked once against Leeds; I was also booked twice against Bolton (once while playing for Middlesbrough) and three times each against Birmingham and Sunderland (on five of the six occasions while playing for Boro). My record scarcely paints a picture of a real desperado who goes about kicking everything that moves above grass level.

Indoctrination into the seamier side of football often begins at schooldays where the so-called great players are often the biggest, strongest and most violent players. The big lad often shines as brightly as the North Star but the other kids gradually catch him up and then, thank God, the skill factor takes over.

Personally, I was not, as I have already mentioned, large for my age and more often than not it was me who was on the wrong end of a kicking, which taught me how to avoid those lunging boots. Not that you are terribly aware of it at that stage as, more often than not, the fouls are born out of clumsiness rather than being done on purpose.

In fact, the first time I really came across the very physical side of things was as a youth at Tottenham, and especially when we played indoors in the club gymnasium among ourselves. That sort of football is all about bodily contact and it was often a case of knock 'em over or be knocked over yourself. There is definitely an art to playing that sort of football, particularly when you have players like Dave Mackay, Terry Naylor, Roger Hoy, Phil Holder and Cyril Knowles bouncing you off walls. No wonder there were always black eyes, when fights would break out regularly.

I even swapped a few punches with my mate Micky Dillon. We would clash a few times, call each other names, act like big girls and then forget all about it by the time we got out of the bath. It had to be like that otherwise we would never have coped with living in each other's pockets the way we did.

But even that did not prepare me fully for my first taste of the real rough stuff in the later stages of the Youth Club. At local level we were so much better than our rivals that there were no problems, but in the semi-finals against Bristol City, I picked up a few lumps and bumps and then, of course, I had my famous running battle with Dennis Mortimer which led to me being booked in one game and then, seven days later, being sent off for what the Football Association described in their report as 'persistent infringement'.

The trouble is at that age you don't know how to be nasty even if you want to. Everything you do is so obvious to the referee and to everyone else. The problem then, and probably now, is that I am a bad loser. Aston Villa were in the process of beating us and Dennis had, as their best player, become a personal challenge to me. In the end the referee had enough of our warring and, right on the half-way line, in front of both benches, the directors' box and the press box, I was sent off. My only consolation was that I did not have far to walk.

I suppose it was then, in my first final, that I realized that the game had a little more to it than the best team triumphing. It was my first taste of winning at all costs and that, even in sport, the rules have to be bent now and then to achieve your ends or to combat your opponents' rulebending.

I was blessed with the traditional Scottish nature, a bit on the fiery side, and Spurs Youth team coach Pat Welton would often warn me that opponents would try it on and attempt to upset me. It was Jack Charlton who taught me to be more professional in my approach when I moved up to the north east with Middlesbrough. Never one to stand on ceremony as a player, Jack had exactly the same attitude as a manager and his favourite expression to describe an opponent would be: 'He's an effing chicken, man.' He would pick out players competing in my territory and, if it could influence the direction of the game, get me to sort them out. He believed the odd kick or two was quite legitimate within the framework of football.

In those days I was fairly crude in my tackling, with no

finesse at all and I admit that I did tend to go over the
top in retaliation rather than as an instigator. I was a bit
unruly at Middlesbrough and I had left the referee with
little alternative when I was sent off at Carlisle. What a
waste on that beautiful pitch of theirs. Both Boro and
Carlisle were going for promotion that season and it was
a close game with little being given away. Stan Ternent
and I had already swapped a few verbal punches when
we went down on the half-way line in a tangle of legs.
We kicked out at each other, he hurt me and I gave him
a right hander. This time I had further to walk and longer
to reflect on my selfish stupidity. It could have even cost
us our promotion.

I was beginning to understand how first-class soccer
worked but I really caught on in my first season in the
top grade when we played at Ayresome Park against who
else but Leeds United. It was a typical, grimy November
day and we were indulging in our usual verbal exchanges
with them. I was involved in a ding-dong with Billy
Bremner and Johnny Giles and was going in to challenge
Billy when Terry Yorath came in on my blind side and
took me at knee height. It was some tackle and I knew
straightaway that it was a bad injury. In fact it was my
knee ligaments and I was in plaster for three weeks and
out of action for almost three months.

All I could think of was getting myself fit and ready for
the return match against Don Revie's team. I was going
to gain my revenge on Terry Yorath at all costs and I told
anyone who wanted to listen that, if necessary, I would
feed him a knuckle sandwich off the ball. He couldn't
have failed to get the message that I was after him and,
eventually, he was so busy looking over his shoulder for
me that he played a short ball to John Hickton who went
on to score the only goal of the game. It was at that
moment I saw sense. We were winning and here I was

doing my best to get myself sent off, a move which would have probably meant losing the match. Who would have come out on top then? The goal was revenge enough.

Not that my quarrel with Terry Yorath ended there. It seemed that one or other of us would get our names taken whenever we met, particularly when he was at Coventry and Spurs. It accounts for the fact that I was booked five times against the Midlanders and four times against my old club, as often as I was cautioned playing against Everton for Liverpool in one of Britain's toughest local derbies. It led to suggestions in the press that there was a vendetta between us. It must have looked that way but it wasn't true. We had terrific respect for each other and he would take it as well as give it. Sure he would moan to referees, that was the Leeds style, but he never moaned in public.

Playing against Leeds for Middlesbrough, I often felt isolated in that midfield battle. My goodness it was hard. Take Johnny Giles, a small man, but how he could look after himself. I am not suggesting he was dirty but he was one of the craftiest and most difficult opponents I have ever encountered. He was a gifted passer of the ball but he also had had to learn to look after himself. I cannot even remember getting in a good tackle against him for he was quick and nippy and if there was the slightest chance of him being hurt you would suddenly be confronted by a full set of studs. He knew I was after him and, once, after nipping me, Johnny gave an impish grin and said, 'You will learn.' I did.

Norman Hunter, he of bite-yer-legs fame, was always fair and honest when I played against him and a lovely fellow away from the Park. Billy, nearing the end of his career when I played against him, was easier to catch and not as cute as Giles while Terry was as slow as me. It was Johnny who made enemies and upset people – just like me. But playing against players like him and his team-mates showed me what an awful lot I had to learn about some aspects of the game. I started to look after myself and learned not to be so stupid as to pick up injuries like the one I suffered against Terry Yorath. I tried to be more selective in the balls I went for but, on no account, to go in half-hearted. All or nothing, that is the way it was to be.

I was suspended pretty soon after joining Liverpool, mainly for points picked up while I was with Middles-brough. It threatened my place in a European Cup semi-final and I learned it was not Liverpool's *modus operandi* because you were not a great deal of use to them injured or suspended. It was Joe Fagan who gave me some good advice around that time when he told me that if I stayed on my feet and did not go lunging into the fray I wouldn't get booked so often. I can put my hand on my heart and swear that I have never tried to put someone out of football and when the Argentinian Ricky Villa was off for a long while after we had clashed I felt far from proud. I was upset even though there had been no malevolent intent in the challenge.

I seem to have more than my share of trouble with Spurs, probably because sub-consciously I am always thinking that I have something to prove. It even happened at Wembley in the Milk Cup Final against them when I nipped Glen Hoddle and Garth Crooks came steaming in to protect his team-mate from big, bad Souness. He stuck his face aggressively into mine and I just brushed my forehead against his. It provoked an instant response and as he tried to butt me I pulled away so he was left assaulting thin air and succeeding only in getting himself into trouble with the referee. I felt like telling Garth what Johnny Giles had told me.

Those two incidents were highlighted by television and,

often, the slow motion replays and the opinions of the commentators can make incidents appear far worse than they really are. There was a classic case at Sunderland when their big centre-half Shaun Elliott, who I had had problems with while at Middlesbrough, was kicking Ian Rush and David Hodgson black and blue. My chance to put him in his place came when he challenged for a ball near the tunnel, I turned into him and caught him in the chest with my shoulder, almost sending him into Alan Durban's lap. That, I admit, was deliberate; I wanted him to know I was there and that I also knew what he was up to.

I knew Shaun from our local derbies in the north east and games between neighbouring clubs are always reputed to be the most bruising of the season. This is usually because they are played at such a tremendous pace and people are inevitably going to get caught. In the end it is normally about who is going to tire first and, needless to say, you don't want it to be you.

The Merseyside games are always difficult, blood-and-thunder affairs in a city which is completely divided into red and blue. Even those who never go to watch a game of professional football have their preference. I have been booked in four of them but, fortunately, I had nothing to do with the incident which ended the career of poor Geoff Nulty. It was the result of a tackle by Jimmy Case who was vilified for it, yet I was just a few yards away and swear to this day that it was not a foul tackle.

Not that Jim was, or is, any blue-eyed boy. He is the sort of player whom I would always rather play with than against. When he got angry he would turn as white as chalk and the opposition knew that they should watch out. He gave no other indication and would never utter a threat or say a word, he would just do as he had done in a pre-season friendly in Austria when one member of the opposition who had been putting himself about suddenly found himself prostrate on the ground with Jimmy 50 yards away and totally expressionless.

He also had a very hard friend in Ray Kennedy who was not averse to a little skirmish here and there. I recall seeking a little vengeance on Ray's behalf in a Milk Cup duel with Arsenal after Peter Nicholas got our big fellow sent off. With the tie going to a replay it was all a bit tense and I went after him with such obvious intent that Peter turned to Ian Rush and asked him why I didn't like him! The Welsh international eventually had to go off after a rather high tackle in the first half of the second game from Graeme Souness but that was a case of live by the sword – die by the sword and I felt little remorse at the time.

Not that Ray Kennedy usually needed much looking after. But when he couldn't do it himself his room-mate Jimmy Case would – and vice versa. You would not believe how close those two were, they would even help each other on with their jackets. There was also the famous night in Tblisi in the Soviet Union when, after being knocked out of the European Cup by the Georgian side, one or two drowned their sorrows in the nightclub in the basement of the hotel. Jimmy was particularly distraught at the defeat and was in danger of making a nuisance of himself until Ray clipped him with a short right cross, threw him over his shoulder and put him to bed. That's true friendship.

I must admit that I don't normally go around minding other people though, on one or two occasions, I have taken offence at the treatment meted out to my own room-mate Kenny Dalglish. Where he and Ian Rush rule is the hardest place to survive, that is, where you really get kicked just trying to do your job. They play where it gets positively naughty and the truly great strikers often have a quality the fans don't see – a large heart that keeps them going even when they are carrying injuries.

Playing against Pompey at Fratton Park in another of those so-called friendlies, a young Scot was trying to make a name for himself by kicking Kenny and anyone else who came within range. When the chance came I gave him a little nip only to be severely reprimanded by Bob Paisley for not letting people sort out their own battles. There are plenty of defenders around the world who would testify to Kenny being quite capable of doing that.

However, you are always likely to get caught yourself playing in my area of the pitch and when you do there is no use moaning about it. Even with my experience, I was clobbered about as badly as you can be when we played Real Madrid in the European Cup Final in Paris. Camacho was diving about, going over the ball to everyone with the game only a few minutes old. I decided I ought to try and sort things out early on but after I had gone over the top to him the German Stielike came in from behind and kicked me. I limped for the rest of the game cursing myself for not remembering that lesson at Leeds.

Liverpool always used to have some right battles with Ipswich when they were going well under Bobby Robson and they sometimes got a little teethy. But I didn't always get my own way and in one particular game Paul Mariner went over the top, through my stocking, through my pads and through my skin. Ronnie Moran came running on and told me to lie back and not to look but I did and I didn't let it upset me. It wouldn't have done to show Paul and his Ipswich colleagues that he had hurt me and I didn't even bother to have the half-dozen stitches inserted until after the game.

I have also had a bit of fun over the years with Kenny Burns when he was with Forest, for even though I roomed with him and we became friends, sparks would fly when we clashed. I am certainly not as hard as him or the Spurs centre back Graham Roberts who is as tough a player as I have come across in recent years. Manchester United's Remi Moses is another who will tackle hard to win the ball and developing along the same lines is the young Southampton player Reuben Agboola, a good player but still with a lot to learn.

The ones I don't worry about are the ones who tell you what they are going to do to you. A classic example was when Martin O'Neill, who likes to think of himself as a busy player, got himself into a situation he couldn't handle and had to leave the field for treatment. He couldn't play on but he came out with us in his civvies in the second half and he started to tell me what he was going to do to me. I was listening to him and laughing when Notts County's last man, Ian McCulloch, turned round and glared. Naturally I thought it was directed at me but then I heard the Scot say: 'He wants to do it on the pitch instead of off it.'

I was, however, guilty of a similar, but worse, outburst myself after a game against, of all teams, Everton. We had played well and deserved to win but Andy King, so often a thorn in Liverpool's side, knocked in a late goal to snatch a draw. I was even more annoyed than usual because we had been in direct opposition that afternoon. We were going at each other hammer and tongs when he threatened to sort me out after the game. It was the sort of thing which is often said in the heat of the moment but this time I would not let it pass and when I saw him standing with his wife at the bar in the players' lounge I went up to him and told him I was ready. I was red in the face and boiling inside and I snapped: 'I don't want to embarrass you in front of your wife – are you coming out onto the pitch or not?' Andy saw I was in earnest and sensibly would not budge and I went home seething but gradually feeling more and more foolish. When I think of it now I feel embarrassed.

But, fortunately, I seldom bear a grudge and it has never entered my head to keep a little black book of names as my former manager Jack Charlton was reputed to do – but I dare say that my name might be in a few other players' books. I don't just mean opponents I have tangled with but youngsters who are seeking a reputation. Because of my notoriety built up through publicity I know I would be a fair old scalp for someone, probably the most desirable, for an instant reputation.

There have already been a few who have tried and one or two waiting for their chance. I know who some of them are but I wouldn't give them the satisfaction of naming them. I have no doubt that one or two managers give their instructions just as Jack Charlton used to with me and I swear one or two of them would like a go themselves judging by some of the torrents of abuse I have heard coming from the touchlines.

In the end, however, it is all down to that poor man in black, the much maligned referee. I am afraid that a large percentage of them don't even know when a serious foul has been committed. Too many see only the obvious and are more likely to book you for swearing than for going over the top on someone. I will say now that the standard of officiating in Britain is as high as anywhere in the world. I have been booked unfairly many times but, equally, I have often escaped when I should have been cautioned. The referees I cannot stand are the schoolmasterly types who beckon you to them and then treat you like a naughty boy.

We are all fully-grown men earning our living and I wish they would treat us like adults in the way that Gordon Hill used to. He was the best. Swear at him and he was just as likely to swear back at you and he would also tell you if you had a good game or a bad game. Of the current crop George Tyson impresses me most. We don't always make it easy for our referees. A lot of duping goes on with a great deal of appealing and chat. The worst team I have ever come across for this is not Leeds, as you may imagine, but the more recent Sheffield Wednesday side who have five or six players regularly appealing *en masse* for offsides every time the ball is played through. It is so regimented that it looks as if they have been specially coached in how to con officials and it must intimidate referees.

Mind you, we all indulge in a little of that with officials even if it is only checking out their Christian names before a game. Michael Robinson, an intelligent young man, had the patter down to a fine art. He not only knew the referees' Christian names but also the names of their wives, how many children they had and what they did for a living. Michael would trot over at the start of a game and ask how the newspaper shop was going or how was the latest addition to the family. We are all human and even if it never gains you a single marginal decision, at least it means the game gets off to a reasonably happy start and that can't be bad.

Just before the Milk Cup Final against Everton at Wembley I was more than aware that a booking in a certain match would push the number of points against me over the top and force me to miss the game. I knew it and I also wanted the referee to know it. One of the problems was that the game was against Spurs when I was, as you know, always a little shall we say enthusiastic. When I shook hands with the referee I told him that he would get no trouble from me and I even explained the reason why. I soon got caught up in the game and, before long, I was tangling with fellow Scot Steve Archibald. It could have cost me my place at Wembley but the referee ran alongside and said quietly: 'I thought you were not going to give me any trouble'. That was enough to jog my memory and cool my ardour. It was a piece of excellent refereeing.

I got my game at Wembley and I would have been particularly annoyed to miss it as the teams were to be presented to the Queen Mother. That was a big thrill to me as I am a devoted royal fan and when she came across the red carpet to be introduced to Liverpool and Everton I found myself applauding the gracious lady. It was a great experience and the Queen Mum lived up to all expectations. She sounded really concerned when she asked me about the weather – it was throwing it down – and how it would affect the pitch and the game. She also remarked how cold it was and I suggested, as politely as I could, that she should keep on her gloves. 'Oh no', she smiled as she replied, 'I always take off my gloves when I am shaking hands.' When I took her down the line of players to introduce her to the individual members of the team, I mentioned that Bruce Grobbelaar was from Zimbabwe and that Craig Johnston had come to England from Australia. She responded that it was nice to see the Commonwealth so well represented. She seemed genuinely interested.

I relate this only to paint the background to the scene because it was an undeniably big day for me and I almost had it wrecked by an official who went even further than Frank Worthington. This time I did not find it funny when, on the very morning of the game, I picked up the biggest selling Sunday newspaper of all, the *News of the World*, to read the headline: 'I accuse Dalglish'. It was an article by the controversial, publicity-seeking Welsh referee Clive Thomas saying that Kenny was cantankerous and difficult while Souness was a hard man whom he had booked on a number of occasions, and there was a picture of me to emphasize the point.

As far as I am concerned it was a set-up and disgraceful that a current official, as he was then, could provoke such an inflammatory situation. As Kenny and I read it in our Hertfordshire hotel that morning, I said that one of us would be booked for certain that afternoon.

That was the last thing I wanted to happen in the first-ever Wembley Merseyside derby watched by 100,000 fans in the ground and 500 million others around the world – not to mention the Queen Mother. It was something I would rather had not have happened but, sure enough, just before half-time Portsmouth referee Alan Robinson called me over after a foul tackle on Richardson and asked me my name. It was sickening, not least of all because it was basically my own fault for becoming frustrated as the game was going against us. But neither that first game nor the replay was ever in any shape or form dirty.

The daftest thing of all to get booked for is dissent. Apart from a silly spell at Middlesbrough when I was a bit too eager to argue three times in the space of six months, I have been cautioned on four other occasions only for what they now term verbal abuse. That, however, is seven times too many because you can never win by playing that game and it serves only to put the referee's back up with the likelihood of any other close decisions going against your team.

These days I try to go the opposite way and make light of the situation whenever I can. But in global terms we British are non-starters when it comes to the seamier side of the game. We are mere novices compared with, say, the notorious Spaniards or the volatile South Americans and when we do foul it tends to be blatantly obvious to anyone with the slightest knowledge of the game.

In only my second international game I played against Spain and finished head to toe with a little opponent. Tiny he may have been but harmless he was not, since he kicked me straight in the windpipe before I could move and it was 15 minutes until I could get my breath. I thought that I was going to choke to death. Our fouling tends to be straightforward but on the Continent it includes body checking, shirt pulling, spitting, fingers in the eye, hair pulling and other nasty little habits like the one Steve Coppell tells about in an international against Italy when he suddenly found himself completely immobilized by a hand firmly gripping his testicles. Steve, more than anyone, knows about that side of the game having had his outstanding career ended in its prime as a direct result of an over the top tackle by a Hungarian at Wembley . . . and they call Graeme Souness dirty? They have got to be joking.

7
Middlesbrough

When I joined Middlesbrough I was flash, fancied myself with the birds and consequently made one or two enemies. Usually the vitriol was confined to an abusive remark or, now and again, a poisoned letter until one day while quietly dozing in my digs I received a telephone call warning me that there was a bomb in my car.

My first reaction was to ignore the whole thing and put it down to a crank but gradually the nagging feeling grew that it might just be the real thing, especially as there was then a spate of IRA bombings around Britain. I tried to persuade myself that it was one of the lads playing a prank but in the end I telephoned a pal of mine who, sensibly, told me to get in touch with the police and be safe rather than sorry.

I looked out of the window at my white BMW 2000 parked some 25 yards down the road and decided he was right and I called in the cops. Their response was immediate and within minutes our little street of terraced houses was sealed off at both ends with the inquisitive neighbours being ushered back into their houses as the police surrounded my car, opened the bonnet, looked inside the boot and felt under the chassis. By now every window in the street was filled by a fascinated audience when suddenly the policeman searching inside the car shouted that he had found a white plastic bag under the seat.

The senior officer urgently called down the street, asking me if I knew anything about the suspicious article to which I replied that it was fine, I knew what it was.

This, however, did not satisfy the diligent man of the law who, four times, asked me what it was until, face scarlet, I had to yell back that it was a bag full of Durex supplied by a hairdresser friend of mine.

God knows my reputation was bad enough in that close-knit little community but now they had had it confirmed in front of witnesses that I was a womanizer. Well, why not? I was a single lad and becoming a big fish in a little pond and my clever answer to the inevitable question of what my hobbies were was always squash and birds, not always in that order.

Yes, I thought I was the tops, modelling clothes and generally being seen in the right places. By then Jack Charlton had convinced me that it is a much better life for a footballer if you are successful. He told me that no girl would be interested in a failure and so I worked hard at my game and at my image.

Jack soon had us whipped into shape and by Christmas of his first full year he had us at the top of the Second Division and I had discovered that you could get away with almost anything if you were playing well in a successful team. There was none of the glamour of Tottenham but since I had signed in December 1972 I was relishing playing first-team football and, even more, playing winning football after Jack had taken over and licked me into shape.

Owing to the fact that I left Ayresome Park for Anfield under something of a cloud many assume I did not like Middlesbrough. That is simply not true, I liked the club, the place and the people and I often pop back to see friends while they have regularly come to watch me play. There were a great many influences during that period. Obviously Jack Charlton was the main driving force, as I have already explained, pulling me back once from the verge of tossing away any hopes I had of a professional career. However, even he couldn't keep an eye on me all the time. That was down to my landlady and second mother Phoebe. If anyone put me on the right tracks, it was Phoebe who wouldn't hesitate in telling me I had been out too often and that it was time for a quiet night indoors. She was a tremendous influence on me and played a bigger part in shaping me into a true professional than most of the qualified coaches I came across. Football talent, or most of it, is inherent but developing the right attitude depends on outside forces. I now honestly believe that no one has a better or more professional approach to the game than I have.

In those days, however, perhaps Phoebe should have come with me on a couple of close season tours I had with Middlesbrough. I celebrated my twenty-first birthday on a trip to Australia with them and as my birthday came a little close to a game I didn't shout about it too much. Instead Willie Maddren, Stuart Boam and me got together for a quiet glass of Great Western champagne. At first it was hush this and shush that but as the night wore on we forgot our inhibitions and launched into a few songs from the shows.

The next thing we knew was that Big Jack was storming through the door and demanding to know what was going on in no uncertain terms. Unfortunately our room was directly above his and he was unable to get to sleep. It was no use making excuses we were caught red handed and we owned up. Jack promptly sent down to room service for more champagne and joined in the celebrations. That was Jack. It was my first major tour and I was taking the football very seriously by then but Jack made it clear that it was also something of a holiday and actively encouraged us to mix socially and to get to know a few of the local Sheilas.

I returned to Australia in 1977 when Boro were managerless. This time we stopped off for a game in Hong Kong on the way out and after we had played, Phil Boersma and I became deeply involved in a serious discussion with two English dancers. Somewhere along the way Phil and I split up and he made the plane to Australia the next morning. I did not.

I was stuck. I had no ticket, no money and no visa to get into Australia. I went back to the hotel and persuaded them to put me up for another night on the club's account, passing the time by telling my tale of woe to an English pilot. I arrived at the airport early the next morning in an attempt to convince them that I was who I said and not some tramp trying to cadge a free ride. I must have been fairly plausible for when I managed to get hold of a British Airways' representative they let me on the aircraft but at the risk of being turned away in Australia because of the lack of a visa.

I handed over my few possessions to one of the local airport workers who promptly demanded ten dollars' airport tax despite knowing my dilemma. He had great pleasure in handing me back my bags and turning me away. It was then that I spotted the pilot who I had been talking to the night before and, swallowing my pride, I went up to him. He stopped but so did every one of the Jumbo's crew and, in front of them all, I had to ask for a loan.

That man was exceptionally kind and made sure I was looked after all the way to Australia where fears over the missing visa were dispelled as Middlesbrough had left word that a stray footballer may turn up looking lost and helpless. They let me in and I jumped into a taxi and sweet-talked the driver so that he would wait at the team hotel while I fetched the money to pay him.

I should have been carpeted for that or maybe even

sent straight home but Middlesbrough were trying to persuade me to sign a new contract at the time and neither the chairman Charles Amer nor coach Harold Shepherdson said a word about it. It was on this trip that I was asked to stay and play a few guest matches and the club tried to blackmail me into signing the contract before they would give me permission. It made me realize then how small-minded and petty football clubs can be.

But at least my career was now beginning to take shape and it developed even further when Bobby Murdoch was signed. He came along at just the right time, not only for me but for the whole team. His experience settled us down as we went for promotion and he also proved to be a big influence on my career. Bobby was a great passer of the ball and he had an excellent attitude. He would always pull me to one side to pass on advice or to tell me when he thought I was acting wrongly.

Celtic boss, Jock Stein, long before he became the National Manager, could see similarities between us and he was quoted as saying, 'There are so many likenesses. As soon as Graeme touched the ball he showed all of the control. He does the same things as Bobby in so many ways. As far as I am concerned Murdoch was just about the best player I had as a manager. I only let him move because he had run out of challenges with Celtic. His career needed the impetus he got from a change of club. I see Souness becoming as good a player as Bobby Murdoch. He has poise, elegance and class. He is a longer passer of the ball than Billy Bremner. He generally plays it short and builds it up gradually to an opponents' home but Souness releases the ball quicker and that is what Scotland have needed. He is cocky and arrogant, but not too much to become big headed.'

If there were similarities it was pure coincidence for I never consciously copied anyone, though some of Bobby's style must have rubbed off along the way. When I played for Scotland I was the first player since the War that the Teesside club had supplied to the Scottish National side while playing at Ayresome Park. My career, it seemed, was taking off at last and I was beginning to shake off that troublemaker tag. It was my first taste of popularity and I was enjoying it as, under Jack, we stayed at the top of the Second Division, beating Oxford in front of a 26,877 crowd to clinch promotion before winning the Championship at Luton.

The big time beckoned. Manchester United, Spurs, Liverpool . . . we not only played them but beat them and suddenly there were dreams of major honours. But the nearest we came was when we lost in the semi-finals of the League Cup to Manchester City. I have always maintained that it was partly down to Jack Charlton and one of his rare errors of judgement that we failed to reach the final. We stayed overnight outside Manchester and we were so late leaving for the ground that we had to start getting changed on the coach. We were in no frame of mind to play a cup tie and within minutes our single-goal lead from the first leg had been wiped out and City were two up. They were a good team in those days with players like Asa Hartford and a very young and very promising Peter Barnes but I have always felt we should have made it to the final.

I was becoming anxious to succeed and I made the first of my three transfer requests. If the club were not going to continue to improve then I was determined to do it on my own. I was beginning to get noticed and as I picked up a few local awards I began, once again, to believe that the game owed me a living. The club's cause was not helped when my fellow Scot Lou Macari of Manchester United came out with a strong piece which was splashed across the back pages of the national newspapers.

Lou said: 'Middlesbrough have made a flying start to the season. Souness is up there at the top of the First Division but I still feel sorry for him. What is more I definitely would not swap places with him. He happens to be in a team with a dead end attitude. They won't win a thing and that's a promise. I suspect it was fear that made Graeme so desperate to get away. Deep down he knows he can't pick up trophies or recognition while at Ayresome Park. It must be like a knife in the guts. A player like Souness, who loves to go forward and create, must be almost in tears at the goal scoring record. He is being asked to carry out a defensive job alien to his football ideas. It is vital he is given more freedom now or any ambitions of a return to the Scottish team must be remote.'

You can imagine how I felt reading that, as a young, big-headed footballer who believed that there were greater things waiting for him. Jack Charlton, determined to keep the club in the black, would not venture into the transfer market and neither would he listen to me when my rumblings first began.

Eventually Jack, as he always promised he would, quit the club saying he had been with them long enough and that both they and he needed a change of scenery. The new man, John Neal, joined us on our tour of Australia and assured me that the necessary money and players would be found to ensure that Boro's bid for honours did not fade towards the end of the season as it had the year before. John bought Billy Ashcroft to show he meant business and I was happy to have signed a contract as I eagerly waited for more players to arrive to bolster our lightweight squad.

However, nothing more happened and, to make matters worse, my mate Willie Maddren was injured and we struggled to replace him. All my illusions were gradually shattered and, prompted by articles like Lou's as well as a gentle tap from a couple of big clubs, I was ready to rebel and in went my second and then my third transfer requests. In the middle of the transfer row between the club and me, John Neal, becoming exasperated with the whole thing, dropped me saying, 'Souness has been doing more talking than training.'

It was true. I had made some outrageous statements in the press and generally went around making my feelings known. It was even reported that I had walked out and gone home to Edinburgh just as I had done as a kid at Tottenham but that was complete rubbish.

John Neal dropped me twice during that period of conflict but I can put my hand on my heart and swear that never once did I deliberately play badly, play to get away or give anything less than one hundred per cent. With my mind in such turmoil I have no doubt that I did not reproduce my best form but then it was inevitable. Judging by the atmosphere I wasn't too popular in the dressing room though there is not one of those players who would have behaved any differently if the likes of Liverpool had been making offers for them which were being turned down. The Middlesbrough crowd left me in no doubt as to their feelings.

One way and another the whole thing built up until something had to happen and it came on New Year's Eve in a game against Norwich City. A pal of mine, Erick Fedderson, brought his wife to her first-ever game of football and I also knew that Tom Saunders of Liverpool was, once more, sitting in the stand watching me. With the holiday spirit and the knowledge I was being watched, I was determined to put my troubles behind me and show Tom Saunders, the crowd, my friends and everyone else just how well Graeme Souness could play. Instead it was a total disaster. It was more like the European Cup tie in

Bucharest with the crowd booing and jeering my every touch. It grew steadily worse as the game progressed and as I left the pitch the abuse was so bad that I took off my shirt and threw it at the mouthiest members of the crowd near the tunnel, stormed into the dressing room and swore that I would never play for the club again.

I thought that Saunders and Liverpool would have been put off by my exhibition but, fortunately, they weren't and Boro clearly thought that they would be better off with the cash than they were with such a dissatisfied and unpopular player. I played 205 games and scored 22 goals for Middlesbrough and it may surprise people to know that it was one of the happiest periods of my life and I still have the highest regard for the area and the people of Teesside. I have never replaced people like my landlady Phoebe, oil rig worker Colin Wood, brewer Alan Murray and many others. I still see them regularly.

Liverpool was very much a place for work even though I met my wife Danny there and settled down with our two children Chantelle and Fraser. Middlesbrough was much more relaxed and is a nice place to live. The countryside around there is beautiful and so are the people – well, most of them. The first time I went back to Ayresome Park was to watch an FA Cup replay involving Boro and Everton. I telephoned to ask the club secretary Harry Green for two tickets and he said yes, providing I paid for them.

The crowd, too, are pretty unforgiving and whenever I return to play – I haven't been back to watch since the Everton episode – I get the usual reject chant blasted out with full fervour. That's fine, they pay their money for the privilege but I am sure that they would not have acted any differently if similar circumstances arose in their lives. Obviously I have never once regretted my move from Boro to Liverpool but I just wish that it could have happened without the bad taste it left in the mouth.

8

Chasing Pots at Liverpool

I joined Liverpool from Middlesbrough early in 1978 because they were the best club side in Europe and, I thought, they would give me my best chance of being successful not just as an individual but also as a member of a winning team. My ambitions were realized beyond my wildest expectations and in almost seven sensational years I was involved in winning twelve major trophies – six of them as captain – and that is not counting: the almost annual pilgrimage to Wembley for the Charity Shield; the European Supercup, and a tilt at the World Club Championship in Tokyo.

In those seven seasons we won five League Championships, in what is still thought to be the most demanding domestic League in the world because the depth of quality and the volume of games exceeds that of the closest rivals Italy and West Germany. We also won one League Cup, three Milk Cups and three European Cups climaxing in that unbelievable 1983–84 season when we won the European Cup, the Championship and the Milk Cup.

I suppose that the European Cup triumph at the Olympic Stadium in Rome, which gave us the seemingly impossible treble, should be considered the ultimate achievement but as a committed, dedicated professional I still follow the Liverpool line that the League title is the one which counts the most in the English League. You are made aware of the need to win it from the moment you become a Liverpool player. In my case when I signed in the New Year of 1978, Liverpool had lost an FA Cup tie to Chelsea and were clinging to third place in the First

Division. I knew how desperate they were to close the gap on Brian Clough's Nottingham Forest because, after telling everyone they had lost interest due to Middlesbrough's reluctance to sell, they had paid a record fee between two English clubs for my services.

Despite their reputation for putting expensive players in the reserves I went straight into the side against West Bromwich Albion. I must confess to licking dry lips and feeling the butterflies fluttering as I looked around at the players who were now my colleagues. But it was no time for self doubt and I set to against Albion and made a good enough start in a single-goal victory given to us by Doc Johnson.

Not that I was to prove to be Liverpool's instant answer to success – far from it! My very first home game saw the Red Machine lose a magnificent unbeaten home record to Birmingham City. The only saving grace was that we fought back from a three-goal deficit to 3–2 and I hit the crossbar with a free kick. It is strange how you remember little things like that.

I was keen to create an impression in those first few days, drinking orange juice at the Holiday Inn, going to bed early and training as hard as I could. One of my first nights out with my new team-mates was when a local radio man left to join television and Terry McDermott and Phil Thompson dragged me along to drink him on his way. I kept up the image and diligently ordered a half pint of lager every time an order was taken. Phil and Terry looked at me a little strangely and carried on drinking pints. By the end of the evening they were mocking me terribly, asking what had happened to the Middlesbrough playboy.

By the time I arrived in the dressing room the next morning I had earned myself a reputation as a bit of a poser. I soon set about changing that and it was soon afterwards that I was nicknamed Champagne Charlie. But it wasn't always champagne football on the pitch and when we lost to Coventry City in February we were eight points behind Forest. Liverpool, however, would not admit that the chase was over even when, a month later, we lost 3–1 to Chelsea while Forest were exposing West Ham United's frailties.

Four days later the game was up. Derby County roasted us 4–2. We were beaten out of sight, completely outplayed and afterwards a very angry Bob Paisley dug his hands in his pockets and told the waiting journalists: 'If I were in the horseracing world I would be dragged before the stewards for putting out non-triers.' The papers lapped it up and it was decided then and there that the Anfield bubble had burst. But I need not have worried. We proceeded to string together a sequence of a dozen games without defeat to the end of the season and a Kenny Dalglish hat trick against Manchester City at Maine Road was enough to assure us of second place, making it three wins and three second places for the club in six seasons.

Even though we were seven points behind the Champions Nottingham Forest and had lost nine League games that season, I knew well enough that the club would not be satisfied with anything less than the title next season. How right I was. Liverpool may have conceded the European Cup to Nottingham Forest in the 1978–79 season but we turned the tables on them totally in the League as we regained the title by finishing eight points above Clough's lot.

That 1978–79 season was sensational and I am tempted to say that the team was the best I have ever played in, even though five years later we won the lot with the exception of the FA Cup. It was not a case of winning games but a question of how many we were going to win by. We were knocking the ball about so well and enjoying so much possession that it was almost boring.

We won ten of our first eleven matches, scoring seven times against Spurs (including a Terry McDermott goal which began in our penalty area and finished with a spectacular effort that made it the goal of that season and of most others as well), five against Derby and four each against Manchester City and Norwich.

Liverpool stayed top throughout the 1978–79 season apart from a brief moment when Everton crept above us during a spell of bad weather when we did not play because of iced-over and snowed-under pitches. However, Everton were not the problem but, once again, Forest were. They stuck hard to their task and to us. They promised a great deal when they equalled Leeds United's record of 34 League games without defeat with a 2–1 win at Villa late in September. They stretched it to 42, a full season until, fittingly, we ended it on 9 December with two Terry McDermott goals.

Any hopes Forest had of keeping their title or even of staying with us ended with another crushing Liverpool finish to the season when, from Boxing Day, we played 22 games, winning 17, losing only once (3–1 to Aston Villa), scoring 41 goals and conceding only 7. We clinched the return of the League Championship to Anfield on 8 May, the fortieth anniversary of Bob Paisley's arrival at Anfield, when we avenged the defeat by Villa with a three-goal victory.

That Liverpool side carried all before them in the League that season with a record number of points (68) and the fewest goals against (16) of which only 4 were at home where we did not lose a single game. Bob Paisley was named Bells' Manager of the Year and Kenny Dalglish was the undisputed Footballer of the Year. The oddity was that we used only 15 players all season, something which is still discussed in some disbelief.

Ray Clemence, Phil Neal, Ray Kennedy and Kenny Dalglish played in every game; I missed one; Phil Thompson three; Alan Kennedy and Jimmy Case five each and Terry McDermott and Alan Hansen missed eight each. Of the rest, Steve Heighway and Dave Johnson both played 26 with a couple of substitutions thrown in for good measure, Emlyn Hughes 16, David Fairclough 3 and little Sammy Lee played just the once with one other sub's appearance.

One of the highlights was a prize of £50,000 given by the *Sun* for scoring a certain number of goals. We went to Leeds for the last game of the season still needing two. Doc Johnson scored the first and I bagged the second only to have it disallowed. Jimmy Case, however, clinched it and, for good measure, Doc Johnson added a third to give us a total of 85 League goals for the season. We danced around like kids and insisted on the cheque going straight to the players and not through the club. Our crowd-pulling power spoke volumes for the quality of our play as we packed grounds all over the country. We even had 62,000 people paying £80,000 plus in a testimonial game for Jock Stein when we beat Celtic 3–2.

For years people have said 'follow that' after Liverpool touched the heights – and we usually did. Looking back it was as if we were building up for that treble in 1984. Despite having the runaway success with that great team in 1978–79 we were knocked out of the European Cup in the first round, the League Cup in the second round and the FA Cup in the semi-final.

The next season we won the League again, reached the semi-finals of the FA and League Cups but were still knocked out of Europe at the first attempt. There were changes. The Japanese electrical firm Hitachi was shrewd enough to jump on the sponsorship bandwaggon with us in tow and on 2 August Emlyn Hughes departed for a £90,000 fee to Wolves. No matter what you have done for the club they never allow sentiment to interfere and you stay on after your usefulness as a player has gone only if you can offer something on the inside.

There is no room for sentimentality in football although it can be difficult when you are closely involved. I experienced just how hard it can be at the European Cup triumph in Rome. While everyone else was leaping about celebrating, our former skipper Phil Thompson was practically destroyed. We had taken a party of 17 with us to Italy and Phil was bitterly disappointed when he was the odd man out and not even on the substitutes' bench. As if that was not enough, when he went to get on the team coach from the hotel to the Olympic Stadium, he was told by manager Joe Fagan that as the bus was going straight into the tunnel on arrival and he was in the stand it would be better if he went with the VIPs on the second coach.

Phil pointed out that the recently signed Paul Walsh was on the team bus, but Joe was equal to that and told Paul to keep Phil company on the other bus. They couldn't have told him he was not wanted more frankly than if they had put it up in neon lights on the Olympic Stadium. Yet, despite his frustration and anger, Phil and his wife came along to the after-match celebrations as though nothing had happened. He joined in the sing-song and shared in our triumph. Phil, like Emlyn, was Red through and through, straight off their beloved Kop but when their time came . . .

The 1979–80 season started well enough when we beat Arsenal 3–1 for the Charity Shield in front of a record 92,000 crowd at Wembley with the previous season's pattern being perpetuated by a couple of goals from

Terry McDermott and another from Kenny Dalglish. But if we expected to romp away with it again we were soon put in our place.

We opened our home League programme with a dreadful, boring goalless draw with Bolton and there was nothing to suggest we were going to win the League title again when, after three games, we were in sixteenth place. By the end of September we had lost to Southampton and Forest as well as drawing with Bolton, Leeds and Norwich. It was all bets off. But, before Christmas, we got our form back again, touching the top for a moment when we beat Spurs 2–1 in front of 51,092 fans and then going back again soon afterwards to stay there for the rest of the season.

Manchester United caught up with us around March but just when the pundits began to fancy them they were hammered by six goals at Ipswich – and were lucky to get off so lightly as Gary Bailey saved two penalties. Just to rub it in we beat Everton 2–1 at Goodison Park on the same day. Even so it was not until 3 May that we finally shook United off when we beat Aston Villa 4–1 while they lost by two goals at Leeds. It certainly was not a vintage goalscoring season for me in the League for I scored only once in a 2–0 home win over Manchester City but we were not short of goals and topped 80 in the League thanks again to: Doc Johnson (21), Kenny Dalglish (16), Terry McDermott (11) and Ray Kennedy (9). I mention that only because in April of that season we were all amazed when the club splashed out £300,000 for a skinny Welsh lad who few of us thought would make it. Were the club losing their touch? Who the hell was Ian Rush anyway?

We had a problem in 1980–81. We were winning the League with no difficulty but, since taking the European Cup in my first season, we had done nothing in the knock-out competitions. So, we promptly regained our European title, won the League Cup – and had our worst season in the League for years! It is one for the records that, in the 1980–81 season, we could finish only fifth with 51 points not just behind the new Champions Aston Villa but also behind Ipswich, Arsenal and West Bromwich Albion. Perhaps it is significant that Liverpool used 23 players and our legendary finish to the season was almost non-existent with our record from January reading: played 17, won 6, drawn 5, lost 6, 16 for and 15 against.

The 1981–82 season was one of the most significant in my career for it was the year I was made captain and I felt the exhilaration of lifting not only the League title, which we regained, but also the first-ever Milk Cup. But the season started the way the last one had finished when we lost our opening game away to Wolves and then scraped only a 1–1 draw with Middlesbrough thanks to a Phil Neal penalty. By the end of the year we had lost to Ipswich, Manchester United, Southampton and Manchester City while drawing with Aston Villa, West Ham, Swansea, Brighton and West Bromwich Albion.

It was then that Bob Paisley offered me the captaincy and, once again, I landed on my feet as we won our next five games in succession and lost only two more League games (away to our old boys at Swansea and at home to Brighton) during the remainder of the season. Only a fool would suggest that the transformation was due to my brilliant leadership. It was of critical importance that, the month the season opened, we sold our goalkeeper Ray Clemence to Spurs leaving Bruce Grobbelaar to step into the breach at least a season before he was ready. Understandably he had a nightmare, not just conceding daft goals but also taking abuse from those same fans who have now elevated him to the role of hero and clown prince. Then it was just clown and that was one of the milder terms he was called in the sackfuls of poisonous letters he received. It amazed me that he never once let it get him down. He is either blessed with the skin of a rhinoceros or he has an outstanding character. Maybe it is just a bit of both.

Whatever the reasons, by January we were ninth with 27 points from 18 matches and when we finally clinched Liverpool's thirteenth title manager Bob Paisley said: 'I am proudest of this one because there was so much to do.' We were forever having meetings early in that campaign about what was wrong and then, after losing to Manchester City 3–1 on Boxing Day 1981, coach Joe Fagan suddenly exerted his authority, banning further meetings. He said: 'Go out and celebrate Christmas with a glass or two. We've talked enough and all that is really wrong is that the ball has not run for us.'

However, while we were thrilled with our 'double' of League and Milk Cup, our supporters were evidently not so ecstatic for gates that season were down 25 per cent on the two previous seasons and one of the results was that the staff was cut from 31 to 23. The recession was biting deeply. It was also the year that former manager Bill Shankly died and everyone at the club was affected by the sad loss in varying amounts of grief.

On 24 August 1982 Bob Paisley confirmed to the general public what the players already knew, that this would be his last season. It was suggested that, because of this, our main objective would be to win the one trophy he had never held – the FA Cup. It was nonsense for, as usual, it was the League title that Bob Paisley wanted and we gave it to him, wrapped up in red ribbon by 19 April. The Professional Footballers' Association already decided the month before that Liverpool were going to be the Team of the Season by naming Kenny

Dalglish the Player of the Year, Ian Rush the Young Player of the Year and giving Bob Paisley a special award, one of many he was going to pick up that season, including yet another Bells' Manager of the Year award.

The only time there looked to be any doubt over the destination of the League title was when we lost successive games to Ipswich and West Ham early in October and slipped from first to fifth. We lost again in December, away to Norwich, and then did not lose again until Southampton beat us on their own little ground in April. But after Everton had beaten Manchester United to ensure us of the club's fourteenth title, we received a lot of criticism for going through the last seven games without winning one of them. We were called everything from fools to cheats but we had won and that was it as far as we were concerned. It was so easy that we still beat second-placed Watford by nine points.

I can't say that it thrilled Bob Paisley to see his last days as manager fizzle out like that but I think even he got the message when he called us into a team meeting and, stern faced, pulled the curtains to with a sharp tug bringing them crashing down on his head. It got so bad that before one away game we popped out for a lunch-time glass of wine and were still drinking at 5 P.M. There were one or two who would have struggled to pass the breathalyzer test when we trotted out that night – but we still managed a draw. That, however, was not typical. Although we went out for most of those games with the intention of turning on the style and winning, the motivation was missing. The bootroom, always looking to turn an adverse situation to their own benefit, used our results to show what could happen with the wrong attitude.

I missed only one League game that season, a 2–2 draw with Brighton, and I managed to knock in 9 goals, although that was a long way behind Ian Rush's 24 (he was just beginning to get going) and Kenny Dalglish's 18. At least I scored more goals than Terry McDermott for Liverpool that season – even though this was because my old sparring partner had left for Newcastle United at the end of September. However, the individual goalscoring feat of the season came from Rushy who potted four in the local derby against Everton of which we were five-goal winners. Just for good measure Ian scored a hat-trick the next week at Coventry. But, in comparison to Kenny Dalglish, he was still a novice. Kenny, who had been named by Paisley as Liverpool's best player of all time, scored his three hundredth goal at club level. Small wonder that Kenny went on to sweep the awards pool that season as the Football Writers named him as their top player while he also won his ninetieth cap for Scotland.

The FA Cup? Oh yes. Bob Paisley was destined never to pick that one up and in those seven glorious years the nearest we came was two very close, very tense semi-finals. Make no mistake we would have loved to have won it, for the FA Cup still has a special mystique about it while the Milk Cup has neither the history nor the glamour. Liverpool, being so business-conscious, were usually away on some money-earning tour when the final was played and we used to watch it from some odd corner of the globe with open envy. The nearest I came was when I added my weight to the commentary team at Wembley after Brighton had beaten us and gone all the way, and yet in my first two full seasons with the club I was involved in four FA Cup semi-final replays.

We definitely fancied our chances in that 1978–79 season when the Cup was thrown into chaos by the weather, yet we were lucky not to go out in the third round at Roots Hall when only the awful conditions stopped a Southend forward adding to Liverpool's Cup woes after he had broken through our defence. After that we went through nicely with Dalglish, Case and Ray Kennedy giving us an easy win in the replay, while a goal from Kenny was enough to see off a brave Blackburn side in the fourth round. When we beat Burnley by three clear goals at home and Ipswich away by a single Kenny Dalglish goal, we really felt we were on a winning streak, capable of beating any side on a neutral ground.

We drew Manchester United and levelled with them 2–2 at Maine Road, after Terry McDermott had missed a penalty. We went to Goodison Park for the replay full of hope but lost to a seventy-eighth minute goal from Jimmy Greenhoff. Brother Brian had scored one of United's goals in the first game. It is hard to explain the feeling after losing in an FA Cup semi-final and afterwards we went for a meal with Kenny Dalglish and his wife Marina. Not four words were spoken throughout the entire evening but the supporters were not short of words and we received sackfuls of abusive letters.

We were doubly determined to go one better in the 1979–80 season as we emphasized in our opening five-goal win over unfortunate Grimsby, but the euphoria quickly drained away when I heard the draw for the fourth round. I was sitting in the back of my father-in-law's Rolls Royce heading for the sea air of Blackpool when it came over the radio that we had to travel to meet our old rivals Nottingham Forest. We beat them by two goals, scored by Kenny Dalglish and Terry McDermott. Then, riding on a wave of success, we put out first Bury with two David Fairclough goals and second Spurs at White Hart Lane thanks to a Terry McDermott spectacular when he picked up a bad pass from Ardiles in the outside right position, flicked it up and volleyed it into the top corner. Having beaten one North London team we then faced another as we drew Arsenal at Hillsbrough.

We shared a goalless draw in Sheffield and drew 1–1 twice at Villa Park before losing to a Brian Talbot goal in the third replay at Coventry.

It was no consolation at all that we had been watched by almost 180,000 people paying more than £620,000 for our four semi-finals and I was close to tears and in a fighting mood when we boarded the coach for home. Kenny Dalglish had to physically restrain me from attacking my own players when they started singing and laughing at the back of the coach. I couldn't understand why they were so happy when I was so sad. When I calmed down Roy Evans explained to me that he had started off the singing to relieve the tension, especially as we had a vital League game against Aston Villa on the following Saturday and spirits needed lifting. It was a lesson well learned and one I will not forget. Neither will I forget the performances of the wonderful goalkeeper Pat Jennings in all of the games. He was absolutely magnificent and he, more than anyone, stopped us from reaching that final.

Apart from the last game we had had enough chances to win the Cup twice over. To compound that feeling we eventually lost to a goal given away by Mr Reliable himself, Ray Kennedy, who lost possession in the left back position. It was one of the few times I had seen him caught like that in all our games together and it helped to convince me that we were not destined to win the FA Cup.

The next year was almost worse, for after beating top non-League side Altrincham 4–1, we lost 2–1 at Everton with a freak goal helping us on our way out as our Israeli international Avi Cohen thought that the ball had crossed the line for a goal and casually put it back into his own net, when in fact Phil Neal had scrambled the actual shot clear. My very first game as captain was in the third round tie at Swansea in 1982 and I celebrated as we won 4–0 and followed it up with a three goal victory over Sunderland, but if anyone thought I could change the Cup hoodoo they were mistaken, for on 13 February we gave away two goals to lose at Chelsea.

It was the same story next season as we dismissed Blackburn and Stoke. Although the League was our prime target in Bob Paisley's last season as team manager we still wanted the Cup for him as well. The bad vibrations started when it was decided that we would play the game on Sunday to avoid Everton's home game with Spurs. It put us out of our routine and with our ex-player Jimmy Case scoring one of the goals we lost 2–1 to Brighton.

Why we should have been so successful in the Milk Cup and so useless in the FA Cup defies explanation. After all it is the same teams that are involved at the top level.

I was ineligible for Liverpool's first-ever League Cup Final and had to watch from the Wembley stands as 18-year-old Chris Woods, standing in for Peter Shilton, had a blinder and forced a replay at Old Trafford which Forest won with a John Robertson penalty given away by Phil Thompson. An indication of how frustrating the game was for Liverpool is the fact that during it Ian Callaghan picked up the one and only booking of his career.

We didn't get a chance to get into trouble the next season as we lost 1–0 at Sheffield United in our first match, but in the 1970–80 competition we struck our old Nottingham Forest jinx again to lose one of three semi-finals in the space of two years. We were then given a fairly pleasant little run-through to the two-legged semi-final by being drawn against Tranmere, Chesterfield, Exeter and Norwich.

Again it was my old pal, John Robertson, who finished us off. Robbo, of the ever-present cigarette in the corner of his mouth and the dirty Hush Puppies, was ice-cool to shoot home a penalty in each tie. What a penalty taker the man was, as he ran up you always felt that the odds were stacked in his favour against the goalkeeper, especially when he took them against Liverpool. I felt it sad that Robbo never did as well as he deserved. He won plenty of medals and Scottish caps, but to me he could have been one of the greats. In my opinion he never played at above 60 per cent of his true abilities. Having said that, he was tremendous to have both on and off the field; one of the most likeable men in football except, of course, when he was pushing those penalties past Ray Clemence.

Who could have guessed that a 1–0 defeat at Bradford City in 1980–81 could mark the start of one of the most amazing runs in the history of professional soccer. There was scarcely a blemish after that first hiccup at Bradford as we went on to put six past them in the second leg; beat Swindon 5–0; Pompey 4–1 and Birmingham City 3–1. The first stroke of luck we had was when Manchester City had a perfectly good goal disallowed in the first leg of the semi-final at Maine Road and it meant that we took a 1–0 lead to Anfield.

The second leg was not one of our best performances either and we came back to the dressing room to face a barrage of criticism from Bob Paisley. He spared us absolutely nothing until Ray Kennedy pointed out: 'What does it matter? We are at Wembley.' But that was typical Liverpool. While other teams would have been shouting and dancing we hardly paused for breath. We needed breath, for West Ham took us to the limits in the final, drawing 1–1 after extra time before we beat them 2–1 in

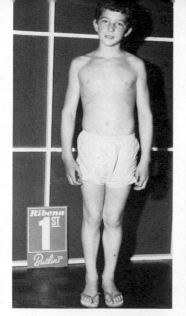

TOP LEFT: Winning the Butlins' Tarzan competition aged nine. I hate to think what the rest were like

TOP RIGHT: My schoolboy hero, the legendary Dave Mackay

ABOVE: Learning to be petulant! I'm on the extreme left of the back row as my team line up for a photograph after winning a cup

TOP: At least someone at Spurs thought I could play. Winning the Spurs supporters' Lewis Trophy but playing second fiddle to Pat Jennings *(centre)* and Alan Gilzean *(right)*

ABOVE: Living up to my nickname of Champagne Charlie as I help my old Middlesbrough team-mate, Willie Maddren, to celebrate the opening of his sports' shop at Stockton with the assistance of an obviously thirsty Ray Kennedy and Liverpool team-mates, Phil Neal and Steve Heighway

TOP LEFT: Jack Charlton, the manager who put me back on the right path
TOP RIGHT: Jock Stein, one of the great managers
ABOVE LEFT: Bob Paisley, the Football League's most successful manager
ABOVE RIGHT: The lull before the storm for Ally MacLeod as Scotland
qualify for the 1978 Argentine World Cup

TOP: Rod Stewart achieving his lifelong ambition by wearing Scotland's shirt and joining in a practice match before the team's departure to Argentina
ABOVE: Kevin Keegan, still a legend at Anfield, and Kenny Dalglish, the man who succeeded him in every way

TOP LEFT: I've never been one for the Home International Championships
but that didn't mean there were any half measures as I show here in a
challenge with former Liverpool captain, John Toshack, whom many
thought would be my manager at Anfield after Bob Paisley's retirement
TOP RIGHT: Bob Paisley disappearing down the tunnel after collecting his
last trophy as manager of Liverpool in 1983. Fittingly, it was the League
Championship which he always claimed was the most important
ABOVE LEFT: The day the jeers turned to cheers. I had been booed by the
Walsall supporters after being booked in the 1984 Milk Cup semi-final
when a wall collapsed. I just did the natural thing
ABOVE RIGHT: The boys from the bootroom: Joe Fagan and Ronnie Moran

TOP: Perhaps this is why Liverpool signed John Wark in the same season I left

ABOVE: Proud Dad with son Fraser at his christening. Flanked on the left by my parents and brother and on the right by my father- and mother-in-law, Austin and June, their son Damien, wife Danny and daughter Chantelle

TOP: Controversial referee Clive Thomas was not going to let this one pass and neither was Everton's Kevin Ratcliffe who tells us both exactly what he thinks of the tackle

CENTRE: The toughest battles were always with Leeds and this one with my Scottish team-mate, Kenny Burns, was obviously no exception

ABOVE: The day Merseyside came together. The 1984 Milk Cup Final at Wembley which ended in an honourable draw before we won the replay at Maine Road. The game was as much a triumph for the fans as the players for their magnificent behaviour

ABOVE: A beef sandwich.
Argentina's most famous export since corned beef Diego Maradona is caught between Trevor Francis and me in our Italian League meeting in Naples

LEFT: Somewhere at the bottom of the pile there's me after scoring the only goal of the 1984 Milk Cup Replay to win the first of Liverpool's treble that season. Ronnie Whelan (No 5), Phil Neal, Craig Johnston and Ian Rush offer their congratulations

the replay with goals from Hansen and Dalglish, which I missed because of a bad back.

It was while I was watching that game that it was first suggested I should play abroad as I was quietly tapped by a senior representative of Bayern Munich. I listened politely but my mind was already on the prospect of playing in the European Cup Final and of winning more honours for Liverpool. By the time we began our defence of the League Cup, now called the Milk Cup as part of the sponsorship deal, I was captain. And I must have been the first to have picked up two cups in one go as they gave us not only the new Milk Cup but also the old League Cup to keep as well, after a marvellous competition. We crushed Exeter 11–0 on aggregate; beat my old side Middlesbrough 4–1; Arsenal 3–1 after a goalless draw at Highbury; Barnsley 3–1 after being held to a draw at home; and Ipswich 4–2 on aggregate in the semi-final.

The final against Spurs was built up by the press as a contest between the abrasive Souness and the delicate skills of Glenn Hoddle. As it turned out it was a superb game to play in and nothing particularly to do with either of us. We won 3–1 after extra time when it had looked for a while as though we would lose. Hoddle might have swung it for Spurs if he had enjoyed a little more help from the rest of his midfield and I couldn't help thinking to myself during the course of the game how well he would have done in our side. Not that we needed him, for it was our own midfielder Ronnie Whelan who popped up with two goals to clinch our double-headed win.

I suffered some criticism in that final for a tackle on Tony Galvin. It was a fair challenge in a game marked by the commitment of both sides. It seemed I was always in trouble against Spurs and it was assumed in some quarters that it was because I was continually seeking revenge for what they had done to me as a kid. Nothing could be further from the truth for I have always considered them to be a great club.

We were already beginning to think of the competition as our own when we went for the hat-trick the next season. We appreciated the value of winning the Milk Cup in March as it took off some of the pressure for the remainder of the season, with a place in Europe assured, and we also knew that the season could not end in total failure. There was a tough enough start to our battle when we drew Ipswich in the opening round but wc beat them home and away. We then sailed serenely through, past Rotherham, Norwich and West Ham before making sure of a place at Wembley with a 3–0 first leg win over the then struggling Second Division club Burnley in the semi-final. It was all too easy and we lost the second leg 1–0. It seemed relatively unimportant at the time but it took us a long time to pull ourselves together which shows just how vital it is to keep a winning momentum going.

It was the final everyone wanted, Liverpool against Manchester United and this, according to our critics, was to be the moment that the team from Old Trafford would begin their takeover. This was to be their springboard to greater things and it looked that way when Norman Whiteside turned Alan Hansen to score the opening goal.

Predictably we carried the final into extra time, as we had done in the two previous years and were to do again a year later against Everton, when Alan Kennedy came up with one of his invaluable goals. Some of the great strikers dream of scoring a critical Cup Final goal but Alan, an unpredictable full-back, did it almost for fun. He scored the goal which gave us a draw against West Ham in our first Milk Cup Final; knocked in the only goal of the European Cup Final against Real Madrid in

Paris; set us up for this one and then gave us the European crown again with the decisive penalty in the shoot-out against Roma. Alan takes some stick from within the club but we are all indebted to him for those goals. This time it set up Ronnie Whelan to become the extra-time hero for the second year in succession, and Bob Paisley was a winner on his last visit to Wembley.

9

European Challenge

There was a time in soccer's murky past when European football was riddled with stories of bribery, corruption and plain, simple cheating. I have certainly come across plenty of gamesmanship in the top competition of them all, the European Cup, and I even had wind there of an attempt to bribe Liverpool. The odd thing about the affair was that it was bribery in reverse, for this particular East European club told one of our senior officials that they would take money to lose.

If that sounds double Dutch then it needs explaining that foreign currency was of considerably more benefit to these poor people than the honour of winning a piece of silverware which had to be returned at the end of the season and it would have been seen as no disgrace to lose to Liverpool.

Needless to say Liverpool refused any sort of deal but the great irony of it was that we ended up losing to this unfancied team anyway! Those of us who knew of the offer were stunned to say the least because, though there was never any question at all of the deal being considered, it made us wonder whether other teams in other countries would share our morals. For, make no mistake, Europe is big business and there was an almost audible sigh of relief from the Anfield boardroom when we made sure of our place for the next season.

European football also means a great deal to the players and it was something I had yearned for before joining Liverpool. I remember when the bug first bit. I was in Australia of all places on tour with Middlesbrough and I watched Liverpool beat Borussia Moenchengladbach 3–1 in Rome on a television in a bar full of German expatriots in a little mining town just outside Sydney. That day I became a Liverpool supporter. I was proud to be British among the Germans who were so sure that their team were going to knock seven kinds of stuffing out of Kevin Keegan and his boys.

The nearest I had been to European competition before was watching the Eurovision Song Contest so it was a dream come true when I won a European Champion's medal within four months of signing for Liverpool in 1978. Not that my first experience was exactly the prelude to a glory march. Because I had not completed my transfer to Anfield until after January, I was not eligible to play in the quarter-finals against Benfica and I was petrified that my chance would be gone before I could even kick a ball in anger. I needn't have worried as, in a torrential downpour, Liverpool won at the Stadium of Light and while the team celebrated I had to make myself useful picking up soggy socks and muddy shorts. It was hardly an auspicious start but I did my chores with a smile on my face, knowing I would get my chance in the semi-finals.

However, I nearly did not make it at all. There I was, all set to make my début against the team Liverpool beat in the final the year before, and my place was in doubt. The problem lay in a couple of cautions I had received while playing for Middlesbrough and suddenly I was faced with a three-match ban for totting up twenty points. Not that the ban affected Europe but the game against Borussia Moenchengladbach fell right in the middle of my suspension and manager Bob Paisley worried that I was short of match practice. I was then robbed of my European début when I was named substitute.

Fortunately my anguish was relieved when I was sent

on with the team trailing to a Hannes goal. The prize of a place in the final at Wembley beckoned when 'Doc' Johnson scored three minutes from the end, only for Bonhof to beat Ray Clemence with a free kick. We made our usual dash for home after the game with a long coach drive from Düsseldorf, where the airport had closed, to Cologne and I couldn't get it out of my mind that we had let the match slip.

However, I had not yet fully realized the importance of the away goal and, sure enough, we destroyed the West Germans 3–0 in the second leg at Anfield. It was a memorable night as it was the first time my parents had watched me play for my new club and to celebrate I combined with Terry McDermott to set up the first goal for Kenny Dalglish. Ray Kennedy and Jimmy Case added the other goals in a truly superb performance. We won with something in hand and I was in my first big final.

The date was 10 May 1978; the venue was Wembley Stadium and our opponents were the Belgian Champions, Bruges, and though it was never a distinguished match it meant a great deal to me. Bruges had one or two key players missing through injury and seemed totally content to hold us, so much so that our manager Bob Paisley was convinced that they were trying to win it on a penalty shoot-out after extra time. Dour Bruges' coach Ernst Happel had come to London with that sort of reputation.

Their packed defence and brilliant Danish goalkeeper Birgir Jensen held us out until I squeezed in a pass for my room-mate Kenny Dalglish to score. I didn't have a bad game and the papers gave me a very good write-up, particularly over the ball which led to the goal. I wouldn't say it was a fluke but there was a small element of luck about it. If I am honest I have to say that I went to block the ball in a tackle, fully expecting to be kicked for my troubles. Fortunately the Bruges' player pulled out and, without a great deal of finesse, I somehow managed to guide it to Kenny who did the rest.

Bruges might have snatched an equalizer when Alan Hansen, in the team that night because our iron man, Tommy Smith, had dropped something on his foot in his garage, made a mistake which let in Sorensen and then Simeon but, with Clemence beaten, Phil Thompson cleared off the line.

The celebrations went on long and hard that night with most of the photographers concentrating on me and my companion, Miss World Mary Stavin. However, the gossipmongers were way off the mark for next morning my companions were – my Mum and Dad. I had jumped into a cab and woken up my parents because I wanted to share that moment with them.

No one had taken much notice when, in the middle of the celebrations, Bob Paisley, already thinking forward to the next season, warned everyone that the biggest danger to Liverpool winning the Cup three times in a row would be Nottingham Forest, the team who were to beat us for the title.

We did not even bother too much when we drew Brian Clough's team in the first round in the defence of our hard-won trophy the next season. After all we had made a magnificent start to the 1979–80 season as we knocked in goals all over the place, including hitting seven against poor old Spurs.

As far as we were concerned it was just a question of how many we were going to score against this team with no experience of the niceties of European football. It was to be one of the biggest lessons I have ever received in European football. The boss, as usual, was right but instead of playing Forest as a European side we played them just as we would have done in a League match and went chasing after goals and a victory. We were on top all right but could not score and then, as our frustration grew, Emlyn Hughes and Phil Thompson were caught square and an unknown carpetlayer named Garry Birtles nipped in between them to score. Even then we could not get it right and I went tearing off down the right flank looking for an equalizer. The move broke down and I was caught hopelessly out of position and could look on only in anguish as their full-back Colin Barrett added the second.

The way we were playing in the League made it probable that we could pull those two goals back at Anfield but Brian Clough's shrewd tactical brain added to the formidable presence of Peter Shilton, Larry Lloyd and Kenny Burns, kept us dangling on the end of a string. That was how it was with Forest in those days. Whatever the competition we seemed to spend 85 minutes in their half only to lose; we couldn't even beat them when Peter Shilton was missing in the League Cup Final, though I wasn't eligible to play and watched from the stands. But that first game at the City Ground was my growing-up game as far as European football was concerned. It taught me when to go and when to hold. Bob Paisley realized this and has since said so but he did not criticize at the time for he knew that I was fully aware of my failings and he expected me to put them right myself.

As for Brian Clough, it was another display of his tactical skills and his ability to make the best use of the limited resources available and we were all delighted when Forest went on to best Malmo in the final with a Trevor Francis goal. It not only meant that the Cup stayed in England but, as League Champions again, it gave us another crack at keeping it here.

We told ourselves how much we had learned from our defeat against Forest but we discovered we were still babes in the wood when we drew the Soviet Union Champions Tblisi in the first round and then prepared ourselves to lay siege on their goal in the first leg at Anfield. But Tblisi turned out to be a good side who were prepared to play football and take us on and their reward was a crucial away goal from Chivadze to offset our two from Doc Johnson and Jimmy Case.

Tblisi is the capital of Georgia in the Soviet Union and to get there you have to go via Moscow, making it the longest, most arduous and unwelcome trip in Europe. It was as if the Soviets were determined to make playing against one of Europe's outstanding teams even harder than it already was for us. To begin with, we were forced to use Aeroflot instead of our usual carriers and I will never forget the smell that greeted us as we boarded the aircraft. I do not know whether it was the disinfectant they used or a deliberate ploy but it will live with me forever – And that is just about how long the flight seemed to take as they routed us via Moscow where they searched every item of our luggage and held us for an unnecessary length of time in a tiny room while they put us through immigration procedures.

Matters did not improve on arrival in the deep south when we were given a poor hotel. We took most of our own food and I did not eat a meal the whole time I was there as I lived on chocolate, biscuits, shortbread and crisps. I even took my own soap and toilet paper; precautions which proved to be worth while. Then the press and officials discovered that the beef was horsemeat, and not very fresh horsemeat at that, and the sarcasm I had taken for carrying my own little stock of food soon turned to pure envy. It was hardly what every good professional carries to a game but under the circumstances, it proved to be a useful survival pack.

The trip out to the Soviet Union had been shattering

and we all went to our uncomfortable beds on the eve of the match very early indeed. Considering public meetings are banned out there, you can imagine how we felt when we were woken in the early hours of the morning by hundreds of people carrying torches and marching round the hotel chanting, 'Dinamo, Dinamo'. It is hard to believe that it was a spontaneous welcome, as the marchers were escorted by police, and when our Chief Executive Peter Robinson rushed downstairs to complain he was told he was not allowed out of the door. Our futile response was to throw a few pieces of fruit out of the window at them.

It was a bleary-eyed team that went down to breakfast next morning to be greeted by the blank, expressionless stares of the Georgians who were looking at us as though we were monkeys in a zoo. These were supposed to be the happy, bouncing Georgians.

There was plenty of atmosphere, however, in the stadium that night. It was packed long before the kick-off despite a day of torrential rain. The pitch was surrounded by young ball boys who, we discovered were there to play a very precise role in the game. While we dug in and held on to our slender lead until half-time these ten- and eleven-year-olds tore around the touchline whipping the ball back into play in seconds. When the Russians were in front they strolled, stopped to chat to each other and even kicked the ball away. How sad, I thought, that children of that age were being taught gamesmanship and how to cheat. What made it even dafter was that Tblisi were undoubtedly the better side and good value for their eventual three-goal victory with Gutsaev, Chivadze, from the penalty spot, and Shengeliya rubbing our noses in the mud.

Our experiences were by no means unique for Kevin Keegan told us that his Hamburg team had suffered similar problems and West Ham were later subjected to the same treatment. UEFA are quick to act when English fans misbehave and they also fine the Europeans when they let off their firecrackers yet, despite the presence of official observers, nothing is done about these blatant contraventions of the spirit of the game. It would soon be stopped if teams were banned. The main problem appears to be the Eastern European teams, certainly in my own experience. When they come over to England we offer them every hospitality but when we go over there they create a hostile environment.

My dislike of the Russians has nothing to do with their politics or the fact that their poor economies mean inferior hotels and food – but is due simply to the fact that they will cheat to win. England manager Bobby Robson said to me on our return from a violent encounter with Dinamo Bucharest in Romania, that we were babies when it came to skulduggery on the European scene and I am sure he is right. We play it fair and square and must be looked on as a soft touch by those teams who wine and dine referees and do everything they can to tip the scales in their favour before a ball is even kicked.

All the time we were in the Soviet Union we were followed around by this so-called interpreter who had a pure American accent and a wardrobe of clothes that would not have been out of place in Stringfellows. He stood by after the game when Jimmy Case, having over-done the drowning of the sorrows, told one or two of the pressmen what he thought of them. A glass or two was broken in the process and Ray Kennedy had to be quite firm before slinging his mate over his shoulder and seeing him off to bed. Perhaps it was a good thing that we lost that one.

However, it was Forest again, not Tblisi, that won the European Cup that year, beating Hamburg in the final in

Madrid. Although they had equalled our achievement in retaining the trophy for the second year it was more stimulating than upsetting and, as Champions again, we were determined to make a real bid to regain the European Cup.

It looked as though we were being a little over-ambitious when, in the first round, we stumbled again, being held to a 1–1 draw by the Finnish part-timers of Oulu. All in all it was a disappointing trip for, to cap it all, I sat up half the night waiting to see the Aurora Borealis lighting up the northern sky. It was, they told us in our Lapland hotel, the perfect night, cold and clear. But nothing, not a flash. The only thing that saved the trip was the sauna and pool at the back of the stand.

We made up for our mistakes in the return leg when we ran up a 10–1 victory with myself scoring a distinctly unmemorable hat-trick and Terry McDermott and David Fairclough scoring two goals each. At last we had cleared the first hurdle and we were on our way.

We were off towards those elusive Northern Lights again in the second round when we were drawn with the Scottish Champions Aberdeen. How the papers, particularly those from north of the Border, loved that one. This was to be the big game for them and Aberdeen were going to knock Liverpool off their perch to claim the prize as British Champions.

The Aberdeen players were quoted at length on how they could match us man-for-man and beat us by their superior teamwork. The whole thing stimulated us tremendously and we were very keyed up for it. The whole of my family watched us play our hearts out and saw Terry McDermott score one of Europe's great goals as he chipped Jim Leighton from a very fine angle. It was one of the best goals I have ever seen. Bob Paisley had seen enough, however, to know that Aberdeen still had a challenge to offer and it was then that the cunning old fox put about the story of Gordon Strachan being worth a couple of million pounds on the transfer market. Gordon took the bait and tried to hold onto the ball all night.

The result was that we took Aberdeen to the cleaners. Willie Miller put through his own goal while Phil Neal, Alan Hansen and Kenny Dalglish added the goals that put us through to the quarter-finals. It must have been a bitter pill for Alex Ferguson and his team to swallow but, to their credit, they digested it and turned the experience to their benefit. We did them a big favour that night and I am sure it played a part in their eventual triumph in the European Cup Winners' Cup and their continued success in domestic competitions.

I managed to write my name into the record books in the quarter-final when I scored three times in a 5–1 victory over CSKA Sofia of Bulgaria at Anfield. I am not noted as one of the world's great goalscorers but I became the first player to score two hat-tricks in one season in the European Cup. The first I took past a defender and slid it around the goalkeeper as he came off his line, while the other two were both hit from outside the penalty area. Sammy Lee and Terry McDermott added the others and, for good measure, David Johnson scored an early goal to give us a victory in the away leg for a 6–1 aggregate passage into the semi-final.

We drew the favourites Bayern Munich in the semi-finals and one of the most frustrating nights of my life was when I was forced to watch the home leg from the bench to which I had been confined because of a back injury. I had been out for three weeks and had been unable to continue in training just the day before we were due to meet West Germany's most famous team. We struggled to break them down and, after hitting the bar, Bayern's loud-mouthed skipper Paul Breitner told the world just how poor English football was, how predictable a side Liverpool were and how the second leg in Munich's Olympic Stadium was nothing more than a formality, a lap of honour for the home fans to celebrate.

The Germans were so convinced that they would be in Paris for the final that they distributed leaflets throughout the stadium telling their fans how to apply for tickets to the final and informing them of the travel arrangements.

That night belonged to Bob Paisley. For the first time, to my knowledge, he adopted a man-for-man marking system, telling little Sammy Lee to stick with Breitner just before we ran out for the game. Sam never gave the Bayern skipper a kick of the ball but we were still in difficulties when Kenny Dalglish limped off injured early in the game. Bob surprised everyone by sending on reserve winger Howard Gayle who proceeded to tear the very heart out of the Bayern defence. They could stop him only by kicking and holding, so much so that Howard began to lose his temper and retaliate, looking in serious danger of an early bath. But Bob could see it coming and substituted the substitute.

The rest of us had run ourselves into the ground and there were more than a few of us suffering as Doc Johnson, limping on the right wing, found Ray Kennedy running with great effort. Razor called on all of the skills that made him Arsenal's top goalscorer before Liverpool transformed him into an international midfield player and he scored what was surely one of his most valuable goals.

Although Karl-Heinz Rummenigge snatched an equalizer near the end the Germans were already a beaten team and we were on our way to Paris. I have rarely derived such pleasure from a victory and I could not resist the impulse to put my head round the Bayern dressing-room door to ask them what had happened to Paris.

They couldn't get us out of the bath that night. We were like kids with a rubber duck singing 'Gay Paris' over and over again and soaking anyone who came in to try and end our childlike fun and games. A couple of us hijacked the bus and its driver to continue the celebrations as the night sank into total oblivion. Somewhere along the way I lost a gold bracelet. I didn't know how and I didn't care.

The stage was set for a classic in the magnificent Parc des Princes Stadium in Paris with Liverpool ready to take on the most successful team in Europe, Spain's legendary Real Madrid. The only concern was over the English supporters and whether there would be rioting as when Leeds lost to Bayern Munich at the same stadium. Real Madrid, it turned out, were worse than the fans. Some of their tackling deserved an X Certificate and in the first few minutes we were knocked out of our stride by the violence of their challenge. I decided that they needed a little of their own medicine to slow them down and to show that we could not be intimidated. It was then that I picked out the nasty Camacho, but as I closed in to give him a little nip, the German Stielike came in on my blindside and left me a limping passenger for the remainder of the game.

I was beginning to wonder whether I would survive extra time when Alan Kennedy collected a throw in from Ray Kennedy, put his head down, went past two scything tackles and almost ripped the net with a shot from an impossible angle. No one has given Alan more stick than me over the years but that night all I wanted to do was hug him. The only problem was that we couldn't catch him.

I was more than ready to join the celebrations at a

Parisian hotel but Phil Neal and I were pulled away for a dope test. As might be expected, neither of us could raise a drop, we were so dehydrated. They poured beer down our throats until we were reeling but not even all the taps running at full flow could induce me to provide more than a trickle. In the end an official, quite against all the rules I am sure, topped it up with a drop of water and we went off in search of a groundsman to let us out of the locked and unlit stadium.

The only transport we could find at that time was a press bus and, would you believe it, they refused to take us any further than the other side of the ground. There we stood trying to flag down a taxi until, totally frustrated, I stepped in front of a police van and flagged them to stop. We were about to be arrested when a French-speaking journalist came to our rescue and explained who we were and what we were doing. We went in style to our reception, blue light flashing, siren wailing and the happy gendarmes passing round our European Champions' medals. It was a satisfactory conclusion to a successful night. I was delighted to have put one over the violent Spaniards who have earned themselves the undisputed title of the dirtiest footballing nation in Europe.

What a pity they cannot do what the Italians did. They recognized that they were on the wrong track, altered their ways and not only won the World Cup but turned their previously stodgy and violent League into one of the best in the world, certainly in terms of quality of players. The Spanish possess a similar natural talent and if it were channelled properly they would be considerably more successful at international and club level.

The omens were good when we drew our old friends Oulu in the first round of the defence of our hard-won Cup. And again, the gallant Finnish part-timers found themselves on the end of a hammering after almost upsetting us at their own little ground. The nearest we got to the Northern Lights were Oulu's floodlights but Kenny Dalglish's goal sent us off to the sauna in a pleasant frame of mind and set us up for a seven-goal victory in the return leg, although this time there were no goals for me.

Liverpool's reputation in Europe had been built on a solid defence but there were signs that times were changing in the next round which pitted us against the Dutch Champions AZ 67 Alkmaar. For an hour we produced some of our best football and fully deserved the two-goal lead given to us by Doc Johnson and Sammy Lee. But then fighting broke out in the crowd and we lost our concentration.

Liverpool supporters, while I was at Anfield, behaved themselves pretty well but there are a group of no-gooders whom Liverpool and the game could do without. They cannot be genuine fans of the team otherwise they would not have caused us so much distraction. The result was that, after being in command, we blundered among our back four and allowed Kist and Tol to pull the game back to even stevens. The same thing almost happened in the second leg in which, though we won 3–2, we gave away silly goals including a farcical own goal which hit the bar, bounced against Phil Thompson and into the net. Phil stood there shaking his head at the crossbar in disbelief.

We were back on familiar territory for the quarter-final when we were paired with CSKA Sofia once more – a team we had beaten a year earlier with five goals to spare. We went off to the second leg in the Levski Stadium with only a Ronnie Whelan goal behind us instead of the 5–1 cushion we took previously. Despite that we played well and should have had the match

wrapped up when Ian Rush scored – only for the unbelievably bad Austrian referee Frans Woehrer to wave
play on as the goalkeeper pulled the ball back out of the
net.

Even so Whelan's goal looked as though it would be
enough until Bruce Grobbelaar, who had replaced Ray
Clemence only that season, came for a cross that he had
no chance of making and left Mladenov a free header
into an empty goal. Worse was to follow as the Austrian
official sent off Mark Lawrenson for an off-the-ball incident in which Mark was more sinned against than sinning.
We were left to play extra time with ten men and against
increasingly violent tackling which had Terry McDermott
nursing an injury in the dressing room already. It was
never meant to be our night and we hit the woodwork
three times in all and, in the end, conceding another
sloppy goal to Mladenov we were out. We were all sick
at going out like that and no one more so than Bruce
Grobbelaar. But he had been plunged into the team
when Ray Clemence left and no one blamed him for the
defeat after the game. The only consolation was that
Aston Villa beat Bayern Munich to keep the Cup in
England yet again and we set about making sure we
would be around to challenge it once more the next
season.

We were, and a 4–1 away victory against the Irishmen
of Dundalk gave us a flying start. Everyone expects you
to win these games by a distance but, like international
football, the European scene has changed and there are
no longer many naïve or poor sides against whom to
score in double figures. These are the sort of games in
which you can ruin your whole season and the value of
that away win was shown when we could only add a goal
from Ronnie Whelan to our winning margin in the return
leg at Anfield.

The point was proved again in the next round when the unfancied HJK Helsinki beat us by a single goal over there and although we put five past them in the return, the writing was on the wall. We found ourselves again behind the Iron Curtain, this time travelling to Poland to face the dangerous Widzew Lodz and, sure enough, we lost 2–0 with Bruce again having a nightmare and taking the blame for both. His problem then was purely one of concentration and experience and it says a lot of him that he survived two disasters like that to come back so brilliantly.

We still felt we had a great chance of pulling it out of the fire at Anfield and, indeed, when Phil Neal scored from the penalty spot we had them against the ropes and were on our way. All we had to do was keep pushing them onto their heels until the goal came but, instead, they restored their two-goal margin and it was all down to me. I won a ball in the midfield and as I went past a player I was fouled. Instead of claiming the free kick I stayed on my feet because I had seen Phil Neal breaking down the right. But by the time I had recovered my balance there was a defender between him and me and as I looked for an alternative, I slipped, lost possession and Bruce was forced to bring down the man who robbed me for Tlokinski to score from the penalty spot. We had to abandon ourselves to total attack after that with four goals now the minimum requirement and although we scored through Rush and Hodgson, they took advantage of our stretched defence for Smolarek to give them a 4–3 overall advantage.

Bruce might have been to blame in Poland but I felt the burden of responsibility for our eventual defeat and it left a sour taste that only winning the League to qualify again for the competition could sweeten. We did, maintaining my record of having played in the competition every season I had been with Liverpool. I loved it and, after all, it was one of the main reasons I had yearned to move to the best team in Europe. I enjoyed the big stage, the pace of the game and the challenge of playing against unknown players and fresh tactics. Europe is not only rewarding financially but also culturally and that is why playing abroad, particularly in Italy, gradually became a fixation.

I was not disappointed. The quality of the football was as good as the quality of life and I enjoyed a marvellous first season as my new club Sampdoria enjoyed their best-ever season by winning the Italian Cup and finishing fourth. Had they done things right we could have built on that and maybe won the League the next season, but football rarely works out the way you expect.

10
The Treble

One moment of blind anger almost cost me the greatest climax to a season any professional footballer could wish for. I could so easily have been sent off and suspended for the game against Roma which brought Liverpool the European Cup and a glorious treble. Had the Swiss referee seen me he would have had little choice but to send me off for I threw a short right hook which broke the jaw of Romanian international Lica Movila in two places during one of the most violent ties I have ever played in.

Without question, the Romanian Champions Dinamo Bucharest were the nastiest, most physical team I have played against and their European campaign was littered with yellow cards and suspensions. In the first leg at Anfield, Movila was the worst of the lot. He was a disgrace. He kicked everything that moved and three times caught me with punches off the ball. I went completely crazy when he came in late and high yet again and as he half turned I let loose with the best punch I have delivered in my life.

I must admit that I felt nothing at all for him as he was helped off but later, when I was confronted by a leather-coated Romanian at the entrance to the tunnel and was told the extent of the injuries I was full of remorse. Even if it was understandable to retaliate, it was unprofessional in the circumstances and foolish. I meant the man no real harm other than to warn him he had picked the wrong person to intimidate.

Much of the blame must be levelled at the Swiss referee

Daina and his linesmen for not curbing a notoriously dirty team. He allowed them to get away with far too much and had the rest of our team not been so controlled it could have ended in a bloodbath.

The odd thing was that we had played the Romanian Champions in a pre-season tournament and had been impressed with their football abilities and particularly by Movila who was their best player. Now here he was playing the other game, leaving his foot there, going in late, throwing punches and spitting at people. You can stand only so much of that.

It did not help that Dinamo, who had put out reigning Champions Hamburg and the difficult Soviet side Minsk, sat back and defended really well in the first leg. As in all of our home European games during that triumphant season we were desperately aware of the importance of not conceding a home goal, believing that we were always capable of scoring goals in away games – which proved to be so. In the end we had to settle for a rare Sammy Lee goal, made even more extraordinary by the fact that the little man headed it past goalkeeper Dimitri Moraru.

After I had thrown that punch I got out of the referee's way as quickly as I could and I am sure that there was only one other player on the pitch who saw exactly what happened apart from the victim – even the television cameras missed it. However, Movila could have left the bench in no doubt as to the perpetrator of the crime for within seconds the substitute came on, pointed a finger at me, muttered 'Bucharest' and then tackled me waist high. I denied all knowledge of the incident after the game because it would have only stirred up an already heated situation. But the Romanians made it clear that, if they had anything to do with it, I would be returning on a stretcher a fortnight later.

Sure enough, when we arrived in Bucharest for the

return leg, a group of four raincoated policemen pushed their way through the crowd towards me. They repeated my name over and over again, pointed at my chest, mentioned Movila's name and signalled that death would be a light escape for me. Even when I was on the bus another policeman, after consulting a team picture, knocked on the window and indicated that I would have my eyes gouged out. I was amazed to see this coming from a uniformed official and invited him to repeat the gesture in front of a few of the lads so that they could see I was not making the whole thing up. He did.

I scarcely set foot outside our hotel, not because I was afraid of the crowd of Dinamo fans outside, but because I had left an unseasonally sunny England wearing summer clothes and was not going to ruin them in the torrential rain. But as I walked out into the packed stadium I was greeted by a chorus of booing which became louder every time I touched the ball in the warm-up. The lads soon realized what was happening and every time I knocked off the ball it would come straight back to me. I thought I would give the fans some value for their money and did a bit of juggling. That really made them hysterical and when the next pass came towards me the jeering was building to a deafening crescendo until I lifted my foot and cut them off in mid-boo. It was the best dummy I had ever thrown in my career.

What the Dinamo supporters did not realize was that it served only to give both the team and me a terrific lift, as did Dinamo's tactics in the opening minutes when Ion Andone, who had been without question their best player in the first leg, dropped off and sent me somersaulting twice in the opening minutes. As Andone had almost put us out in the first leg when he broke clear and hit the post, the decision to have him kicking lumps out of me took away the pressure from our defence. It was lessened even further after ten minutes when a weak clearance from a Sammy Lee corner dropped sweetly for me to volley a pass into the path of Ian Rush who skipped past his marker in sensational fashion and then surprised even us with a fabulous chipped shot.

It was just the start we needed in this hostile environment especially as we thought that West German referee Pauly would give us the protection we had missed in the first leg. How wrong we were. Dinamo were even rougher in the second leg than they were at Anfield and over the top tackles were the order of the day.

Yet when I committed my first foul the referee ran up, spoke to me by name and told me that the next one would be a red card. I would have laughed if it had not been quite so serious as the thought struck me how ironic it would be to be sent off and miss the final for something comparatively petty after what I had done in the first leg. Some would call it justice.

I am sure that if the game had been three or four years earlier, I would not have held out but I had learned self control and knew that the referee had had his card marked. I held my breath when I accidentally handled the ball in the second half but survived. The only other problem was whether I would last the match in one piece. The tackles became progressively worse, going from shin to knee to thigh and if ever there was proof of the value of shin pads it was in that game. My socks were in shreds and one pad, made of sturdy stuff, was split from top to bottom.

Costel Orac pulled back our early goal just before half-time with a highly doubtful free kick awarded against Mark Lawrenson. But Dinamo gradually ran out of steam and Ian Rush sealed their fate with another unruffled goal as his marker failed to clear the ball. That was it. With the Milk Cup already in the bag and the League

Championship coming our way, we were in another European Cup Final and had a chance of doing what all the critics said was an impossibility – winning three major trophies in one season – something not even the legendary Real Madrid had achieved.

We had set our sights on the final early in the season but when we set off for Denmark and our first round match against OB in the quaint Hans Christian Andersen city of Odense, we did not realize just how difficult we were going to make it for ourselves. We certainly did not underestimate the Danish Champions as their National team was then on the point of putting out England and qualifying for the finals of the European Championships for the first time in their history.

Years ago this team of willing part-timers would have been treated with something close to contempt but we were happy to pot an away goal through Kenny Dalglish and then give ourselves a nice little boost by scoring five times in the second leg. This was not so much due to the margin as to the fact that Michael Robinson matched Kenny Dalglish by scoring two of the goals. It was a great relief to this willing player who, though lacking the finer skills of Kenny and the world-class stature of Ian Rush, was doing a great job for his illustrious team-mates. He was the willing workhorse for the two of them and, despite finishing as our second top scorer that season, he took a lot of unfair criticism not only from the media but also from the fans.

The real rough ride, however, began in the second round when we drew the Spanish Champions Bilbao. To all intents and purposes we were on our way out when the team of Basques played so well at Anfield and shut us out completely. It was such a polished performance that, as we agreed afterwards in the dressing room, we would have been proud of it ourselves.

But it was then that the confidence which was eventually to bring us the cup began to blossom for we, to a man, thought that we could catch Bilbao on their own ground when they opened up and came out at us. We got it exactly right and produced a superb team performance with Ian Rush scoring the only goal of the game with a downward header. It was at a time when most people, myself included, thought that Rush's head was just for nodding and shaking to questions from the press, but that goal sparked off a spell of superbly-headed goals that eventually ran into double figures and earned Rushy the temporary nickname of 'Tosh' after John Toshack.

It was a night when everything went right, particularly for me as I performed as well as I had anywhere. The moment we looked at the pitch, the good weather and took in the tense atmosphere we fancied our chances. That feeling increased when we discovered that they had soaked the ground before the kick off; it was so wet that I wouldn't risk spoiling my Gucci shoes by walking on it, though I couldn't wait to get my boots on and ping the ball about on its surface.

I remember saying to Roy Evans before the game that I thought if we won this one we would go all the way. We knew it would be tough but we went out determined to quieten the crowd by knocking the ball about, giving Bilbao nothing and not being antagonistic by conceding silly fouls. We did it in record time and gradually brought the fans round to our side. That was a real bonus for us and so was the fact that Bilbao were so gentlemanly and very unSpanish in their approach. It is my belief that we were helped by the cloud hanging over their heads after a violent match with Barcelona when Maradona was put out of football for three months after a clash with Goicoechea, the Beast of Bilbao. He was like a lamb with us and, indeed, played very well in that first game.

The most memorable moment, apart from Ian's goal, came after the game when we sat on the coach waiting for our usual night dash to the airport. There must have been a thousand Basque supporters gathered outside the ground. They clapped us onto the bus and then passed around their leather drinking bottles in a magnificent gesture of friendship. I recall turning to Phil Neal and saying, 'What do you have to do to get highs like this when you finish playing football?'

A few critics suggested that Bilbao were not such a good side as people imagined, thus devaluing our performance. But I noted, with some satisfaction, that they went on to complete the Spanish Cup and League double in the same season. There were a few more highs still to come in that memorable season and if there were any doubts that this was the year of the away match for Liverpool FC in Europe, they were dispelled in the quarter-finals against the Eagles of Lisbon, Benfica.

Once more we failed to produce a conclusive and convincing performance in front of our own supporters at Anfield. The atmosphere was again lacking and all we had to show for our efforts was yet another Ian Rush goal 66 minutes into the game. But the most important thing was that Bruce Grobbelaar had once more kept a clean sheet. Benfica had a prolific record for scoring goals at their magnificent Stadium of Light and, judging by their reaction at the end of the game at Anfield, they thought they had done enough to reach the last four. Certainly they had our respect but we also knew that the Portuguese League was hardly the strongest in Europe and, while they were proficient at defending, we doubted their ability to do so when forced to go forward.

It was a game I could easily have missed. I was stunned by the death of my mother back home in Edinburgh and I was not even sure whether or not I was going to make

Lisbon in time and when I did I had to go straight to bed with what felt like the flu. I was hot and cold alternately and sweating profusely but a friend told me it was probably a physical reaction to the emotional shock I had just suffered and, sure enough, I was fit to train next morning and to play in the evening.

In contrast to the Basques of Bilbao, Benfica supporters were not a nice lot. When we had played them previously we had been turned away from the local ground in Estoril and though they allowed us to train this time our coach was hemmed in by cars and we couldn't get out for some time. No one seemed to own them and I wondered whether it was a deliberate attempt to disrupt us a few hours before the game. That opinion hardened when we arrived at the Stadium later in the evening. As was our custom we went out early to get used to the pitch and, on this occasion, to the atmosphere and the abuse that we knew would come our way. It did, and in spectacular fashion, not just whistles and jeers but oranges and coins. It was our policy not to add to the antagonism but, just as I couldn't resist a little showmanship before the semi-final in Bucharest, neither could Bruce Grobbelaar in Lisbon when he picked up the oranges and threw them back.

The atmosphere was unpleasant and our fans were attacked without provocation. Those 70,000 passionate, totally-biased Benfica fans were silenced in just nine minutes when Ronnie Whelan got our habitual away goal. Craig Johnston scored an absolute cracker before the experienced Nene pulled one back. It gave the Portuguese a glimmer of hope only for we threatened to score with every attack and eventually finished up 5–1 aggregate winners with further goals from Rush and Whelan. Not only were the fans quietened but the famous Stadium of Light darkened considerably as one of the lights flickered and failed towards the end of the game. It was almost as if the groundsman had had enough and wanted to get off home as soon as he could.

We got back to Estoril as quickly as we could with a small group of us heading into the old fishing port of Cascais for a celebration with local lobster and vinho verde. The head waiter, who had kept the restaurant open specially for us, showed us a tangled mess of plastic and wires, explaining that it was the shattered radio of the distraught chef who had hurled his prized possession against the kitchen wall at just about the time that Craig Johnston had scored our second. He didn't come out to see if we enjoyed the meal but neither did he poison us.

The trip back from Lisbon was surpassed only by our return from the semi-finals in Bucharest when we knew we had made it into the final, Liverpool's fourth and my third.

The build-up to the final was tense to say the least as speculation grew about my possible transfer abroad, until it was generally agreed that the European Cup Final would be my last serious game for Liverpool – unless I played badly in Rome. In truth, the possibility of a move to Italy, Germany, Spain or even London was little more than gossip apart from a genuine approach by Chelsea and the first tentative tickle from Sampdoria via the Leeds lawyer who had dealt so well with the transfers of the likes of Liam Brady, Joe Jordan and Trevor Francis.

I was determined to put it all out of my mind and to concentrate on the job in hand, though nagging at the back of my mind was the knowledge that I would be putting myself on show to all the potential buyers against the successful Brazilian combination of Roberto Falcao and Toninho Cerezo. In direct contrast to our frenetic arrival at Rome's international airport there was no big farewell at Speke's Liverpool airport from the fans, they left it to the photographers and television crews. For the first time the wives were on our outward flight but they had to sit at the back of the aircraft while we occupied our usual three rows at the front and, of course, they had separate rooms for that first night.

We were met off the aircraft in Rome by a phalanx of police buses because the coach drivers were on strike and, while the baggage was being unloaded, we were taken to a press conference in the main terminal where we were herded into pens like cattle. We were told we would be required for half an hour but within a couple of minutes Ronnie Moran had us back on our bus. Not that it did us much good for it just meant that the cases came off the plane slower than ever while we sat and stewed. We expected some disturbance on the eve of the final against the local side on their own ground and we were surprised when our escort whipped us through to the hotel in double quick time.

Once inside the hotel our floor was guarded by armed police and a 'minder' brought specially from England. But Kenny Dalglish and I thought that the elaborate plans had backfired when we were woken from our slumbers just before midnight on this night before the final by a television blaring out next door. We banged on the wall; we telephoned the offending room and even went outside to hammer on the door. All to no avail and, in the end, we were forced to call Roy Evans. He tried with no success and he had just decided to batter the door down when the television was abruptly turned off. 'If it happens again,' said Roy, 'call me and we will sort them out.'

As I went out of my room next morning to go down to breakfast, the next door opened at the same time and the identity of the man who had woken two of the European Cup Final side was revealed. It was our own manager Joe

Fagan! 'Didn't you hear the telephone ringing?' I asked him.

'Yes,' replied the boss, 'but I thought it would be another Italian journalist looking for an interview so I ignored it.'

'Did you hear someone at the door?' I persisted. 'Of course,' he responded, 'but I wasn't expecting anyone and I was ready for bed.' With more than a hint of desperation creeping in, I asked: 'Didn't you hear Kenny and I banging on the wall?' 'No,' said Joe shaking his head thoughtfully, 'probably because I had the television on rather loud.'

Throughout the preparation we were remarkably relaxed, leaving the worrying to AC Roma who were being put under enormous pressure from their own fans and the media to beat us and win the European Cup for the first time. They had been feeling the strain for three weeks while we had prepared by going to Israel to play their national side and getting quietly drunk. We did well at both, beating the Israel national side 4–1 and drinking enough to put us thoroughly at ease.

It stood us in good stead for, despite the proliferation of guards, the hotel was besieged by a variety of people including some Swedish friends of mine. I was delighted to see them and when we realized that it would be a Swedish referee, they suggested a few simple phrases to help butter him up. Unfortunately we had no paper at the time, so I scribbled them down on a twenty pound note which I then gave to my wife Danny to spend in the Via Veneto! Not that any Swedish words were needed for referee Erik Frederiksson spoke better English than my room-mate Kenny Dalglish.

I accept the premise that it is wrong for a European Cup finalist to play the final on their own ground but I will say it created a phenomenal atmosphere. I soaked it all up when a handful of us went out to warm-up but that was nothing compared with the explosion of noise and colour as we ran out for the game. Just before we left the dressing room I did my captain's bit and turned to the team and said: 'Come on lads, let's buzz.' I should have known better for, within seconds, it sounded like a hive of honeybees as we all went buzzzzzz – literally. The boss had been equally low key in his pre-match speech. Joe pulled out a piece of paper with Roma's team list written on it and ripped it up. 'If we play,' he said, 'there is nothing in this for them.' He was as calm and unworried as we all were even though he stood on the threshold of winning his third trophy in his first season as manager of Liverpool.

We all knew the stage suited us. The Olympic Stadium was a perfect setting with a great surface and we were quite happy to let others tell us that the odds were stacked against us and that we were the underdogs. I also knew that, sitting up in the stands, were the people who were going to help me decide my immediate future and, Brazilians or not, I was going to show them all that Graeme Souness had come a long way from his prefab in Edinburgh.

Those who feared that it would be a bruising, physical affair were proved wrong. There were just the usual incidents with Cerezo almost castrating me with a tackle that ripped into my groin. It was a good thing that he was wearing rubber-soled boots or I would have been out of the final then and there. I quietly mentioned to him that I owed him one which I duly returned. I also nipped his countryman Falcao a little but he retaliated with a late tackle on Ronnie Whelan rather than me.

I noticed, however, that Cerezo changed his rubbers for studded boots at half-time and I made a mental note to watch him. But the only kick I received was a sly one from Bonetti who got in his twopennyworth after a bit of pushing and shoving which involved Whelan who had got his own back on Falcao. We looked to be on our way when a dreadful mix-up by the home side gave Phil Neal the chance to score in his fourth European final but Roma came back well and deserved their equalizer from Roberto Pruzzo just before half-time. But that effort took a great deal out of them and after a flurry at the start of the second half I always fancied we would beat them – though not quite in the way we did.

At the end of extra time, we all went round congratulating each other but secretly believing that we were going to lose the penalty shoot-out. Liverpool are notoriously bad penalty takers and, just a few days before, we had carefully rehearsed the possibility of a shoot-out against our youth players. Although Alan Kennedy and Steve Nicol scored, Dalglish, Neal and Souness missed and the kids beat us 5–2.

When Steve Nicol missed the first penalty, after insisting he should bear the responsibility, it seemed our innermost fears were being realized but the drama was only just beginning. I complained to the officials that the photographers behind the goal were using flashlights while we were taking penalties but not when a Roma player stepped up. Roma, however, moaned that our extrovert goalkeeper, Bruce Grobbelaar, was waggling his backside, pulling faces and moving up and down his line.

Fortunately none of us was aware of the penalty-saving reputation of Franco Tancredi, who had stopped half of the last 16 spot kicks taken against him, and we thought that the agile Bruce might put us back with a chance. As it was, the experienced Bruno Conti blazed one over the bar. I had lost the toss for penalties and it meant that we were kicking right into the teeth of the Roma fans but I did not even notice them as I concentrated on striking my penalty as firmly and cleanly as I could. Phil Neal and Ian Rush also scored but Francesco Graziani hit Roma's fourth against the top of the crossbar and suddenly it was left to Alan Kennedy to take the penalty that could give us the treble. There were a few of the team who didn't fancy Alan's chances but the man who had won us the Cup with his goal against Real Madrid in Paris did it again and we went wild.

I went berserk. For the first time I wept tears of joy and I was alternately laughing and crying along with a few other senior professionals and we launched into our famous victory celebration song as we lined up for a team picture. The words are too dirty to repeat but they seemed to delight the Italian photographers who kicked each other while fighting over the best spot to take their pictures.

The only moment that spoiled our celebrations was when a line of policemen refused to let us show the cup to our supporters who, despite being outnumbered by more than five to one had shouted and cheered as loudly and for as long as I have ever heard them. They were magnificent that night and for their efforts they were attacked after the game by a certain bitter section of the Roma fans who had raised their hopes too high.

Remembering our experiences in Madrid, we waited for Kenny Dalglish and Sammy Lee to complete the formalities of their drug tests, before we headed off for the magnificent Villa Miani on top of one of Rome's seven hills for a party laid on by the club's sponsors Crown Paints. It turned into the biggest sing-song of all time with each and every player joining in. It was 5 A.M. when we danced our way back into the hotel to be greeted by a crowd of our supporters who had waited up all night for our return. But, despite the champagne and singing, I couldn't help reflecting on how differently it could have turned out had the penalty shoot-out gone against us. That is no way to end a game of football. It was heartbreaking. I appreciate that the problem of policing fans in a foreign city rules out a replay nowadays but a result should be decided by two teams playing football.

It was an emotional return to Liverpool with more than 300,000 lining the route from Speke Airport to the Town Hall. Two little ten-year-old scallywags will never forget it either. They talked their way on to the open bus which was to carry us on our tour and when I asked them who they were with, they pointed in the general direction of the photographers. But none of them had ever clapped eyes on the kids before and they prepared themselves to be thrown off. Instead I shook their hands and let them join in. They deserved it for their cheek and, moreover, they reminded me of myself at their age.

People in Liverpool talk about the first time the team went to Rome and won the European Cup, saying it could never be repeated. I wasn't there but I cannot believe that it could compare with our entire campaign consisting of a string of brilliant away performances against all odds; the dramatic penalty finish and the boss winning three trophies in his first season as manager.

Three trophies! At the start of the season, I thought we would be struggling to win one. I felt that we were not as strong as either we had been or we should be. I foresaw that we would give too much away to win the biggest and most important prize of them all, the Football League Championship. There were times during the season when I was convinced that my early judgement was correct for we gave away some ludicrous points.

We began by drawing with newly-promoted but soon to be relegated Wolves. We even contrived to lose to them at home as we did to Sunderland but the worst and, eventually, the most significant result was our four-goal defeat at Coventry on 10 December. To be fair it shouldn't have been so heavy but we deserved to be beaten. The loss came after a run of 15 games without defeat and we were becoming a little complacent. We needed to be brought to our senses and that result was just the trick. The critics slammed us and hailed Coventry City as the team to watch as Bobby Gould's reshaped squad clawed their way towards the top. The rest is history. We went on to win the League while Coventry struggled to avoid relegation.

Right from the start of the season, the Charity Shield in fact, we knew that Manchester United's expensive squad would be our biggest threat. And so it seemed when they beat us by a single goal at Old Trafford and then snatched a draw at Anfield with a late goal after we had camped out in their half for 85 minutes of the game. That was a memorable day for me but even more so for Kenny Dalglish. It was the first game of 1984 and I was sickened by the injury to Kenny which was to keep him out and affect his form for the rest of the season. Maybe it was that which fuelled my anger as, after the game, and for the first time as captain, I had words with the manager Joe Fagan. They were rather loud words as well as I rather forcibly put over my opinion that Liverpool had gone soft. If we had beaten Manchester United that day I am sure we would have put them out of contention then and there but, having been continuously at the top, we were not professional enough to finish them off.

I actually told Joe Fagan, Ronnie Moran and Roy Evans that I thought Manchester United would win the League and that we would get absolutely nothing. They disagreed and, as events turned out, they were right and I was wrong. After all you can hardly argue with three trophies. They put it down to luck but, at one stage, I

could have been proved horribly right. I was in Southampton and we needed to win to get back above United.

It was on the eve of the Friday night live televised
game that I received the shattering news that my mother
Elizabeth had passed away in Scotland. She had been
very poorly for some time but it still came as a terrible
shock and there was no question of me playing against
the Saints. The club urged me to catch a flight home from
Heathrow which I did. We went on to lose the game with
two goals from Danny Wallace and United were suddenly
faced with the prospect of opening up a five-point gap if
they could win at Nottingham Forest the next day. As
Ron Atkinson said at the time United could not be caught
if they won all of their remaining games.

Fate was on our side that day, however, as unbeknown
to me in Edinburgh with my mind occupied on sadder
events, and to the players back in Liverpool it had been
raining heavily in Nottingham and the game was called
off. The long and the short of it was that United picked
up ten points only from those remaining ten games and
every time we slipped they slipped too. There was even
talk of Nottingham Forest or Southampton pipping us
both to the crown but I knew the day we lost at Stoke
and United lost at Notts County that the title would be
ours.

In the end winning is all down to attitude. Those games
we lost were down to us, the players, and not the
management. In fact, the blame must be shouldered by
the senior players because, with all due respect, no side
that fancies its chances to win League titles should drop
home points to Wolves and Sunderland. Manchester
United blamed the loss of their influential captain Bryan
Robson for their collapse but, when you are chasing titles
over a season as long as ours, those are the sort of set-
backs you have to take in your stride just as we did over
the loss of the skills of Dalglish.

For me Manchester United's bid for the title was undermined by other factors, such as the talk of a takeover by Robert Maxwell which dragged on for weeks and, even worse, speculation over the possible transfers of Bryan Robson and Ray Wilkins to Italy. They are all distractions you do not need when your sights are set firmly on a big one like the League title.

Our advantage was that we had won it before and while United were looking ten games ahead, we were divorcing each one from the next. Taking it game by game may be an old cliché but it is a truism as far as I am concerned. Our only distraction was a piece of nonsense from Craig Johnson who tried to twist the boss's arm by saying he wanted to move if he couldn't be guaranteed a first-team place. Now, I like Craig but he is a bit scatter-brained and outbursts like that helped no one, least of all himself. My only fear was that Joe Fagan was too nice to cope with it. I should have known better because he used Craig far more than Craig ever used him.

Joe, incidentally, was very good to me after we had clinched the League title for him with a fairly stagnant goalless draw at Notts County, when he said that I was his Man of the Season. Joe was being kind for he, more than anyone, knows that this is a team game and all of the cogs have to mesh together precisely.

There are, however, key players and they are not always the ones the fans salute. Take Ronnie Whelan for example. While players like Craig are whizzing around and covering every inch of the ground, Ronnie watches and thinks, makes runs and when in possession uses the ball to its most telling effect. There was no talk of transfers or dissent when Ronnie was fighting his way back into the side that season after injury. He just got on with the game until he became a regular part of the team again. During one game in which he was being barracked by the Kemlin Road End, I turned to him and said that players like us would always get abuse thrown at them because of our style. He uses his head as well as he does the ball and in my opinion he is a great player and likely to become even better. He could become a very famous footballer indeed.

It is ironic that the player he eventually replaced midway through the season was Steve Nicol. I was delighted when Steve got his chance to come on and win himself a European Cup medal for replacing Craig Johnston, even if he did miss that penalty. This lad can play anywhere in the midfield or the back four. He can defend, he can tackle, he can head the ball, he can take players on and he can score goals and not only would it not surprise me if he eventually finished up in my old position for Liverpool but also I see him as a natural captain, lifting up the trophies for them as well. He is two footed and, talking of his feet, they are size twelve and make their presence felt. His only problem is that he is so honest and nice that he is too easily wound up – and that can be fatal at Anfield.

Steve let himself in for a ribbing right from the start when he turned up for an away match at the team hotel with a teddy bear on top of his bag which read something like, 'I am Sad Sam, will you cuddle me and love me and make me happy.' The Jocks were particularly unmerciful, telling him they had taken seven years to install the Tartan Mafia and here he was undermining it all in a matter of minutes because he was too nice. The worst trick we pulled on him was on one of Liverpool's money-making trips to Israel when Alan Hansen, a great practical joker, revealed that Kenny Dalglish was suffering from a terminal disease and did not have long to live. All the necessary people were instantly wired in and wherever the unfortunate Nicol checked he received confirmation.

In the end he approached Kenny himself and he was almost in tears as Kenny confirmed it, asking if Steve hadn't noticed the change in him, the loss of weight and everything else. What made it really funny and caused us to give the game away was when Kenny asked Steve if he hadn't recognized Kenny's poor form of late.

To his credit he took it well as he did the disappointment and horror of missing that penalty in Rome. A lesser person might have broken down, upsetting the players who still had their moment of pressure to come. He was obviously feeling dreadful but he kept it to himself. That is the sort of stuff of which captains are made.

Other key players in our success were Ian Rush and his 49 goals, the improved goalkeeping of Bruce Grobbelaar and the brilliance of Jocky Hansen. What a good player that man is. One of the best central defenders there has ever been. One of the many reasons why Liverpool seem able to maintain the momentum is knowing when to sign new players and when to get rid of the old ones. The signing of my fellow Scottish international John Wark and, later, Paul Walsh, was nothing short of brilliant. I would go as far as to say that the arrival of John from Ipswich gave us that final push, the impetus to win the League, not just from his presence on the field but off it as well. It made competition for places just that bit keener. He is, of course, one of the best midfield goalscorers, able to time late runs to perfection.

The joke when Paul Walsh arrived from Luton Town after months of speculation, was that he must be able to play because he came with a trail of adverse publicity in his wake. That is nothing new for Liverpool when you look at the stories surrounding players like myself, Alan Hansen and Terry McDermott. It is what you do for the club that counts and it is my guess that Walsh, with his tight control and quicksilver turns, is going to be a very good player indeed for both Liverpool and England. He makes me wish I was five years younger. In fact, when I looked at the team and their ages after the treble, I began to wonder when it was all going to end for that side could be together for a long time. Perhaps they won't win three in a season again but they will certainly continue to pick up trophies for a club who consider they have had a bad season if they win only a couple of pots.

There was a time when Liverpool and a few other clubs did not even bother to enter the League Cup because it was seen as a further complication in an already congested season. But then it became an early entry for Europe and a very nice moneyspinner in hard times. Having claimed the old League Cup we set about winning the Milk Cup for the third time and making that our own too. We did but there were times when it looked as though it would take us all season to do it.

Our bid for the Milk Cup began on an October evening in Brentford and ended 13 games later when we beat our local rivals Everton in a replay at Maine Road at the end of March. By then we had played 21 hours of football and had been watched by more than 400,000 people who had paid somewhere in the region of a million and a half pounds for the privilege.

We opened our account with a 4–1 win over Brentford in the first leg of the second round, but it was not as easy as the score implies. They were an aggressive, busy side who were determined to make life as difficult as possible for us in front of the all-seeing eyes of the television cameras. Even after Ian Rush scored the first of his two goals, Brentford popped back with an equalizer less than a minute later through Roberts. And it was with some relief that we settled back to our usual feast of fish and chips on the coach after the game, having scored further

goals through Rush, again, Michael Robinson and myself
to give us a cushion for the return. Not that the club can
have been too overjoyed for it meant that a crowd of less
than 10,000 turned up for the second leg when I scored
from a first-half penalty with Hodgson, Dalglish and
Robinson giving us an 8–1 aggregate win. It should also
have meant the end of the two-legged games until the
semi-final.

Some hope. It was just the beginning of our marathon
trail back to Wembley. We had to play Fulham three
times before we scraped through the next round and, to
be honest, we would have had no cause for complaint if
we had lost to the London club. All three were difficult
games and a great credit to Fulham and their then
manager Malcolm MacDonald. I, for one, didn't believe
him when he said that they would knock the ball about
and play football. They did and, what is more, matched
us completely. It was against the run of play when Rush
scored and Fulham were full value when Lock scored
from the spot a minute later.

They did it to us again at Anfield, scoring from the
penalty spot after we had taken the lead through Dalglish.
They won the toss to stage the second replay and that
was decided only after extra time when I scored in the
114th minute, the ball bouncing in off my shin and
scarcely reaching the back of the net. My estimation of
MacDonald had risen by several points during those three
weeks and we were more than pleased to see the back of
his team.

I followed up my goals against Brentford and Fulham
with another in the next round against Birmingham City
at St Andrews. We murdered them in that first half and
were looking forward to a comfortable win especially as
the date of any possible replay had been set for 22
December, the night of the players' Christmas party and

the highlight of our season. But Harford scored a quarter of an hour from the end and we finished up cursing our folly. We were in party mood for the replay and although only a handful of people turned up at Anfield we won 3–0 and I was completely taken in. We were awarded a penalty towards the end and as I went to take it Ronnie Whelan came up and said that it would be a good idea to let Ian Rush have it to complete his hat-trick. I was all for that and called Rushy over. It was only when he scored and we were running back to the middle that I realized that Steve Nicol had scored the first and the lads, to their obvious glee, had tricked me out of my penalty.

The management are not supposed to know about our party but it must have been obvious to everyone what was going on as we fled out of the ground in double quick time and dived into the team bus which was to take us to Tommy Smith's club. Within minutes the Liverpool team had been transformed into a motley bunch of Roman Emperors, American footballers, schoolboys and drag artists. We even had Michael Robinson looking the spitting image of Rod Stewart. God knows what people thought as we drove through the streets of Liverpool with clothes flying everywhere. Our win against Birmingham gave the party an extra bit of spice even though it meant we had lost a few hours' drinking time. The evening went off perfectly, including the traditional cabaret given by the new signings with the most expensive topping the bill.

There was no party spirit in the fifth round when we drew Second Division promotion chasers Sheffield Wednesday away from home. The only similarity was the headaches we had next morning after heading away so many aerial balls. I reckon they must have practised appealing for offside for, as the back four pushed up, the whole team would be waving their arms and looking at the linesmen. It was not good to play in and I know, from the spectators I spoke to, that it was not good to watch. It is not my idea of football but it won them a 2–1 lead and, again, we faced a replay when Phil Neal scored from the penalty spot. I suppose their argument would be that their tactics were successful though I was pleased to see the superior footballing side, Chelsea, win the Second Division Championship.

In the replay I got a finger in my eye in the opening minutes and ran round for most of the first half wondering which ball to head. To give Wednesday their due, they played better football on our quality surface at Anfield although we were also in much improved form and won with a brace from Ian Rush and a single from Michael Robinson.

I was injured and missed the first leg of the semi-final against the surprise package from the Third Division, Walsall. It was as frustrating to watch as it was to play with the West Midland side battling away and twice cancelling out the lead given to us by Ronnie Whelan. The second Walsall goal was scored by Summerfield after a mistake by Alan 'Jocky' Hansen. I remember that well for television pundit, Barry Davies, criticized him on the highlights which were shown later that night and I thought how unjustified it was to infer that Jocky was always making errors like that. He is the best defender around by a mile and is rarely pushed as far as he can go.

Walsall obviously thought they had it made but we knew that two mistakes had brought them their two goals and that, for all their commendable huffing and puffing, they had done little else to threaten us. Our biggest problem in the second leg was when Ronnie Whelan scored our second goal and a wall containing our own supporters collapsed. I realized what was going to happen and I was already on my way when the fans came tumbling down the terraces. It could have been a major disaster had the terraces been high ones but fortunately this was at the old Laundry End and only a few steps high. I shouted to those at the back to ease the pressure because they did not know what had happened. I received a lot of publicity for carrying a little boy to safety but all I did was take him off someone else who had lifted him out and was staggering under the weight.

The funny thing was that earlier I had been booked for a rather harmless body check and was being booed every time I touched the ball. The crowd finished up cheering me off when the players went into the dressing room on a bitterly cold night while order was restored behind the goal. We suffered somewhat because of the break but survived some gritty pressure from Walsall to book our place back to Wembley, against of all teams, our local neighbours Everton who had come through their semi-final against Aston Villa, winning 2–1 on aggregate. Earlier in the season we had crushed Everton 3–0 in a match which was televised live and, probably because of that, everyone assumed it was going to be a walk-over. Our record in the competition should have told them better.

Maybe a few of the team believed what they read because we certainly did not function on all cylinders that day. Everton were full of conviction and confidence while we were still rubbing the sleep out of our eyes having been woken up at four in the morning by some lunatic running through the hotel chanting, 'Everton, Everton'.

We did not play at all in the first half during which Everton claimed they were robbed of a penalty when Jocky Hansen handled. To this day he swears that he did not and he is the sort who would have owned up – afterwards that is!

It was a difficult game with Everton conceding nothing and, in the end, I let my frustrations get the better of me and I was cautioned for sticking my elbow in Ian Richardson's face. We got the slating we deserved at half-time with Joe Fagan telling us that it looked as though only two or three of us wanted to play. He did not single out any one player but used the Liverpool psychology of letting the players answer for themselves so even the two or three who had acquitted themselves well would feel unsure and would try that much harder in the second period.

Although we improved in the second half we were still grateful for another chance at Maine Road on the following Wednesday. The nice thing was that the public enjoyed it and I am sure that it was largely due to the outstanding behaviour by the supporters of both clubs. It was a throwback to the old, pre-violence days as supporters wearing their blue and red colours flooded into London to enjoy themselves with the maximum amount of fun and the minimum of trouble. If only the supporters realized how much we appreciate this and how much we hate the idiots who cause trouble. We were all of one mind, Liverpool and Everton, and wished that they would always behave like that. The atmosphere was amazing and listening to the two groups of supporters chanting 'Merseyside' in unison made it memorable.

The worst hooliganism I saw that day was on the train going back to Liverpool. It was back to school for the lads as spirits were restored with the bread rolls flying about the dining car. Even the British Rail representative joined in the fun after a couple of soggy rolls had bounced off his head. It was also at that final that we decided we were something of a male voice choir and so sing-songs became a feature of the rest of the season though they were more of the rugby variety than the sort boy scouts sing around the campfire.

The replay was altogether better as far as we were

concerned. We played a lot closer to our best form and I felt we were never going to lose. I know I had quite a good game that night and, though I would love to take the credit for the turn which brought me the winning goal, I must admit it was a touch of poor control which led to the turn that lost Kevin Ratcliffe rather than any Brazilian-like skills though I will take full credit for the shot.

I felt that we were good value for that win but Everton really impressed us and we were all delighted at Anfield when they went on to win the FA Cup. In fact, they made it a clean sweep for Merseyside by winning the Youth Cup as well. What about the FA Cup? The one that escaped Bob Paisley and has always avoided me. One of our songs was: *You can stick the FA Cup up your jumper* or something like that, but we would have all liked a taste of that glory.

We thought we were on our way when we whipped Newcastle in front of live television cameras, winning by four clear goals and persuading Kevin Keegan to think about retirement in the process. Then we drew Brighton, the team who had beaten us the year before and there was no possibility of lightning striking twice, especially since they had been relegated after beating us the previous season.

Just as the season before, the game was live on television on a Sunday and though you try to put these superstitions out of your mind they nag away at your subconscious. In the warm-up I felt a niggle at the back of my right knee and then, once the game got under way, I ran into a cameraman and felt it again. One more tackle was enough to convince me that it was not worth risking my knee any further with the Milk Cup semi-finals looming. I went off to be replaced by Ronnie Whelan. It was just one of those days and we went on to lose 2–0. The strange thing is that I came out of it with credit. It was like the game for Scotland against Holland in Argentina. My timing was good, coming into the side when things could only improve and then being given the credit for it. I am sure that had I stayed on we would still have lost to Brighton but everyone said that it was because I was missing.

It was that sort of season. Had I played every game I would probably not have gained the recognition I did. Apart from the Brighton defeat, I was lucky to miss a goalless draw at Sunderland; the 2–2 draw with Walsall; the 2–0 defeat at Southampton and the 2–2 draw at home to the then struggling Ipswich. It was kind of people to say that the team did not function as well without me but Liverpool simply do not operate that way.

I have no doubt that my missing games had as much to do with the votes cast for me by the Football Writers who voted me into third place behind Ian Rush and Bryan Robson for Footballer of the Year, but the opinion poll which really surprised me was when my fellow professionals voted me second to Rushy in the PFA awards. I wondered for a while if I was becoming soft or something. Awards came pouring in for Liverpool again with Joe Fagan being named Bob Paisley's successor as Manager of the Year, and that after winning only one of the monthly Bell's awards.

What a year. Hoisting three trophies in one season is something no one would dream of and yet, for me, it came true. We had, at last, stepped out of the shadow of the great Liverpool teams of past years. Maybe we were not the best team ever to wear the Liverpool shirts but our experience and character ensured that we were the most successful.

11

This is Anfield

Every player, every coach, every manager wants to know the secret of Liverpool Football Club – and the more they are told there is no secret the greater becomes the mystique which surrounds this remarkable club. When I was at Middlesbrough and daydreaming of playing for the team they called the greatest in the world I harboured my own ideas of what it was going to be like.

I had no illusions at all of how hard training was going to be for weren't Liverpool a team of superfit sportsmen who were always likely to win games in the last five minutes and who always ended the season with a sprint finish while the others floundered and tired.

You had only to watch them to see the outstanding technique which spoke volumes for the coaching staff, while the complete lack of scandal demonstrated the highly-organized, highly-professional manner in which the entire club was run.

That first day at Anfield – 10 January 1978 – was a revelation. It seems a long time ago now but I remember how normal and ordinary it all was, no prima donnas, no superstars. They talked about the same things every other player talks about in every other dressing room; with the emphasis on money! I made only one error on that first morning, I asked Tommy Smith if I could borrow his hairdryer (I know it is hard to imagine tough guy Smithy with a hairdryer but it's absolutely true) and he turned to Phil Neal and said pointedly: 'Everyone is allowed one mistake.' I took my own in future.

From then on Liverpool went about exploding the

myths that surround them. I discovered in that first season why Liverpool finish fresher than all the rest – it is because they do less training than their rivals. That takes care of the physical strain while the mental pressure takes care of itself because the club do not play to tactics and rarely worry about the opposition. The whole thing is built on a tremendous belief that everything they do is right, that their players are the best and that if they go out and do their stuff then there is no one capable of living with them.

The only time I can remember this golden rule being broken was that time when Bob Paisley told Sammy Lee to do a man-for-man job on Breitner in the critical 1982 European Cup semi-final. It was all done so quietly that the majority of the team was in the dark as to what the boss had devised until the game unfolded. Coaching, in fact, is an absolute no-no at Anfield with Bob Paisley and Joe Fagan pouring scorn on modern jargon for making the game appear more difficult than it really is. While Ronnie Moran and Roy Evans have come back from preliminary coaching courses laughing and taking the mickey. I cannot think of anyone at Liverpool who is in possession of a full coaching badge.

The dietitians would not believe how mighty Liverpool eat after an away game (come to that, neither would those friends who know my favourite meal to be oysters natural, followed by grilled lobster and washed down with a bottle of the best Sancerre). Just before the game our coach driver John would nip down to the local chippie and order twenty portions of cod and chips to be picked up after the game. There we would sit on the coach, eating our dinner out of newspapers and washing it down with lager, orange juice or lemonade until recently when we really went up-market and added a German hock to our wine list. Diet is something the club has never studied in depth despite the intense research on the eating habits of athletes in other sports.

There are a few basic Liverpool rules to follow, like not drinking too much fizzy pop and eating toast rather than bread but there was never any objection to our having the odd alcoholic drink. Bob Paisley used to say: 'Watch what you are pouching,' but he never objected, for example, to Ray Kennedy and Jimmy Case taking a bottle of wine with them to drink in their room on a Friday night before a game.

Dinner before an away game would consist of tomato or mushroom soup, followed by either fish, steak or eggs, usually with chips and milk, orange or tea to drink with it. Nothing too exotic! One thing they would watch very carefully, however, was bread. That was stodge and it took too long to digest. The staff would eat with us and follow the same rules other than treating themselves to a rice pudding or something similar afterwards. Even those players not involved the next day were bound by the no bread ruling – as Alan Kennedy discovered to his cost and embarrassment one lunch-time.

What Liverpool have that other clubs do not is continuity and that stems from a set of volumes stored at the ground and kept up-to-date without fail every day. It is the football bible as far as the Anfield backroom staff are concerned and contains the answer to almost every problem and every situation which could arise in the day-to-day running of a successful club. Every detail is noted from the temperature and ground conditions to the physical and mental state of the players. Injuries are logged, including how and why it happened as well as how it responded to treatment. There are volumes and volumes, maintained ever since Joe Fagan first introduced them under Bill Shankly.

The books even dictate what type of training we should

do according to the time in the season and the prevailing weather. The books come out even before the season begins when the backroom staff arrive at the bootroom and consult the oracle against the weather to see what sort of programme we should undertake. If it's hot then not too much is done but, in any case, it is a slow start during that first week of pre-season, just a question of the players opening their lungs and nice, easy action.

During the summer months muscles quickly become soft and get out-of-condition. It amazes me that some clubs return after the holidays, see how unfit their players are and promptly make them jump through the hoop with cross-country runs and similar exercises. Then they wonder why they are so unlucky to start the season with two or three injuries. At Liverpool they work the other way and if anyone goes too mad they deliberately slow them down. Personally I never had that problem but players like Craig Johnston and Bruce Grobbelaar were always enthusiastic and eager to charge about.

Another unusual ploy, again introduced under Bill Shankly and carried on by both Bob Paisley and Joe Fagan, is for the players to report and change at Anfield and then travel to the training ground at Melwood by coach. This is done partly for *esprit de corps* but also to allow for a cooling-off period. The bootroom boys reckon that if everyone just got showered, changed and left the ground they would catch colds. It all makes sense.

Everything possible would be done to avoid injuries and it was for this reason that any running we did was always on grass and never on roads or cross country. Come the second week and we would be seeing a lot more of the ball although midweek we would have our hardest day with, depending on the temperature, a couple of laps around the pitches at Melwood.

It was always a question of being eased in with gentle

sessions in the morning and again in the afternoon. No one ever knew what the schedule would be except for the training staff who had already checked out those big black books. As soon as possible the competitive element is introduced with the seniors and the reserves mixing together to form two- and three-man teams. These mini-games were taken very seriously with the kids determined to show that they were ready to challenge for first-team places and the seniors equally determined to resist.

The third week is usually set aside for a pre-season tour. My first with the club was to Austria and West Germany and I was staggered at how relaxed everyone was. In Munich we stayed at the Holiday Inn with its famous Yellow Submarine Disco in which sharks and other large fish swim in vast tanks which form the walls around the bars and dance floor. The staff were quite happy to give us a couple of days off and turned a blind eye to the late night visits to the unusual night spot. The players are always treated like adults but there is also enough rope to hang yourself and if anyone is daft enough to overstep the mark and let down the rest they have their wrists slapped and find themselves in the reserves. Everyone knows that Terry McDermott, Ray Kennedy and Jimmy Case left the club earlier than their talents demanded because they occasionally over-did the leisure time! They were players we missed badly when they first went but, in each case, the management decided that it was time.

Due to their timing, those pre-season games were always a little unpredictable and I will never forget Bob Paisley's face when we arrived at our hotel headquarters for one tournament in the Spanish resort of Marbella. I swear that he did not realize what type of place it was until we stepped off our coach and walked past the pool on our way into the hotel. The arrival of a group of reasonably fit, tanned, young men caused quite a stir among the topless beauties around the resort – and we did not complain either.

Bob shrugged his shoulders and accepted the situation for what it was, realizing it was too late in the day to do anything about it. Liverpool are very flexible like that as they showed on that same trip when they were told that kick-off time was to be 10 P.M. 'No way,' the organizers were told firmly, 'our lads have to get ready for a tough season.' But as soon as the ante was upped agreement was reached.

Bayer Leverkusen were staying at the same hotel and their approach was in direct contrast to our own. They trained at the crack of dawn, returned to have breakfast and were back in their beds before the heat of the sun could get at them. We preferred to relax around the pool, enjoying a lager or two and then, after dinner, go back to the bar for a nightcap. The German team's coach and trainer could not believe their eyes.

What made it a lot worse was that they lost their opening game against Malaga while we went out and put three past Betis to reach the final. It was just too much for their coach when we returned from our game and went straight to the bar. 'Is this the way all English teams prepare?' he demanded wide-eyed. We assured him that this was how all teams behaved back home. We eventually lost the final to Malaga on penalties but I have often wondered since what happened to that German coach and his training methods.

Far more serious and testing is the full-scale practice game against the reserves when we return home. Now that was, and still is, a serious game of football. It is a game in which you don't forget to wear your shinpads because those reserves have an awful lot of enthusiasm and a great deal to prove. If the first team get a draw it constitutes a good performance but I also remember a five-goal stuffing. It is a real kick up the backside just before the season starts.

Once the season is under way Liverpool can usually reckon on a couple of games every week and if they don't have a game it is on the plane and away for a quick friendly to top up the club coffers with the £23,000 or whatever guarantee they are asking at the time. With this in mind, the training is scarcely stepped up.

Reporting time on a normal day is around 10 A.M., ready to leave Anfield for Melwood a quarter of an hour later. Even then there is a marked reluctance to start training as the lads linger to tie up boots, make a telephone call or snatch a last quick look at the newspapers that have been thieved off the apprentices or anyone else who buys them at the ground.

That little flurry, however, is often more energetic than the opening routine which consists of a gentle walk around the three pitches followed by a jog over the same course. Muscles are loosened up gently by stretching exercises and now and again a spell on the multi-gym circuit indoors using very light weights. There are short, sharp sprints, depending again on the prevailing conditions and on what day of the week it is. If there is no midweek fixture we usually have Monday off altogether with a leisurely return to training on Tuesday. Wednesday would be the hard day but never anything too long.

One common denominator of every day's training with Liverpool is that there would be a game of some kind, whether a five-a-side or bigger. Maybe a couple of times a season Ronnie Moran would detect a slight flagging in enthusiasm and say, 'Right, if you don't want to play we will go on a run.' Even then it would become fiercely competitive with Moran stirring everyone up, telling them that he could beat them even at his age. Ronnie also figured prominently in the practice games, always picking his own team. In my early days he would make sure he had Ray Kennedy and Jimmy Case on his side and in latter years he would have Dalglish, myself and Neal so that every time he would have the players who would see things early and give him a chance to play. With their strong element of competition, these games were encouraged to be taken seriously. This, they reckoned, is all part of the character building at the club and it begins very early.

There is a marvellous stretch of turf at Melwood which has been christened Wembley. It has two sets of portable goals and the senior training staff use it to play matches against the young apprentices. I named these games 'kick-a-kid' day because the boys were bounced all over the field and, to make matters worse, would have blatantly obvious refereeing decisions given against them just to test their reactions. This works two ways; it helps make a kid stand up for himself and not withdraw into his shell as soon as something goes against him and, at the same time, conditions the players not to go chasing referees and finish up in the book for dissent. There is no better test for frustration especially as the old campaigners always win or draw in the last minute – no matter how long they have to play to achieve their wicked ends!

They stoop as low as possible, even to the extent of using injured senior players, on their way back to fitness, to do all the running for them. You could always tell who was injured at Liverpool for these were the only ones allowed to wear tracksuit bottoms to keep the damaged parts warm. No one else wears them, playing or training, however cold the conditions.

No one objects, however, to a bit of extra clothing around the top of the body and the odd investment of £15 for a roll of drycleaning polythene bags to help get a sweat on. Ray Kennedy used to keep a roll in the boot of his car because of his weight problem (he would always bring an extra one for Jimmy Case) and there was always a roll in the bootroom. It was a real giveaway when someone who did not normally use one pulled on their plastic bag for a training session because we all knew who had just had a good night out. I wore a plastic bag almost everyday so no one knew when that applied to me.

Occasionally the daily game would be changed to possession or one touch and at the end of a session we might indulge in some shooting practice. But, in all my time at Liverpool, I can honestly say that I have never been coached. The attitude is that if you can play you get out and do it and, of course, you must be able to play if you are in Liverpool's first team.

I will never forget one pre-season training match when Phil Thompson, fresh from an England tour, suddenly shouted: 'Drop off and give depth.' The whole game stopped and everyone was completely dumbfounded. That was the attitude towards technical terms and though you would sometimes have an exchange of opinions that would be as far as it would go. The theory put forward is: 'If you don't know, we can't tell you.' Training is geared towards what happens on Saturday afternoons and doing in practice what you do in those games. That tunes up the body while the dressing room sharpens the mind. You have to be quick of wit in there or you will be destroyed.

The worst thing to be at Liverpool is injured. There was a time, I am reliably informed, when Bill Shankly would completely ignore injured players. It is not as bad these days but it is still looked on as downright careless to be hurt badly enough to miss games. For a start you have to go in on Sunday morning, almost like a punishment, and then at 9.30 A.M. on subsequent days.

You have your prescribed treatment and then drive your own car to Melwood where, according to how bad your injury is, you work out in the gym or maybe even have a sauna.

There is enough experience around to recognize the seriousness of a sore muscle or a pull and to know who will be off with the slightest complaint. You don't get too many of those at Anfield, though, because you might have to struggle to get your place back if you miss a game. There are more than a few who play on with injuries. The amazing thing is that there is not one full-time physiotherapist employed at Anfield. A lot of clubs are shocked at this seemingly obvious gap in standard requirements but Liverpool's fantastic medical record speaks for itself.

Once again it is all down to experience and those black books. By referring to them, the staff can recognize the type of player by his shape and the sort of injury he is most likely to suffer. They know within minutes if the injury has happened before and exactly how it happened. I imagine that those books reveal some very interesting facts about certain people. Anything the staff don't understand and the player is sent straight to hospital and to the top man in that particular field.

Not that it always goes according to plan, as I found to my cost, when I picked up an injury against Ipswich when Paul Mariner sliced open my right shin. I eventually had the stitches out but the wound did not heal properly and when I played against Wolves in the next game, it was weeping and running down my leg. It felt sore when I went for a Christmas Eve drink with my mate Jimmy McCurley. It became so bad that I went home early and collapsed in the doorway.

A specialist was called and he wanted to send me straight to hospital, only relenting because it was so close to Christmas day. When I did go in it was diagnosed as gas gangrene and I was put on to some extremely strong antibiotics. All told I lost a stone in weight and was left wondering how close I was to having my career finished by injury. Not that I did myself any good because I misread the prescription and took half the dosage only. That set me back even further and the talk in the dressing room was that I had done it deliberately to get an extra holiday.

It was not true but, as it happened, I did manage to persuade the club that a break in the sun would speed my recovery. My journalist friend, Bob Harris, often took his family for a winter break in the Canary Islands and another pal, Jon Dexter, was just off to Tenerife. I thought that would suit very nicely and when I booked up felt it was almost worth being injured, only for Bob Paisley to ring up at the last minute to block me going because he thought I might be able to train the next week.

You can imagine how sorry I felt for myself especially when Dexter came back to tell me how great the place and the hotel was and how he had primed everyone in Puerto de la Cruz to be ready for my arrival. But, as usual, Bob was right and, after three long weeks, I was back in action. But it goes to prove that things can and do go wrong at Anfield. Just how human the whole set up can be was admirably displayed when I presented a prescription at the chemist to be told that the item mentioned had not been on his shelf for five years! As I said before, the record of injuries and absenteeism speaks for itself. The system can't be that bad. The same can be said about the bootroom boys. You simply cannot argue with the history books.

As the name suggests this little room, in the corridors between the dressing room and the manager's office, is where they keep the first team players' match boots. They look after them in the way Alex Higgins would care for his snooker cue or Geoffrey Boycott would love his cricket bat. That – and a lot more.

The room is not very big and the carpet could do with replacing but it has an atmosphere all of its own and it is a big honour to be invited inside. Sometimes the players might wander in to beg a glass of pop, which they pay for, but if the door is closed you stay out. This is where all the playing decisions are made and where the big pow-wow takes place after every home game when it is strictly out-of-bounds to us poor players.

Opposition coaches and managers would be invited in for a beer, on the house. Then they could look round this rather cramped room with kit on the shelves, cupboards containing the bootroom boys' private bits and pieces and all the latest calendars displaying fit, young girls with more athletic bodies than you will find in any dressing room.

When that door is locked and bolted you can imagine what goes on inside only for, though you may pause, you never hear a word. It is not a shouting room, it is a place for whispers, secrets and, especially, those black books. The furnishings are ordinary, Joe Fagan's chair is sacrosanct but still only made of plastic, much the same as the one in the manager's office just along the corridor opposite the players' room. But while the bootroom is a hive of activity, often packed with a dozen people, the other one is more often than not empty. Neither Paisley nor Fagan were too keen about moving out of their 'home'.

Inside the bootroom you will find: Ronnie Moran; Roy Evans; Tom Saunders; Reuben Bennett; Chris Lawler; John Bennison and Geoff Twentyman, though rarely all at the same time. I must be honest and say that when I contemplated writing about this part of my life, I did not plan to be particularly benevolent to Ronnie 'Bugsy' Moran. I have had more rows with him than anyone in football. But when I sat down to analyze how I felt, I realized just what a remarkable job this man does for Liverpool Football Club, albeit in a most unusual manner.

I am not the only player to have had words with Bugsy but it was a long time before I discovered that it was all for my own benefit. He is deliberately antagonistic, a personal device used only to motivate players. There are no pats on the back, no congratulations, in fact, in the end you feel that you have done it yourself in spite of him rather than because of him. He is the club's *agent-provocateur*, the man who gets everyone working, not just the players I played with at Liverpool but those who went before. It cannot be a coincidence that he has overseen all of the great teams. At the end of the day Ronnie is all about Liverpool. He got his point home to me and if he has done that with every player before and since, then he has more than done his job. Every club could do with a Bugsy.

His mate, Roy Evans, is just the opposite. He reminds me of a young Joe Fagan in that he is the perfect diplomat, always ready to talk and to listen. He is everyone's friend. Roy's promotion from the reserves to the first team was as expected as it was welcomed, for he fits perfectly into the Liverpool mould and looks set for life if he wants it that way.

Tom Saunders probably knows more about the club and how it works than anyone else involved below stairs because he is the go-between who travels without hitch or hindrance between bootroom and the offices. The funny thing is that Tom, as far as I am aware, is still officially called 'Youth Development Officer' as he was when he left his job as headmaster to join the club. He is a clever and versatile man who handles such matters as cautions, writing after-dinner speeches for Bob Paisley and spying on our European opponents, more lately with Bob Paisley himself.

I suppose I owe Tom a great deal myself for it was he who cast the final eye over me in my last game for Middlesbrough against Norwich in which I was jeered every time I touched the ball and he saw me throw my shirt into the crowd in disgust. There must have been something he liked in that petulant act because he could so easily have stopped the deal by reporting back that I was a spoiled brat who couldn't take stick from the crowd.

The job of watching our domestic opposition falls on the capable head of Reuben Bennett. The boss would often run through his report, touching on aspects like free kicks and corners rather than individual players but always emphasizing that no two games are ever the same. Reuben is another popular figure and particularly among the 'old boys' who come to visit. They call him 'The Fighting Scot' in reference to the dirty work he used to do for Bill Shankly.

Chris Lawler will be remembered as a player with the club. He now takes the reserves and is still a well-liked, nice guy who hasn't changed other than becoming greyer about the temples. John Bennison is in charge of the kids and the hatchet man of those kick-a-kid games on 'little Wembley' while Geoff Twentyman is the chief scout who is obviously a good judge of a player and, like the rest, has worked hard over the years.

What makes the bootroom successful, and different, is that this is the domain of football, of the boots and the ball. Money might be the major topic of conversation in the dressing room but wages or contracts are never discussed, that is taboo downstairs and the business of the Gentleman's Club upstairs.

When it comes to contracts the manager just tells you that they are waiting upstairs. 'They' in this instance would be Peter (PBR) Robinson and the Chairman John W Smith, CBE, JP, DL. Both are outstanding business-men who automatically command tremendous respect both in and out of the club. PBR prefers to stay in the background, rarely quoted in the press and with his picture used even less often. Yet everyone knows him throughout the game and I would venture to say that there is not an administrative job in football which would not be open to him.

John Smith's calm, unflustered approach means that he is in great demand in soccer and also in other sports such as tennis or in racing as a trustee of the Aintree Race-course in Liverpool along with Lord Derby and Dick Francis. There are never any arguments over contractual difficulties. If you hit a snag the chairman would turn to the secretary and say, 'Can that be done, Peter?' PBR would reply noncommittally: 'We will have to look into it', and away they would go for their private conflab before coming up with the answer. It is because the two departments are kept apart that everything seems to work so well.

I have been asked to compare the running of Liverpool with that of Middlesbrough. I could not because it would not be fair. It would be like putting a corner greengrocer's shop up against a multi-national chain. I remember being dreadfully disappointed with Boro for not buying the two or three extra players they needed to become a great team. They were happy to tread water while Liverpool, despite their success, are always planning years ahead.

It all combines to keep the players on their toes and to

keep them winning trophies. Neither do the fans ever let the players feel they have achieved as much as that which went before. The ghosts from the past are all part of that secret the others are seeking. Well, is it that simple?

12

Sometimes I wish I was English

If I have one major regret in my football career it is that I
should have won at least a dozen more international caps
for Scotland. It has absolutely nothing to do with selection
or managers – it is simply me. I openly admit that I have
pulled out of Scotland games when I have been tired or
carrying the sort of knock which you would normally
shrug off during the course of a League season.

I will say in my defence that the games I have missed
have all been friendlies or games of no account. I have
always been prepared to roll up my sleeves and play
standing on one leg if necessary, if a European Championship or World Cup qualifying game was in the offing. It
has always been my own choice and I must say right away
that Liverpool never put pressure on me or forced me to
pull out of any Scotland game, even though international
football generally makes them gnash their teeth and
prepare themselves to count the cost.

Forget all that drivel about clubs and countries coming
to a growing understanding. It is just lip service and most
clubs would happily do away with the international scene
despite the fact that caps and international performances
can greatly enhance a player's transfer fee (as in the case
of Ray Wilkins when he went from Manchester United to
AC Milan for more than three times the price he would
have fetched on the domestic market).

Apart from the risk of the sort of injury which helped
cut short the careers of players like Roy McFarland and
Steve Coppell, managers simply do not like having their
weekly routine disturbed by their players being taken

away from them. You may as well shut up Anfield altogether when there is an international date which involves the Home countries. As well as the break in routine and habit, an international game invariably means a lot of travelling and two or three days of over-indulging in rich food and drinking too many Cokes at first-class hotels. Managers would seem to have a point for the level of performance and, often, results fall off sharply immediately after these games just as they do after a long trip and a hard game mid-week in Europe.

Some managers do more about it than others. When squads gather, it is common knowledge that certain players have pulled out of games for no reason and are fully backed-up by their clubs. One First Division manager even went as far as to tell one of his enthusiastic players that he had been dropped. The plan backfired when the player telephoned the international manager to be told that it was his own boss who had pulled him out. That confrontation almost led to a transfer but such is the hypocrisy of the game that a few days later the club manager involved was picking up cash writing for a national newspaper saying, 'clubs had got to get behind the international teams.'

Jack Charlton, with 35 caps, a World Cup winner's medal and, at one stage, strongly tipped to become England's boss, once offered my mate at Middlesbrough, Willie Maddren, financial compensation if he agreed not to play in an Under 23 game because Willie had a suspect knee and Jack did not want him to risk aggravating it before an important club game. There is also the some-times imagined problem of the players being out of their managers' hands for four days and being guided along the wrong tactical lines or subject to a lack of the proper disciplinary control. It is true that, sometimes, players come back from international games with rather inflated ideas of their own ability. We had a saying at Anfield if anyone tried to be too smart and would bring them down to earth with the cry of: 'That's an England ball.' From my own point of view I try to keep things as normal as possible, even to the extent of going through my own fitness routine because I know my battle-scarred, old legs will respond to that without strains or pulls.

Things are not going to change, either, while professional footballers are asked to be at their peak for 60 or 70 games a season. I am sure that there would be a better response from everyone concerned if there were fewer games and I am convinced that results would improve accordingly. Look at Italy and West Germany, they can adjust their programmes to fit the circumstances because they have far fewer League and cup commitments than we do.

The whole farcical situation was shown up for what it was when Spurs were due to play Anderlecht in the UEFA Cup Final at the end of the 1983–4 season. While other Leagues around Europe are prepared to cancel games and entire programmes to accommodate a major fixture for club or country, the Football League ordered Spurs to play an away game at Southampton two days before they were due to play in Brussels. Would the Football League have been so insistent if Spurs had been making the arduous journey to Dinamo Tblisi in Georgia via Moscow? Let's be fair, if the Football League cannot reach agreement with their own member clubs, then what chance have the Football Associations with their history of trouble and aggravation.

I suppose I shouldn't complain too much as it was because of injuries, club calls and absenteeism that I got my very first chance to add senior international honours to my schoolboy and youth caps when I played for the Under 23 side against England at Newcastle. To say I was not first choice would be a gross understatement for manager Willie Ormond was forced to find eleven replacements on the eve of the squad meeting in the north east. Admittedly things had been going well for me at Middlesbrough as we chased the Second Division title but I guess that my club's close proximity to Newcastle and the lateness of the hour had quite a bit to do with my selection.

England also had their problems, I recall, with Trevor Francis, then at Birmingham City, and with Kevin Keegan, still at Liverpool, both absent and it meant that I was in company as David Mills was an equally late replacement for England. I suppose I could have been offended at being almost an afterthought but I wasn't. I couldn't get my boots packed quickly enough and get to Geordieland. We lost 2–0 on a pitch which was barely playable because of a pre-match deluge but, in a hastily gathered side, I felt that I acquitted myself well.

Willie Ormond must have thought so too for a few months later he called me up to join the full Scottish squad for the first time to play against East Germany at Hampden Park, making my début along with Celtic striker Dixie Deans. I was, frankly, surprised as the most I had hoped for was a place on the bench. When I joined the squad at Seamill I must confess I did not know what to expect. Everyone talked about the Scottish squad as if they were a wild bunch and I was more than interested to see at first hand what they were like.

As a 21-year-old who had already had a taste of a hedonistic lifestyle, I was determined not to get involved and jeopardize any international future I might have. In any case I had only heard of or seen most of the players in that team on television. There weren't too many Scottish international players in the Second Division at the time for me to get to know.

I was under some pressure as I was wearing the number four shirt favoured at that time by the absent skipper Billy Bremner but things went quite well for the team and for me. We won 3–0 with goals from Tommy Hutchison (from the penalty spot), substitute Kenny Burns who had replaced the injured Jim Holton, and Kenny Dalglish who was then, of course, playing football for Celtic. I was lucky enough to get good reviews for my performance and even the East German manager Georg Buschner told the Scottish press that I was a good player in the making. All in all I went back to my parents' home in Edinburgh that night feeling more than a little pleased with myself.

I kept my place for the European Championship match against Spain at Hampden Park, which we lost 2–1, missed the return in Valencia and then played in the 1–1 draw against Sweden in Gothenburg. That was on 16 April 1975 – it was to be my last international until 22 February 1978 when, as a Liverpool player, I returned for the 2–1 win against Bulgaria. Apart from a couple more Under 23 games, both against the Dutch, that was it. I must confess I was baffled for, according to the critics, I hadn't done badly and even the manager had complimented me. What really surprised me was that there was no explanation at all. No wonder loyalty from the players is in short supply later on in their careers.

At least those early games gave me a chance to play alongside some of the old guard like Bremner, Lorimer, McGrain, Jardine and even Denis Law was in one of the squads. This, I suppose, was the end of an era and I didn't get invited to too many of the parties, if they went on at all. The worst I saw was some very heavy card schools when sums of £300 or £400 would change hands. I watched Billy Bremner lose at one of these sessions, hardly surprising considering that he had already taken his sleeping tablets and was more than ready for bed. The others worked as hard at keeping him awake as they did taking the money off him.

Mind you I should be grateful, I suppose, that I was axed from the team when I was for it meant that I did not see, or more importantly, get involved, in the famous Copenhagen nightclub episode. It was odd but I had been hoping for a recall for that game though I knew I was not in line as Willie Ormond had not even come to watch me. Anyway, Scotland won the game with a Joe Harper goal but he, Billy Bremner, Willie Young, Arthur Graham and Pat McCluskey later faced a disciplinary enquiry by the Scottish FA at which all five were banned for life from playing for their country. An over-reaction which was later amended.

They were no crazier than their English counterparts. After all who was wilder than Terry McDermott? Who enjoyed a good time more than Tony Currie, Emlyn Hughes, Frank Worthington or Mick Channon? I think one of the reasons that the Scots were slammed was because of the different journalists who covered the two teams. Some Scottish journalists felt that they were part of the team – until things went wrong and then they would vent their anger on us, especially the Anglos.

There came another breed of journalist later, the newsman whose sole job was to wait for someone to step out of line. They made the football writers look positively benign. What they did not seem to appreciate was that a drink was often the best way to unwind after the pressures of a major game and how many of the journalists could hold up their hands and say they had never had one too many themselves? I remember the brilliant Spurs and Scottish international striker Alan Gilzean telling me if I didn't drink I would never be a footballer. It is not the sort of advice I would pass on to an aspiring young apprentice but I could see his point. There was a certain logic behind this seemingly crazy statement for it is essential to be able to relax at the right moment. I have always enjoyed a drink, starting off, like most kids, with beer, then progressing through the gin and tonics to champagne. I am not such a fierce animal these days and my relaxation takes the form of a good dinner and a bottle or two of Sancerre.

I must admit that I have sometimes wished I could have played for England instead – but not often! From a purely financial point of view the rewards for being an English international footballer are far greater than for being a Jock. English players are held in much higher esteem than the Scots, the Irish and the Welsh and the commercial market is also much wider, on population alone. The Scottish Football Association were also a little small minded at one stage. The players used to be a secondary consideration. At Liverpool the players were always put first, whether it was getting us on an aircraft, checking us into a hotel or whatever. With the Scots it was the other way round, officials and journalists first, players last.

There is also the permanent problem of the Anglos and the locals. Certain of the home-based players think we are a big-headed lot and let their feelings be known. Aberdeen manager Alex Ferguson joined in the pettiness when he made some cutting remarks about a rather smart llama overcoat I wore to a game in Switzerland. He later apologized which enhanced my opinion of the man. At least Ferguson recognized me, which is more than you can say for some of the officials. I was cornered recently by a Glasgow club's chairman who wanted to discuss some award that Willie Miller had won. Being wicked and having an audience of other players I kept the conversation going without letting on that, in fact, I wasn't Miller. It was a good job he was not trying to sign one or the other of us for his club,

To be fair it happens all the time in football. There was the Scottish team manager who said at a press conference that he couldn't understand why John Giles had never been capped for England while Joe Mercer once brushed the diminutive Duncan McKenzie aside saying he would sign autographs later, not realizing that Duncan was one of the squad he was waiting for. Michael 'Cat' Robinson tells the lovely story of Alan Durban trying to persuade him to sign for Sunderland and promising the ten-times capped Eire international that he would have him in the England side within six months.

It just goes to show how low down international football is on a club manager's list and one day someone must decide exactly how important it is to everyone. Speaking for myself I wish I could have been as successful at international level as I was at club level. There is nothing I would have liked more than to have played in a World Cup Final but the way it looks at the moment, it is going to be a long time before British players can relive the experience the English had in 1966.

One series I was never too enthusiastic about, with the exception of the game against England, was the Home International Championships. There has been a lot of bleating from the Welsh and the Irish about how its axing will bankrupt their football and how unfair it is of England and Scotland to drop the Championship which, through television, they claim used to fund their season. But the world of football has changed dramatically and for how much longer were television companies going to continue paying good money for a tired and worn-out competition which interested no one outside the big two.

It is no use Mike England and Billy Bingham pointing at their recent results because I am sure that the decision to drop the games had nothing to do with how good or how bad the Welsh and the Irish were. Far more significant was how many people watched the games and how useful they were as preparations for World and European Championship matches. In the end the games would have died a death because no one would have wanted to play in or watch them.

Speaking as a player, I could not motivate myself to play against the Welsh or the Irish in a stadium with no atmosphere and in matches which were basically meaningless. Winning the British Championship meant very little to the Scots if they had failed to beat England and I am sure that applied vice versa. It must have been a good competition once when travelling abroad was long and difficult. Now you can be in South America in half a day. It is a far cry from the days when a World Cup qualifying group comprised the four Home International Countries. Now every year has some sort of international significance with either qualifying competitions or, hopefully, the finals of the big two, and with European club competitions thrown in for good measure. It is fine for the First Division reserve or the Second Division player to run and chase the big names who have nothing to gain and everything to lose by playing in the cup tie type of atmosphere that these games generate.

There is little to be learned in preparation for games against the more technical European nations who opt for a slow build-up until the last-third of the field. How often have our National sides lost vital games abroad after a long, hard season made even more difficult by a physical encounter against the type of player you are meeting week in and week out. If we draw Wales or Northern Ireland in a major competition, it will add extra spice, but as for the Home International Championships I can say only good riddance.

13

Argentina Disaster

The weight of the world was on his shoulders but, with a
deep sigh and a shrug, Ally MacLeod watched Scotland's
team doctor throw handfuls of pills into the fields lining
the road from Alta Gracia to Cordoba, pointed at the
horses idly grazing and remarked: 'They will be doing
gambols by the time we return.' You had to admire the
ability for humour in a man who was under attack from
all sides; there he was, the most talked-about manager in
the 1978 World Cup Finals, witnessing the disposal of the
evidence that more than just one of his World Cup squad
were taking pills that were on FIFA's banned list.

For most of the horrendous days of that World Cup
competition I was the outsider looking in, the youngster
on the fringe impatiently waiting his chance. But on this
occasion I was in the best position to see what was going
on as I sat on the coach in the seat behind the manager
and the doctor. Only those who had handed over their
illegal drugs knew for sure if there were other players
apart from the disgraced Willie Johnston taking Fencam-
samin in the form of Reactivan tablets. I watched the
doctor dispose of dozens of tablets as we headed for a
training session just a couple of days before playing Iran,
indicating that at least two or three more of Scotland's
cream were popping pills. But the chaos had started long
before poor wee Willie pressed the self destruct button
that led to the Scottish squad returning home in disgrace.

It was all so different at the outset when Scotland
qualified for Argentina while England and a good few
other top teams failed. Instead of being content with that

and allowing the finals to run their course it was decided by the tartan-eyed media in Scotland, and with support from an enthusiastic and helpful manager, that Scotland would win the World Cup. I was lucky, if that is the right word in retrospect, to be involved at all and it was probably only the fact that I had joined in Liverpool's success that had earned me an international recall for a friendly against Bulgaria at Hampden Park. We won 2–1 and it was enough for me to be included in the 22 bound for South America.

The contrast between club and country was to strike me right from the start because, just before I linked up with Scotland's World Cup squad, I was playing for Liverpool in that European Cup Final against Bruges at Wembley. As usual, at Liverpool, the build-up was very low key with as much of our routine being kept to as possible and the game being treated much the same as any other. Scotland, on the other hand, were jumping. Everyone was on a high. Drugs were not needed, the atmosphere was enough to set the nerves on edge and get the adrenalin flowing fast.

Already, there were ill-omens. For me, personally, they had begun when I was called on as a substitute against England in the Home International Championships. My delight at getting stripped and joining the action was marred, however, by the supporters at the Rangers End of Hampden Park who mistook me for their hero Derek Johnstone. When they discovered it was me instead, they let everyone know exactly how they felt. Even before that, the team had managed to scrape together only a draw against the Irish in front of 64,433 fans at Hampden.

Injuries and experiments saw Ally make a number of changes for the next game against the Welsh who were, naturally, thirsting for revenge after losing to Scotland in

the World Cup qualifying competition by a very controversial penalty. A goal by Derek Johnstone looked as
though it would give the team an important boost but
fate was already playing tricks. Brian Flynn missed a
penalty for the Welsh four minutes from time but we still
managed to concede one of the daftest international goals
of all time as goalkeeper Jim Blyth rolled the ball out to
Willie Donachie who promptly rolled it straight back past
him. Even worse, our big centre-half Gordon McQueen
had run into a post in the first half to sustain a knee
injury that was eventually to keep him out of the World
Cup finals altogether.

A win against England would have put all of that to
rights but, in front of a near 90,000 crowd, we could not
put the ball in the net and a close-range goal from that
little opportunist Steve Coppell gave us a single goal
defeat.

The writing was on the wall and, then and there, we
should have scuttled away and righted the situation but,
instead, the great wave of euphoria carried us forward
with all of the danger signals being studiously ignored.

The most obvious problem was money. The question
of bonuses should have been sorted out long, long before
but money remained the main topic of conversation
among the senior players. Meetings were held and
Tommy Younger gave a little lecture about being proud
to play for Scotland and all the rest of it. But still nothing
was done or decided. Quite frankly, I found the whole
thing puzzling. Had we been talking about thousands of
pounds it might have been different but this was like a
little club squabbling over a player's pool before an FA
Cup semi-final. Maybe it sounds a little blasé, but in
football bonus terms it was all about peanuts.

Lessons should have been learned from the years
before. No one ever gets what's promised to them in

these circumstances and, after tax, it is scarcely worth the effort and certainly not the distraction and disruption it causes. Tommy Younger was right and the players who moaned were wrong in this instance and if the players who did the shouting, all of them senior members of the squad, were not embarrassed at the time they should be now. The Scottish Football Association can be blamed for not settling the matter early on but Ally and the lads must shoulder the larger portion for waiting until the last minute to voice their complaints.

Coming late into the side, because I had not been involved in the qualifying competition, it seemed to me that the whole commercial aspect was taking priority in the last-minute preparations. When my brother Billy came to take me home to Edinburgh one Saturday night, I was glad to get away from it. I picked the right weekend for a break as boredom had begun to take its toll and that night there was trouble involving our players in both Falkirk and Stirling.

Mind you, we all felt a little claustrophobic at that Dunblane Hydro Hotel and I too was involved in an incident when the youngsters who always hung around for autographs and photographs, were pestering Kenny Dalglish. There was no chance of getting any rest at all and Gordon McQueen came into our room to see what all the noise and fuss was about. We decided to have a little game with the kids and grouped them together as if for a photograph before dousing them with water. It was a bit of fun and even the kids laughed but that was not how the incident was reported and we should have sensed then the way things could go if we were not careful.

The whole thing remained a complete shambles, culminating in the daftest moment of all when we returned to Hampden Park, scene of all three of our disastrous British Championship games, to give the fans a chance to say goodbye. Thirty thousand of them had turned up to be entertained by comedian Andy Cameron, pipe bands and majorettes, while each of us had to individually complete the long walk-out to the middle to be introduced. It was all highly embarrassing and not at all spontaneous. As Ally MacLeod pointed out later, it was not so much a salute to what we had already achieved but a celebration before we had even kicked a ball.

Older, wiser and with the benefit of hindsight I would never be party to that kind of foolishness again. Far more impromptu was the drive to Prestwick airport when people came out of their houses to wave to us and wish us well. They included one fellow who had clearly jumped straight from his bath without even time to wrap a towel around him to hide his modesty.

So, even as we boarded our DC 10, there was a feeling of unease, of something not quite right and, maybe, even a premonition of the disaster that was to follow. It was all well hidden on the flight across the Atlantic as the players, manager and doctor relaxed in the first-class section of the aircraft while most of the officials were in tourist. That was a rôle that was to be dramatically reversed on the flight home. Everything continued to go wrong and little of it, at this stage, was the fault of the Scots. A prime example was the coach waiting to pick us up at Cordoba and drive us to our 'luxury' hotel, the Sierras at Alta Gracia. It was a lovely Mercedes, not a clapped-out old wagon, but the clutch burned out in the middle of the village as everyone turned out to greet us. Choking, we all piled on to the officials' bus. We were told that the hotel, selected personally by Ally and SFA secretary Ernie Walker, was a five star wanted by every team in the competition. But when we arrived we found the training pitch was so uneven that you stood a good chance of breaking an ankle while the main source of relaxation, the swimming pool, lacked a rather essential ingredient – water! It was always going to be filled the next day but, eventually, they even let the air out of the balloon which covered the empty, useless pit, clearly deciding that we ought to concentrate on our football instead of swimming.

The hotel was situated not in a town but in a village, thus limiting even further the opportunities for relaxation. Close by, however, was a casino separated from our hotel by a fence. The very first night Alan Rough, Sandy Jardine and Willy Johnstone went out through the main gate to explore and came back over the fence as a short cut. They were instantly apprehended by a gun-toting guard and we were soon to learn that gardeners and even some waiters carried around weapons to protect us.

Pity they could not protect us from some of our own Scottish journalists. Despite the distance and the expense, many a young Scot had made the trip to South America and most seemed to have one thing in common – the complete Scottish strip which they wore day and night. Not surprisingly the locals mistook many of them for us and offered hospitality in every form. The problem was that some of them took advantage of the situation and the drunks and womanizers were portrayed as Scottish International footballers. The stories were so numerous and so bad that many of the players took to locking themselves in their rooms, afraid to telephone home and be told of their latest escapades.

The casino became an ideal den of iniquity for the heavy drinkers and gamblers (if someone had checked they would have found out that it was unlicensed). In fact the only time I saw any of the players worse for wear was when we travelled the thirty odd miles to Cordoba to pick up our identification badges. Even that managed to end badly with big Jim Blyth, our reserve goalkeeper, threatening to knock trainer Jim Haggart through the 'effing window' for slapping him on the back a little too hard.

Consequently, we arrived at the first game against Peru more than a little rattled but convinced that this collection of old men could not halt our progress to the next stage of the competition, an opinion which the selected video tapes of Peru had done little to discourage. Ally, quite rightly, began with the players who had helped the team to get so far and, as a result, I took my place on Saturday, 3 June on the substitutes' bench in the Chateau Carreras Stadium with our heads on a level with the pitch.

It was not the greatest viewing position in the world but neither that, not the troubles of the previous weeks, seemed to matter as we took the Peruvians apart in the opening stages. It was all just as we planned, with Joe Jordan following up a Bruce Rioch shot to put us ahead and with only the goalkeeping of the eccentric and, later controversial, Argentine-born goalkeeper Ramon Quiroga keeping Peru in the game. But football has a habit of kicking you in the teeth and just when everyone on the bench began to wonder aloud how many goals we were going to win by, our game fell to pieces. Just before the interval a quick break and some poor defending let in Ramon Cueto for an equalizer. It could have been put right quickly when, soon after half-time, Bruce Rioch was hauled down in the box only for Don Masson, who had scored from the spot in the vital game against Wales, to fluff it and give the acrobatic Quiroga the chance to cover himself in even more glory.

That was probably the turning point as heads visibly went down and I mentally began to prepare myself to go on, especially when the tubby Teofilio Cubillas put the Peruvians in front. Instead Ally sent on Archie Gemmill and Lou Macari to replace captain Rioch and Don Masson. It made me a long, long way back in the pecking order. But by now Peru were going through the gaps in droves and had I gone on I would probably have been tarred with the same brush. As it was I sat watching with a sinking heart as Cubillas bent one over our wall and into the net. We had simply fallen apart and from being a team in total command Scotland suddenly looked like a bunch of frightened novices.

Ally MacLeod said at his press conference the next day that it felt like the end of the world but little did he know that the nightmare had hardly started for, at that very moment, the samples of Willie Johnston and Kenny Dalglish were being analyzed and the news about to be broken. The trip back to our desolate hotel was bad enough because now all the stories of drinking and womanizing would suddenly carry credence and no one needed telling that a certain section of the Scottish press contingent would turn from 'us' to 'them' and that the knives would start going in with a vengeance.

Whatever Willie has said since, I cannot help but feel that it was all down to him. The doctor came around at least four times to ask what medicines we were taking and to show him whatever we were on so that the decision was up to him. I was taking laxatives at the time and I even declared those before being told that they were safe. I can conclude only that Willie and the others who were taking Reactivan, had not, for whatever the reasons, told the doc. To claim, as Willie did, that he used them regularly as a decongestant was no excuse. He should still have had any medicines cleared even if they had been only smarties.

You can imagine the atmosphere at the hotel after that. Even less was seen of the players. Even though I was then single with no wife to worry about at home and had not taken part personally in the defeat, it was contagious and I hid myself away with my carefully-saved copies of *Playboy* and Harold Robbins' novels.

My one consoling thought was that we would make a recovery in our next game against Iran who were even more unfancied than Peru and that I would be part of the team to do it, as Don Masson had been told by Ally that he would take no further part in the World Cup after falsely confessing to taking the same drugs. Ally had hinted as much to me himself and he had also told Jim Blyth that he would be playing instead of Alan Rough. Jim's chance went when the manager caught him in the act – watching the end of a film on video when he should have been in bed. As for me, I found out I was not in the side when I telephoned home. Ally had told the press before he told his own players and the punters at home knew from their television and radio sets who was in and who was out even before we did.

It was a mistake but, I believe, a genuine one. As he had already shown, Ally was very naïve in terms of international football but he meant well. Even when he set himself up by saying Scotland could win the World Cup he was led on by the media, and particularly by the English national papers who couldn't believe their luck. It was broadcast so widely that, in the end, Ally began to believe it himself while the players were carried along in the swell of publicity.

Ally, in fact, was very popular with the players and I always had the impression that he would have liked to have been one of us instead of having to remain slightly aloof. I am sure he would agree that he got too close but I never came to know him too well myself. Those who did know him did not help as they might have done, indeed more than one stabbed him in the back after he had confided in them. He must have been especially disappointed in Masson who didn't help anyone with his contrived admission.

We were within a whisker of another sensation before we played Peru when, sitting in the hotel's ice cream parlour, Gordon McQueen, still ruled out with injury, took a swig from a bottle of beer only to realize that it was neat bleach. Fortunately he did not take a swallow and spat it out in time but it summed up our sorry situation and warned us of more troubles to come.

Holland had already beaten Iran 3–0 and we were confident that we could restore some of our damaged pride by doing even better. We still had some spirit and there was determination in the air as we waited for the referee to inspect our studs in the tunnel but that soon turned to impatience and anger as we waited and waited.

By the time we got out there the excitement had given way to raw tension. To make it worse the local punters had disowned us and there were only 8,000 in the ground, the lowest attendance of the entire tournament. It was like a practice match.

The best we could do in the first half was an own goal forced by the persistence of Joe Jordan. I was frustrated and itching to join the action but I should have realized that there was no chance for me in this one. Martin Buchan had to come off when he took a kick in the face from Willie Donachie, with Ally bringing on Tom Forsyth even though he had already discovered that he did not play well alongside Kenny Burns. Danaiiford earned himself a small place in his country's football history when he left Archie Gemmill for dead and beat Alan Rough on his near post. Disaster had struck again and though Ally had told me to get ready, he sent on Joe Harper and brought off Kenny Dalglish.

The players, to be fair, shouldered the responsibility themselves in the dressing room after the game and they knew that their humiliation had been witnessed live on television for a second time. The supporters who had travelled so far to watch us win the Cup turned on us viciously, spitting at the players from a ramp above the coach, screaming obscenities and demanding the manager's head on a silver plate. The demonstration continued until we left and, to our disgust, we learned later that some of it had been stagemanaged by the media, though there was obviously no shortage of takers. The one bright spot which went almost unnoticed on the long drive back was that Holland and Peru had shared a goalless draw and that we could still qualify by beating the 1974 runners-up with a three-goal margin. Mind you, it would have meant a place in the funny farm for anyone who had suggested that then.

It was to everyone's relief when we left the Sierras Hotel and Alta Gracia to head for the new surroundings of Mendoza and the little San Francisco Hotel. From a purely personal and selfish point of view, I knew that my chance had come as well. Not that I was fully convinced until the team sheet went up. Stuart Kennedy was in for Sandy Jardine; Tom Forsyth was partnering Kenny Burns and the skipper, Bruce Rioch, came back in place of Lou Macari. Most important of all, Graeme Souness replaced John Robertson as we lined up in a new 4–4–2 formation.

There were all sorts of stories about senior players dictating tactics and approach but it didn't come down to that at all. It was like that bad spell at Liverpool which ended when Joe Fagan announced there would be no more meetings. That is what happened in Mendoza and no manager in the world, Herrera and Paisley included, would have known what to do in the circumstances. The truth was that we knew our play couldn't get any worse and that things could only improve. This was the attitude we took with us onto the pitch.

If ever proof was needed of it being written in the stars that Scotland should fail, it was proven that day. We started well with Rioch hitting the bar and Kenny Dalglish having a goal ruled out. We had shaken the Dutch and they looked even more troubled when their influential, world-class midfield player Johan Neeskens was stretchered off. But, would you believe it, we conceded the first goal when Kennedy and Rough got themselves in a mess and finished up fouling Rep as he cashed in. Rensenbrink, who had already scored three against Iran, did the business from the penalty spot.

To our credit we still kept trying and when Joe Jordan headed down my long ball from the left for Kenny Dalglish to score, we had done enough to have an enthusiastic half-time dressing room for the first time in the tournament. It was well founded and within a few seconds of the restart I had been pushed in the penalty area and Archie Gemmill scored from the penalty spot. Gemmill then produced a solo run and finish for the goal of the tournament and, with more than twenty minutes showing on the stadium clock, it looked as though the miracle was happening.

The Dutch, who had been having almost as much trouble in their camp as we had, were looking resigned until Johnny Rep suddenly aimed a speculative shot at goal, Alan Rough misjudged it and the dream was shattered. Perhaps, on reflection, it was the best result for at least we emerged from the mire with a little pride. If we had qualified for the next round there could have been even more shame heaped on Scotland as certain players had decided they were heading home whatever the result either because of flak from their families over the fabricated tales or because they knew they were out of the team reckoning.

Once things started going wrong it became like a Dutch

auction with players telephoning the press centre in Cordoba offering to sell their exclusive story. As it was the 3–2 win over Holland was a good excuse for a drunken farewell in Mendoza at the foot of the Andes. The lads even put on a cabaret and spirits were still high and the beer still flowing when I left, with full permission, in the early hours of the morning for a beach in Rio.

Another player to get the manager's consent to travel home independently from the party was Lou Macari who was going to join his American wife in New York. When I asked him what time his flight was to the Big Apple, he just laughed. He was heading back to London with his ghost writer from the *Sun*.

The others had their say too and it was while I was lying on the beach in Rio reading a copy of the *Observer* that I saw Archie Gemmill had described me as 'a chocolate soldier'. That was just the medicine I needed. It lifted the gloom and I consoled myself with the thought that I had not let anyone down, least of all myself. I even managed to squeeze myself into one or two of the critics' line-up for the best team at the World Cup competition. How you can be judged on just one game, I don't know.

14
Jock Stein

It was one of the saddest days of my life when Jock Stein died at the end of our World Cup qualifying game against Wales. I felt I had lost far more than a manager, for he was a man whose friendship I cherished – a great man who I really miss.

I was not playing that day because of suspension, but I suspected that something was not quite right with the 'Big Man' at half time when he did not seem as positive or as assured as usual. His death was like a hammer blow, coming within minutes of us rescuing a seemingly lost position to qualify for the Mexico World Cup Finals.

If either Peter Shilton or Ray Clemence had been Scottish, who knows what might have happened in Spain four years after the Argentina disaster. For once in Scotland's chequered international history, lessons had been learned, plans had been laid and there was a squad of ambitious and dedicated players. Alan Rough is a nice man and not nearly as bad a goalkeeper as certain sections of the press would have you believe. He was certainly the best Scotland had in the 1982 World Cup but he was not world class though that was hardly his fault. Neither was it the fault of one of the best managers I have ever come across, the 'Big Man' Jock Stein. I have nothing but admiration for the way he handled both himself and one of the most difficult national teams in the world. The Scots as a nation passionately believe that they should be the best at everything and are disappointed when they are not.

In football, it is inevitably the manager who is blamed

when things go wrong but all he can do is pick the best team available and then cross his fingers, toes and anything else once the players have trotted over the white line. When Jock was appointed I knew what to expect because Kenny Dalglish, who had played under him at Celtic, gave me a tremendous insight into the man. But even those who were not so fortunate quickly discovered what Jock was like and if they did not, they tended not to be around for too long. He knew everything that was going on. He would sit in the hotel foyer or in the restaurant with his back to the wall so that nothing escaped his attention and he ruled with a rod of iron; the iron fist without the velvet glove.

The contrast between Spain and Argentina could not have been stronger. Ally MacLeod was one of the lads, wanting to share the joke and never worrying about being on the receiving end of a crack himself. With Jock, however, you took no liberties. We called him boss and meant it. No one ever had a second chance as Archie Gemmill would testify. As team captain he approached the boss late one Saturday night before a World Cup qualifying game and asked if the lads could go out for a drink. The look precluded any answer and next morning there was a big meeting about attitudes. Jock Stein demanded to know if we would have approached our club managers with the same request, all the time looking very pointedly at the Liverpool contingent and reminding us of Bob Paisley's probable response. I was glad that a hard game and the trip north had tired me out to the extent of having gone to bed early the night before but he certainly made his point. It was driven home in the next team that Big Jock named which did not include Archie Gemmill and he has not been in the squad since.

I almost got into trouble myself some while later in Brussels at a European Championship qualifying match when Kenny Dalglish and I, with full permission from the boss, went out shopping with a Belgian friend of mine. The only stipulation had been that we were back in time for a team meeting. It was a good day out and the only dispute was over the time of our return. Kenny was so convinced that the meeting had been called for 5 P.M. that I readily fell in with him and we even did a little more shopping on the way back.

The moment we saw Jock Stein sitting in the hotel's reception area we knew we had blown it. Even before we had crossed the threshold he tore into me, pointing out that as skipper of the side I should know better and should be setting an example for the rest of the team, particularly the youngsters. Kenny did his best to take the blame but the boss wouldn't let him get a word in edgeways and the tirade carried on through the hotel corridors until we reached the room where the rest of the squad were being weighed and measured. Just to make sure everyone knew that there was not a different set of rules for the captain, he repeated everything he had just said for the benefit of the others.

My pride was damaged and there was no high horse for me to climb on as he was totally justified and, once again, Graeme Souness was in the wrong. Remembering Archie's fate, I spent an anxious time waiting for the next squad to be announced. I don't think I have ever been so pleased to see my name on a team list.

Jock would make his feelings known to his teams right until kick off and I have often seen him put players under pressure in the dressing room before a game. Quite deliberately, he would name players he considered were not playing their best for their country. He was never slow to criticize, or point the finger or afraid to do it in front of everyone to emphasize his viewpoint, regardless of whether you were a youngster feeling your way or a big name like Charlie Nicholas. Most important, it worked. It was not so much a wind but a gale of change when he stepped in and one thing I liked instantly was the way he tempered our tartan enthusiasm. He needed to for the route to Spain and the World Cup finals was pitted with minefields in places like Sweden, Israel, Portugal and Northern Ireland.

Having missed the preliminaries for Argentina I was looking forward to the challenge. Although I made a bad beginning when I missed the opening match against Sweden in Stockholm through injury. Fortunately the rest of the team didn't miss me and a goal from Gordon Strachan gave us a flying start. It is reckoned that to qualify for the finals you need to win at home and draw away. With typical Scottish perversity we reversed the process by drawing with Portugal at Hampden, winning away in Israel and drawing at home with the Irish.

I was back for the game in Glasgow but, for some reason, Jock played me on the right side of midfield. The Portuguese defended well while we huffed and puffed a great deal without ever looking as though we would break them down and satisfy our 60,765 crowd. We put that right four months or so later when we played Israel in Tel Aviv in front of the television cameras relaying the game live to Scotland. It was the classic moment for us to fall flat on our faces as the home side, though unfancied, had strung together a series of fine results. From my own experience of playing against them regularly for Liverpool, I knew that it was going to be no easy task. I was again out on the right but this time things went quite well for me and a good night was capped when Kenny Dalglish scored from a corner to give us a single-goal victory.

It was a tired but happy team that arrived back in Glasgow and I was looking forward to bed as we returned via Rome with the prospect of just three hours' sleep before an early start back to Merseyside. Kenny had opted to stay with relatives which meant a new room-mate for me. I hadn't a clue who it was to be until I overheard Tottenham's Steve Archibald say in a very loud voice that he was not going to share with me. I was too tired to take the bait and discover what this odd young man had against me and, in fact, I was grateful to have a room to myself for once, affording maximum sleeping time. But I have never forgotten nor have I found out what it was that Archibald had against me. Fortunately since then we have talked, played and even roomed together. Being two players abroad we shared common problems and that helped to bridge the gap and bring us together.

A month later, almost 80,000 people turned up at Hampden only to be disappointed again as we dropped a point to the Irish with the goals coming from Wark and Hamilton and Souness again absent through injury! I was back four weeks later in my favourite midfield role, with Scotland, at last, winning at home. The score against Israel was 3-1 but it was nowhere near as comfortable as it looked for we needed a decidedly dodgy penalty to put us on our way and I know that if it had gone against us, there would have been 61,489 rioting Scots.

John Robertson scored twice from the penalty spot that night with Provan adding the other. Robbo was on the spot again in the return game against Sweden in a two-goal win with Souness once more sidelined through injury. It left us needing a single point from our remaining two games in Belfast and Lisbon to send us to Spain and we did it on the first attempt with a goalless draw in Ireland which was a real battle. It was one of those windy nights and it was Pat Jennings' long kicking which gave us as much trouble as anything else.

It may not sound a great result but I derived as much

satisfaction from that performance as from many a better scoreline. Encouraged by the demanding fans, the Scots' game has long been based on the old 'Up And At 'Em' attitude which has often cost us goals and matches. This, however, was a genuine team performance, a rare professional job that got us exactly what we wanted. Although we went on to throw away the last game in Portugal, we qualified for Spain solely on merit while England, as Jock gleefully pointed out, did so with the help of others. It was a tough section to come through as the Irish showed by their exploits in the finals. It was the third time in a row that Scotland had qualified and, this time, we were determined that nothing should go wrong.

The only pity was our last result against Portugal. Jock Stein had quietly suggested that it would be a good psychological boost to get through the year and ten games without a loss against us. We scored first through Sturrock and looked to be cruising our way to a nice win in the magnificent Stadium of Light in Lisbon until St Mirren goalkeeper, Billy Thomson, conceded a soft goal to Manuel Fernandes who then went on to delight a small crowd and sicken us by scoring a second.

However, I wasn't worried and I eagerly looked forward to the draw as television linked up Ireland's Pat Jennings, Kevin Keegan and me. With the competition organized as it was the chances were that even if we drew one of the really big teams, we could qualify for the second phase in second place.

It was hard to keep on a brave face as the draw in Madrid paired us first with the greatest team in the world, Brazil, and then with Europe's on form team of the moment, the Soviet Union. The fact that New Zealand were in with us scarcely registered. I said the right things in front of the cameras while secretly wishing we could swap with either Northern Ireland, who had Yugoslavia,

Honduras and the hosts Spain, or with England who were to meet France, Czechoslovakia and Kuwait. I didn't enjoy dinner that night and felt very low.

The last thing we wanted was for anyone to shout how we were going to conquer the world and, fortunately, as Jock Stein felt the same we approached the finals keeping a very low profile. This was reflected in the Home International Championships. We had drawn yet again with the Irish and only 25,000 supporters turned up to see us beat the Welsh with an Asa Hartford goal although there was the usual full house to see Paul Mariner score the goal that beat us at Hampden. There was no lap of honour this time and as we left the ground Phil Thompson and Phil Neal were given more wishes for good luck than me. My jacket needed dry cleaning after walking through the car park to the car the three of us were sharing. If the fans were subdued so was the commercial world. They seemed to be frightened to death of becoming involved; hardly surprising after the way they had scrambled to disassociate themselves when things started to go wrong four years earlier.

There was no great farewell party, no parades in front of hysterical fans as we slipped quietly away from the pressures of Scotland to prepare in a first-class hotel on Portugal's Algarve. Stein made it immediately clear that it was a working trip and that there was to be no messing around. He said we could indulge in a few beers during the evening but even this was said in such a way that few took him up on his offer, everyone wanting to impress and no one wanting the finger pointed at them at training the next morning.

There was no bickering about money this time as a committee of players, comprising Asa Hartford, Willie Miller and Kenny Dalglish, had sorted it out with the minimum of fuss by the time we boarded our British

Caledonian charter from Glasgow to Faro. The real test of Jock's abilities for organization and discipline was still to come for if there ever was a setting for disaster and the engineering of our own downfall it was in Spain for, instead of being installed in the austere setting of the Basque country in Northern Spain as we were led to believe, we found ourselves in the heart of the holiday area with two of our three games in Malaga.

The predictions, thank God, proved to be unfounded. The Scots' supporters were absolutely marvellous. They mixed with the locals, the holidaymakers and the Brazilians and enjoyed themselves without becoming a nuisance to anyone. They backed us to the hilt and let no one, especially themselves and their country, down. The team were based in Sotto Grande, an hour away from the resort of Marbella and an hour and a half away from the stadium in Malaga. The news reporters from Scotland and England must have licked their lips in anticipation of the front page headlines they were going to get. How we disappointed them.

The hotel was out of the way and sectioned off. There was no other team anywhere near and no one, especially the press, gained entry without Jock Stein's express permission. They spoke to us only when he wanted them to interview us and even little Sammy Lee, not then in the England squad but in Spain on holiday, could not get in. We had to go outside the gates to see him. The only exception was James Bond himself. Sean Connery, a keen soccer fan, joined us to watch Brazil's opening match against the Soviet Union but he was one of the rare guests.

Not that it was like a prison, far from it. There was lots to do, not least of all being able to take advantage of the glorious sunshine. But Jock even organized the sunbathing, keeping a careful eye on the fair-skinned members of the squad and limiting even those of us with somewhat swarthier complexions to 90 minutes or so, and imposing a complete curfew 24 hours before games. We did our training on a magnificent polo field. The grass was as good as Wembley's and it was so big that there was room for at least eight full-size pitches. In other words the preparations were perfect being marred only by the day that Kenny Dalglish sat on a glass table and went straight through it, inflicting a few nasty little cuts in a most inconvenient place. I always said he had the biggest backside in football!

In other words there were no excuses to be found and Group Six got under way just as we hoped it would when Brazil recovered from Bal's 34th minute goal for the Soviet Union to win with two late efforts from Socrates and Eder. We had reckoned that if Brazil won their opening game they would not worry too much against us. We began to fancy ourselves for a draw – but first we had to play New Zealand for the first time in Scotland's history.

We knew that in such a tight grouping, goals could be decisive and we were all geared up to score a few against the Kiwis. The team was as expected and, after little more than half an hour, we were in control with goals from Dalglish and two from John Wark. Then we did it again. Ten crazy minutes saw New Zealand score twice through Summer and Wooddin. It was the old story, sloppy defence, two gift goals and the familiar black feeling of despair began to creep over me. Even further goals from John Robertson and Steve Archibald could not dispel the feeling that we had put ourselves under undue pressure when a five-goal victory, as it could so easily have been, had been there for the taking.

We had three days to put it right before travelling to Seville to meet the tournament favourites Brazil with the manager warning us that there could be no gift goals this time. Even so we were still optimistic that we could get something against the confident Brazilians. There was some controversy over team selection this time as Jock Stein opted to go for Archibald instead of Dalglish but the gamble appeared to be well justified, when, after just 18 minutes, John Wark headed my long ball down for Narey to score. We were ecstatic and not even an equalizer from Zico 12 minutes before half-time, after Alan Rough had made a hash of his defensive wall, could deflate us as we went in to the dressing room.

It was not to be. Zico's free kick had given them the taste for victory and they came out for the second half sizzling. I was guilty of letting Oscar get a yard on me for a near post ball three minutes into the second half and, instead of settling down and holding things together we went chasing goals, and soon conceded another to Eder. Jock immediately sent on McLeish for Hartford and Dalglish for Strachan but Falcao added a fourth. I have always considered myself a good professional and a winner but even through the disappointment of defeat I could see that this game was a great and memorable experience. The stadium was tight and compact, generating a tremendous atmosphere rather like that in an English stadium. But there the similarity ended. The grass was long, the air was hot and humid and half-naked South American women were doing the Samba not three yards from where we were playing.

I looked at Socrates, Zico, Falcao and Eder and thought that this was what the World Cup was really all about. They may not have won the World Cup but they were, without doubt, the best team in the competition and I was pleased to have played against them.

But, despite that defeat, we were still in with a chance if we could beat the Soviet Union. When the Russians coasted to an uncomplicated three-goal win over New

Zealand with goals from Gavrilov, Blokhin and Baltacha, they knew that they needed only to draw with us to secure their place in the second round. It produced tremendous pressure and an electric atmosphere in the dressing room before the game. Jock Stein had told me all along that he thought Joe Jordan would cause havoc against the Russians and, sure enough, he played him and again left out Dalglish. Jock felt that Kenny couldn't perform to full capacity in the heat but, personally, I would have picked him even though he had not been on top form in his game and a bit.

Again it looked as though Jock had read it perfectly when Joe Jordan put us in front and, for a while, I thought we were going to win. Indeed we deserved to but in Dasayev we came up against the goalkeeper who was acknowledged as the best in the competition. And then we were at it again, giving away crucial goals just as Scotland seemed to have done ever since I had been playing for them.

Chivadze put the Russians on terms when Alan Rough dived a split second too early and then failed to come out quickly enough, after a complete mix up between Hansen and Miller, thus allowing Shengelia to score. I could not help thinking at the time that had Ray Clemence been there he would have buried the Russian perhaps not in the way Schumacher had against Patrick Battiston in the semi-final, a foul I could not condone, but would certainly have stopped him with a professional foul.

Even when I scored to make it 2-2 we knew that, short of a miracle, we were on our way home again and, sure enough, soon after my goal the whistle went. It says something about our mental attitude that the overwhelming feeling was that we had not disgraced ourselves. Of course we had wanted to do well, too, but, at least events in Argentina, the nightclub incident in Copenhagen, the boat business and all the other things that had given Scottish international football such a reputation over the years had, for the time being anyway, been put to rest.

My heart went out to Jock Stein for he had done all he could, picking the best players, timed the build-up correctly and could have done no more to give us, the players, the right platform from which to perform. It was us who failed, not him. He was scuppered by the draw which was twice as difficult as that of four years earlier. That is not meant to be a criticism of Ally MacLeod and, perhaps, his enthusiasm together with Jock Stein's discipline and organization might have produced a different result.

But those thoughts counted for nothing. We were out and while Brazil, the Soviet Union and, worse still, England, moved on to the next round we were heading home, or at least joining our families on holidays tentatively arranged beforehand. I was flying to Majorca to join my wife Danny and her parents at their home.

The hotel manager assured me that my journey had been arranged and that my ticket would be waiting for me at the busy Malaga airport for the 40-minute flight. When I arrived no one had heard of me and no one had a ticket for the captain of a defeated team. You can imagine that at the end of June every plane was full and, in the end I was lucky to get a connection to Madrid and what should have been a simple trip took me the whole day. I never did get the chance to thank that hotel manager.

A final word on the 1982 World Cup. I thought it a tragedy that Brazil failed to win the tournament. They were a much better team than either the winners Italy or runners-up West Germany and had a team of their quality been successful it would have been a boost for the game. They finished off the group by putting four past New Zealand (whose only goals were those which beat us).

They beat the holders Argentina 3-1 but then showed that they were, indeed, human by throwing away their advantage and losing to a Paolo Rossi hat-trick. It is nice to know that it is not just Scotland who can blow it!

15
Dalglish and Others

My relationship with Kenny Dalglish did not get off to the best of starts mainly due to the fact that he thought I was a poof! Our paths first crossed on my first trip for Scotland when we played West Germany in Frankfurt just before the 1974 World Cup, and by a strange coincidence, we were instantly marked down as room-mates.

I couldn't understand why I never saw the Celtic striker at night. He was, I supposed, a right stop-out. There I was, all keen and eager to impress, into bed early and always asleep before my room-mate got in.

It wasn't until we joined forces at Liverpool and became regular room partners that he confessed to me that he had heard that I was not quite right, and used to lurk outside the bedroom door until he was sure I was asleep and he was safe. It was, I try to tell myself, understandable in those days when hairdryers and the fashionable hairstyles that went with them were hardly the thing among the short-back-and-side brigade of the football world. Add to that my trim, neat moustache, the deodorant and the French fragrances that I splashed across my face and I suppose I was a little different.

These days the dressing room looks and smells more like Vidal Sassoon's Mayfair salon and it is all taken for granted. But you can imagine what the boy from Glasgow thought of the lad from Edinburgh.

A lot of people assumed that our friendship dates from those formative years but it was hardly surprising that we did not exactly follow each other's careers with careful interest. Indeed, it was some time before we met again when we were both called up for a game against Bulgaria. I made my début for Scotland in that game and, funnily enough, next time I played against Spain in the European Championships while Kenny was on the bench. We didn't get close – he wouldn't let me!

I don't suppose either of us was particularly impressed with the other at that stage because the one thing we had in common as youngsters, apart from both being Scottish, was that we were late developers in the game. Sure we had our schoolboy and youth caps, but we were scarcely earth shakers. Don't get me wrong, Kenny was a good player then but not world class as he was to become in the later years of his career, especially while at Liverpool.

It was only when we linked up at Anfield that we began to get to know each other and, even now, there is no way we would call our friendship close. What we have enjoyed is a good working relationship based on a mutual respect for each other's ability on the football field with the friendship getting only as close as we wanted it. Maybe it would have been different had we been neighbours in our private lives as well as hotel room partners but we lived in different parts of Merseyside and this in itself restricted us to the odd after-match meal together with our wives.

In those early days at Anfield I suppose I was almost Kenny's unofficial interpreter as there weren't many who could understand his broad Glaswegian accent. It made some conversations difficult but has more than once saved him from a booking because a bemused referee could not fathom what he was talking about. Not that Kenny ever went out of his way to chat people up, particularly those outside the game. He was always civil to those in football but would be dreadfully suspicious of anyone he did not know.

Within the club he would be as sharp with his tongue

as he was in his turning on the pitch. He could also be unbelievably irritating, always the one to raise an objection if someone came up with an idea and if a sponsor offered a deal everyone would be happy but him. He would have made the perfect trade union official, and yet he never got involved with the Professional Footballers' Association. Mind you, this perverse attitude often earned the others a few extra quid, particularly for me as his room-mate. He would automatically ask for more if he was offered an outside contract out of habit. If he was offered £500 he would ask for £600 even though he would have done the job for half as much if they had started off at a lower price. Instead the jobs would be passed on to us lesser mortals. Not that Kenny was mean. Sure, he would remember if he had lent you a pound, like any good Scot, but equally, he would always stand his corner, buy the drinks or pay for dinner and he would be generous with his time for charities or children.

Although we nicknamed him 'Super' at Anfield, no one could accuse the man of taking advantage of his fame though at times he would get away with murder simply through being a household name. On trips with Scotland he never abused his seniority and would mix with the young home-based Scots, always ready to give advice, particularly if one of them was contemplating a transfer south of the Border. I recall him talking very seriously to Steve Archibald like a Dutch Uncle before his move to Spurs and, again, with Charlie Nicholas before he went to Arsenal. Obviously Charlie didn't listen too carefully as he went to Highbury instead of Anfield.

Kenny is intensely patriotic. While I pride myself on being British, he is purely and simply a Scot, fiercely proud of every Scottish achievement whether in sport or not. As a player he is one of the greatest competitors I have ever come across. He is exceptionally brave and physically a lot tougher than the critics give him credit for. For me his bravery is often overlooked. He is kicked all game long but I have never once seen him accept it and admit that he was beaten. Even when he is having a nightmare – and even good players do – he never hides. He always shows himself and always wants the ball.

If there is a criticism against him it is that he is greedy but have you ever come across a top goalscorer who was not? From a purely selfish point of view his availability was his greatest asset. Caught in a corner and under pressure on the ball, look up and you would glimpse Kenny's legs. That would be enough. Play it to his feet and you would know that Kenny would hold the ball until you had escaped and were ready to have it back. From an overall viewpoint, his turning and eye for a goal are in a different class and his vision means that he is always aware of players around him.

None of this would be the same, however, without that remarkable courage of his. I recall Kenny being injured in a European Cup semi-final when he was kicked in the opening minutes, and though it was clear to everyone that he would have to be substituted, Ronnie Moran virtually had to drag him off. The same was true when he had his left cheekbone shattered in a clash with Kevin Moran of Manchester United. I was one of the first on the scene and was horrified by what I saw. The injury was so bad that it made me feel physically sick yet there he was, up on one knee and trying to push Moran away once more. The United fans sang with joy at his leaving the arena and even then, as the realization of the extent of the injury sank in, he turned round and gave them a defiant, rude gesture.

Some people were surprised at it, as they were when he kicked the ball away at Wembley in a Milk Cup Final and was criticized by no less a person than Neil

MacFarlane, the Minister with responsibility for Sport, who said that his action was no advertisement for the game. What the politician and other critics failed to appreciate on both occasions was that Kenny is first and foremost a winner.

Don't worry, Kenny can also look after himself out there when the boots are flying. He has to because otherwise he would not survive. He is cute, he uses his whole body, legs, arms and elbows and often sails on the borderline of foul play himself. It is rather like the difference between tax avoidance and tax evasion. When frustration or anger overtake him he tries, now and again, to kick people but usually he ends up getting hurt himself simply because it is not his game. He is just as obstinate off the field and he will argue that black is white. The man thinks that he is a walking encyclopaedia and it usually results in our calling in Alan 'Norris' Hansen, the memory man, to make the final decision.

As a room-mate Kenny was not bad. Because of his accent he used to leave the ordering up to me while he answered the door. What I really objected to was his corny jokes. They were straight out of *The Beano* and *Dandy* and, worse, he used me as his testing ground, invariably as I was trying to get off to sleep.

His popularity at Anfield is, of course, greater than ever but, in goalscoring terms, he developed a rival in fellow goalscorer Ian Rush, a player who has emerged as world class, comparable to the greatest of strikers such as Rossi, Zico, Greaves and Müller. Rushy is raking in the awards and Liverpool eventually had to succumb to a huge offer from Juventus although, typical of Dalglish, Robinson and Liverpool, they got the best of the deal by holding onto him for an extra season. Although I still believe that they will live to regret selling one of the world's greatest goalscorers.

Yet when he arrived at Anfield from Chester a lot of us, myself included, wondered just why the club had invested £350,000 in such an ordinary player. The consensus was that someone had slipped up for once and I certainly couldn't see much there to excite me. How wrong can you be? He seems to improve with every match and who can say where it will stop. Obviously someone saw something, it would be uncharitable to call it luck. He slotted perfectly into the Liverpool style and took total advantage of the service provided for him. Some say he would never have made it at another club but who can predict. Certainly I feel that he was right to resist overtures when he did, from the Continent, and to sign another contract for Liverpool even though he could undoubtedly have earned much more money somewhere like Italy.

Taking everything into account he would have found it difficult to settle in a strange environment as he comes from a big family and lives at home with his parents. Maybe when he is older it might be time to branch out and see whether he can succeed elsewhere although perhaps that chance will come in his international career with Wales. It is going to be fascinating seeing just how far he can go in the game. His pace and finishing were good from the moment he came into the side and he scores goals for fun. But then, as if from nowhere, he began to head goals as if he had been having lessons with John Toshack and executing turns of which Kenny Dalglish would have been proud.

Liverpool have developed, over the years, a reputation for buying players from lower divisions and turning them into stars. Players like Kevin Keegan, Phil Neal and Ray Clemence were bought from small clubs and then went on to have distinguished careers with their country. Ray Clemence was a great professional. Before a big game he would have a look about him. You could see the man psyching himself up and you would know then and there that there was not going to be a lot in it for the opposition. He was still a great goalkeeper when he left Anfield and I am as certain now as I was then that he departed at least a year too soon, not just for himself but for the club and maybe even for his replacement Bruce Grobbelaar. There were a lot of stories as to why Clem suddenly upped camp and left Liverpool for Spurs but I am convinced that the major reason was because he felt threatened by the rave reports that his rival was earning in the stiffs. With the World Cup looming, the risk seemed to prove too great, yet he was too good a goalkeeper to have been replaced that easily.

Bruce, in fact, had a nightmare in his first season and was criticized by his team-mates on the pitch, the backroom staff, the fans and the press. Had Clem stayed, Bruce could have studied at close quarters the best in the game at the art of concentration. It says a great deal for Bruce's character that he was able to survive that first year. I do not know anyone else who would. He is strong, courageous and as good on his line as anyone in the game and the only question mark hanging over him is still in his ability to concentrate and not be distracted by the crowd and everything else happening around him.

One of Liverpool's charms is that they are not, and never will be, a team of superstars. Footballers are not machines, they have their failings. Take, for example, my fellow Scot Alan Hansen. Bright, intelligent and talented but too easy going. If he had any aggression we would have been talking about him in the same breath as Franz Beckenbauer and Rudi Krol. He was capable of becoming one of the greatest sweepers of all time. I will never forget the European Cup Final against Real Madrid at the Parc des Princes Stadium in Paris. It was tense to the point of being breathtaking and to make matters worse the lines were so heavily chalked that they stood off the ground like kerbstones.

It was so bad that Phil Thompson went to trap the ball and it bounced so high off the 18-yard line that he finished up having to head it clear. That might have spread panic in other players but not Jocky. He spent the next ten minutes making fun of the unfortunate Thommo. That was typical of how relaxed Alan Hansen is. A great bloke to have around the dressing room, not only because he could use his retentive memory to settle any argument ranging from what the bonus was in a certain game five years ago to how much you would pick up from a bookmaker on a fifty pence accumulator, but simply because he is such a nice guy.

The same could be said of Phil Thompson. It may surprise a few people to read this coming from me and some may even say that I am being hypocritical but, in all honesty, he was always the sort of man I would want in the trenches with me. I was really disappointed when he refused to speak to me after I had been given the Liverpool captaincy that he treasured so highly. He thought I had stolen it from him and said so to other people in front of me but never behind my back, yet nothing could have been further from the truth.

It was sad to see Phil out of things when we were winning honours and I am convinced that had he been better suited physically to the game he would have been one of the greats. In my years in football I did not come up against many better football brains than his. He would often think five seconds ahead of the others and the higher the grade the better he was. That is why he played so well at international level where a lot of the hustle and bustle is replaced by cold calculation and he could have carried on playing for England for a lot longer than he did.

Footballers, of course, come in all shapes and sizes and it is not only the physical aspect which has to be right but also the mental attitude as well. I often used to think to myself that Sammy Lee and Michael Robinson were far too nice to be in football. For Sammy, in particular, life was difficult because he came through the ranks as a local youngster and he used to feel the criticism even more than Michael. It really used to hurt and yet you could not find two more decent players who would always put the team's interests before their own.

Sam, like Phil Thompson and Emlyn Hughes, was all Liverpool. Everyone's friend, he was not only too nice to be a footballer but also too small. It says an awful lot for him that he overcame these disabilities to do what he did for both Liverpool and England. Whereas Sam was popular with everyone, Emlyn Hughes was not. When I first arrived at Anfield I was surprised at how cliquey the club was and, in particular, the jealousy felt of Emlyn. There seemed to be resentment that he was the big dressing room earner, always called on when a personality was required for television or to earn some extra cash. But why not? He was the personality and had the charisma that was wanted by the agents. I got on fine with him and he never did me any harm.

Jimmy Case and Ray Kennedy were a two-man clique that no one minded. They were so close that they would help each other to dress and even clean each other's shoes. If you wanted to fight one you would have to fight them both. Jimmy, as I have already mentioned, was a genuine hard man as I found out when I tangled with him at Middlesbrough. His face would never change and he was always the man you wanted behind you in a battle. He, like his mate 'Razor', had his problems off the field but both were such good professionals that they never let it affect their performance on the pitch.

The same could be said of Terry McDermott, or the 'Mouthpiece', as I used to call him. Terry's liking for the odd glass of lager or several was no secret but he possessed both natural ability and fitness. He could come in after a session and still run anyone off their feet. That bloke just did not care. Everything in life was a giggle to him. Within football he is something of a legend in his own lunchtime and certainly one of the most popular players in the game.

I would not, however, have liked to have managed him. He is a great mimic and no one was safe from his humour, particularly his old manager Bob Paisley whose distinctive accent and pet phrases made him a natural target. Bob, in fact, took it well and only once did I see him close to exploding with Terry Mac, and that was on a flight to Israel. The man sitting in front of Terry had gone into a deep sleep and Terry could not resist playing a prank when lunch was served. It started with a couple of peas, graduated to mashed potato and by the time the poor fellow woke up he had a full meat and three veg. balancing precariously on his head. The first movement sent the lot crashing down into his lap and Bob, who had spotted what was going on, blew his top and was out of his seat and heading for Terry with murder in his eyes when I intercepted him and managed to calm him down.

This, I am sure, contributed to Terry's premature departure from the club but our regular and lucrative trips for the club to the Middle East used to be packed with incident. I still giggle when I recall Jocky Hansen returning to his hotel in Israel a little tired and emotional after a long evening, picking up his key only to discover he was in the wrong room. He stormed back to the desk to tell them they had given him the wrong key but a quick check confirmed that the room number was right, it was just that our intrepid defender had staggered into the hotel next door!

Another popular player at Anfield, and most other places, was England striker David 'Doc' Johnson. There was no side to that man, he was happy to drift along, ignoring the cliques and being friends with everyone. He was also a very useful man to have around the dressing room due to a bag he carried round with him that contained all the necessities of life. If you were suffering from a cold, a rash, sweaty feet or a hangover David Johnson would have a cure. A razor blade, talcum powder, after shave – whatever you wanted it would be there in that bag. Hence the nickname.

A stranger in the Anfield dressing rooms would think he had gone to the wrong place because of the number of pseudonyms floating around. I, for example, respond not just to 'Charlie' but also to 'Chas' and 'Charles' while there are other *noms de guerre* which come and go within a few days. Like the day it was announced that Bruce was going into the male modelling game, he instantly became 'Burt' because his name was associated with the American actor Burt Reynolds. His other names are 'Slaphead', 'Pally Blue' or 'Blue Boy' – at least until he lets in a soft ball and then he takes on a whole load of new unprintable names.

Phil Neal is, rather boringly, known generally as 'Neally' but the fans on the Kop have nicknamed him 'Zico' after the famous Brazilian. He is happy to acknowledge that, though he is not so pleased about his name of 'Ollie' after Oliver Hardy in the famous American double act of Laurel and Hardy. That, for me, is the most apt and I find myself waiting for him to scratch his head in the time-honoured way. Mind you, I don't think Phil likes it any more than he liked the prank I played on him soon after Scotland had qualified for the Spanish World Cup Finals and it looked as though England had missed their chance. I made a loop tape of 'We're off to Sunny Spain' and played it over and over again until he was tearing out his hair.

It made up, a little, for the ribbing the Jocks used to get. Mind you, young Steve Nicol, likely to be a Liverpool stalwart over the next decade with his two-footed versatility, did our cause no good at all when the story got back about his exploits with some scales in a chemist's shop while on a shopping trip with his wife Eleanor. One of these players who can have a little problem with weight, 'Chipsy' jumped on the machine only to see the needle swing way past his required weight to more than a stone in excess. He demanded to know if the scales were wrong, failing to understand the shop assistant's choked and negative reply, until his long-suffering wife pointed out that he was still carrying the shopping.

Steve was lucky that our defender Alan Kennedy had cornered the market in nicknames like 'Bungalow' (not much upstairs). Poor Alan had more aliases than a master criminal: 'Barney Rubble', 'Bell', 'Moon Man', 'Moony' were just a few. No wonder he kept his mouth shut in the dressing room in case he put his foot in it and earned another.

Football humour can be exceedingly cruel, even though well meant, with Sammy Lee's unathletic shape earning him the pet name of 'Quassi' – short for Quasimodo. There were also the simpler ones like plain 'Lawro' for Mark Lawrenson; 'Jocky' or the 'Big Yin' Hansen; 'Jimbo' Case; 'Razor' Kennedy; 'Tinker' or 'Thommo' Thompson. Others took a little explaining like that of Emlyn Hughes, known universally as 'Crazy Horse' except at Anfield where he was always called 'Edgar'; while Kenny Dalglish preferred 'Super' to his more recent nickname of 'Duggs' which has an obscure and somewhat filthy Scottish connotation.

My old neighbour David Fairclough was called 'The Whip' because of the way he whipped the ball into the middle but on a bad day he answered to the name of 'Bambi'. Steve Heighway was Paddy because he was the most unlikely Irishman to pull on an Eire shirt (I think he qualified because he had a pet goldfish born in Dublin), while Bob Paisley's war exploits and the reprimands he handed out had him known as the 'Gunner' as well as 'Douggie Doings'.

The funny thing is that everyone at Liverpool, apart from Joe Fagan, had at least one other name. He has been just Joe for as long as I can remember. That Anfield dressing room certainly kept you on your toes and one thing I would like to feel I left behind was a closer-knit and far less cliquey dressing room than there was when I joined. The atmosphere, as we crossed that line onto the pitch remains superbly unaltered.

16
The Outer Fringe

Football was once almost exclusively the sport of the working classes with the only exception being the local businessman who chose to become a director either out of love for the game or because it would increase his lot within the community. How the game has changed. Property developers, show-business personalities and front men now take over clubs for many different reasons while the terraces are populated with people from all classes.

The footballers seem to meet most of them in the players' lounge, at the hotel or outside the dressing room. They range from ticket touts to royalty. My first contact with the outer fringe of football was as an apprentice at Spurs. In those days the pop stars and agents were not bothered with the likes of me and my initial dealings were with the touts. They earned a good living from White Hart Lane at that time. With the European matches and the big gates, it was hard for a youngster not to give in to the temptation of doubling his £7 a week wages by flogging his two complimentary tickets. They were good seats, were always wanted and my two for every home match went to a regular contact who was well known at the club and who also dealt with the senior players. A big match in Europe, a local derby against Arsenal or a visit by Manchester United meant I was able to buy a new suit or a couple of shirts.

It was all a bit sleazy in those days: dirty macs, back doors and secretive deals. A friend of mine, then working for Birmingham City, was helping with the tickets for a

Cup replay against Spurs when he tried to put a block on the London touts who were looking for a big killing. They threatened to tip him over the railway bridge at St Andrews. But, like pornography, ticket dealing is a trade which has moved from the back shelf to the front of the shop. It is based on supply and demand and the operators now have offices in the West End and advertise their services in newspapers like *The Times* and the *Telegraph*. They are even welcome at the clubs and deal openly with club secretaries who are in the business of filling seats.

With the stadiums rarely full nowadays there has been a subtle change and a great many of the tickets for First Division matches find their way abroad to bring planeloads of Scandinavians flying over every weekend to get their look at British football. Understandably the dealer expects and gets tickets for the big games as well and, I suppose, that is when he makes his killing. Mind you, it is not so easy for the player as he gets older and better known for the circle of acquaintances gradually widens. There is the man who provides you with fresh fish or meat every week, the man who has your car serviced ahead of the queue, and the payment is always the promise of a ticket for the big game and when you play for a club like Liverpool they tend to come along rather often.

I used to think that Spurs was an Aladdin's cave for the top internationals as they picked up their fancy Italian suits and colour televisions but Liverpool is in a class of its own. There is nothing that is not available to the players and I was even offered a complete sauna recently. Goods seem to fall off lorries with great regularity and you have to be extremely careful to distinguish between a genuine cost price offer and the likelihood of becoming a receiver of stolen property.

Make no mistake, football is not excluded from the law

and I remember when we came back from a European Cup tie in Lisbon in 1984, the whole planeload of players, press and supporters was searched. I discovered later that the players and press were lucky to get away so quickly as some of the club's influential supporters were delayed for two hours or more while the women were strip-searched. Everyone was indignant but it was an eye-opener a few days later when customs officers seized drugs worth £6 million at Liverpool docks.

Sometimes, having a face which is frequently seen in the papers or on television can be extremely annoying if you are trying to have a quiet, intimate meal in a restaurant. Most of the time, however, it is a perk of the job and opens all sorts of doors. For instance, when my wife Danny and I were on our way to the United States for a holiday we were stopped by immigration because the date on Danny's visa was so blurred it was indecipherable. We cursed our luck and prepared ourselves for a long wait in the queue at the American Embassy the next day but as we walked up the stairs a Military Policeman spotted me, recognized the Souness grimace and whisked us straight in. We were in and out within five minutes and on our way to the States. Being 'recognized' can also work with more important things like buying cars and houses. Providing you keep an eye out for the sharp dealer who sees a bit of money coming his way, you can usually get the best deals. Empty tables in full restaurants suddenly materialize and a word with the right person can mean an upgrade from economy to first class on a long and otherwise tiring flight.

All these things add up to make life very comfortable for those professional footballers lucky enough to make it to the top. Don't imagine, however, it is open sesame for one and all. It only falls to a fortunate few and I'm grateful to be numbered among them. How else, for example, could I expect to meet the Queen Mother as I did at the 1984 Milk Cup Final against Everton at Wembley. I am a devoted Royal fan and that experience ranks high on my list. I have also met a number of Middle Eastern potentates through football. There is a growing interest in soccer in that part of the world and Liverpool were not slow to take advantage by sending us out to play matches there, not so much as missionaries, but more to fill up the coffers to help pay our own wages.

Pop stars and show-business personalities, however, are still in greater supply than Sheiks and Kings. Quite a few of the former are ardent fans of football and even the Royal Shakespeare Company's two top directors, Trevor Nunn and Terry Hands, support Ipswich and Liverpool respectively. Terry talks well about the game and obviously has very good taste. What is nice about these people is that they have a genuine love for the game. Elton John and Rod Stewart, for example, hardly need to be seen rubbing shoulders with us old sweats to enhance their reputation yet both devote a tremendous amount of time and energy to soccer. In the case of Elton John, you can also add money to the list and, going by what he has done at Watford, a very shrewd football judgement.

Rod Stewart is one of Scotland's biggest fans and the funny thing is that when he made a record with the Scottish World Cup squad before the Argentina disaster, he was as much in awe of players like Joe Jordan, Kenny Dalglish, Bruce Rioch and Don Masson as they were of him. He need not have been as he proved when he came to our hotel, the Dunblane Hydro, to do some filming to go with the record. He made a dramatic arrival by helicopter and was then even more impressive when he joined in a six-a-side game. He was not so much at home by the swimming pool in Marbella four years later when he came over to swap a few stories. His then wife Alana was definitely not a football fan and poor Rod had this made clear to him before being led off, not quite by the ear, but almost.

There are others like Terry Sylvester, who made his name with groups such as the Swinging Blue Jeans and the Hollies, and Mick Jones of Foreigner, who have shown more than a passing interest in football.

The nearest I came to crossing over to show business was when the brilliant playwright, Alan Bleasdale, invited little Sammy Lee and me to appear in his highly-praised award-winning series, *Boys from the Blackstuff*. I knew Alan as a regular at Liverpool and, indeed, he had a nephew on the Liverpool books for a while but when he approached me I had no idea of the sort of impact his work was going to have. It was all very heavy with strong political overtones which brought home the message of unemployment and its implications for Merseyside.

The whole thing was a great experience and made me realize just how hard actors and entertainers have to work. There is a lot more to it than the finished product, as seen by the public, just as there is with football. I had a total of four lines in one episode and Sammy had a walk-on part. The uninitiated might expect that to take a few moments only but we reported at breakfast time and it was seven in the evening before we finished, and that was not because we kept making mistakes!

The £150 we were paid underlined the long hours that actors work for their money. I shall always remember how the star of the series, Bernard Hill, changed from an articulate Manchester United supporter to a horror of a person. He became a totally different man in a matter of seconds. A nice little footnote to that is that I have, since, received royalties for my performance (if you can call it that) from, of all places, Poland and Hungary. The only other television performances have been the statutory appearances on *Question of Sport* with David Coleman, after-match interviews and once allowing the cameras to invade my house for a Milk Cup Final preliminary.

One thing in football we have in common with our illustrious friends from the pop world are the groupies. They are easy to spot in a sport dominated by men as they hang around outside grounds and hotels but, though it is all very tempting as a young, single player, it is also very frustrating because, unlike those snooker players we read about, footballers are hardly in a position to take advantage. Hotel stays are always before a game when you are under supervision and players are unable to take up the offers which can come with a request for an autograph or even in a letter received before leaving home. I still get letters offering all sorts of services from women and even from the odd, very odd man but, these days, I just show them to my wife and we have a good laugh about them. There is the other sort of football groupie who is not after your body to chalk up as another conquest but, instead, just wants your autograph as often as possible or, preferably, a photograph taken with her. In return she will always remember your birthday and Christmas with little gifts. It is very sweet.

Owing to the very nature of the game most of these brushes with the outside world are brief to say the least. The drink, for example, with former Prime Minister Harold Wilson at the Holiday Inn, talking about football with one eye on his minder, and the five-minute acquaintance with the brilliant American film director Mel Brooks, stand out in my memory. But, however short these meetings, it always delights me to hear of the interest these people have in our sport with its roots still deeply embedded in working-class areas. Even the Queen Mother showed either remarkable knowledge of football or had been very well briefed before the Milk Cup Final. I was more nervous of that meeting than I was of the game to follow but at least I did not let myself down as I did in another incident involving the nobility. It came at a Charity Ball and as a winner of one of the tombola prizes – a bottle of whisky of all things – I was asked to go on stage with the other winners to receive my gift from the celebrity guests, the Duke and Duchess of Westminster. The problem was that I had enjoyed a little too much to drink and instead of a quick shake of her hand or even a polite bow, I got it into my head that I wanted to kiss the attractive lady on the lips. The attending aide-de-camp nearly had hysterics but, fortunately the Duchess saw the funny side and laughed the whole thing off. I don't suppose I will ever get knighted anyway!

Inevitably, the closest encounters are with the people in your own sport. Sometimes the contact is as fleeting as with the outsiders; others you might know only by reputation or from a two-dimensional view from television; while others will go out of their way to shake hands and say hello. Although footballers do not usually mix socially with each other there have been exceptions and because they are rare they are all the more enjoyable. Often there are gatherings to go and watch a concert, normally with members of your own team. There was, however, a classic occasion when there was a meeting, if not of minds, at least of like minds.

I remember that Liverpool were playing Aston Villa at Villa Park and after the game, which we won to put us in exactly the right spirits, half a dozen of us travelled to London by train where we were met by chauffeur-driven limousines and whisked away to the Holiday Inn at Marble Arch where we met up with not only our wives but also players and wives from other teams. There were players like John Robertson, Tony Currie and Martin

O'Neill along with the friend who arranged the tickets and even a trusted journalist. A few drinks in the bar and the big black cars whisked us off to Wembley to watch Paul McCartney and Wings in concert from the very best seats. The cars were waiting right outside the arena doors when the music finished and took us into the West End where football fan Pepé had cleared the Trattoria Imperia, which is a favourite haunt of Members of Parliament and actors, of all customers to lay on a private meal for our group. It was only after the meal which included a considerable quantity of wine that the party broke up and went off, either home, back to the hotel, or on to Tramps. It was a memorable if somewhat expensive night.

Seeing players like John Robertson and Martin O'Neill that night made me wonder just what sort of hold a manager like Brian Clough had over them. Knowing 'Robbo' as I do from international football, it seems inconceivable that he should eat humble pie and that others such as Kenny Burns and Larry Lloyd should treat Clough rather like a headmaster at prep school. I first came across Cloughie when I was an apprentice at Tottenham. I was sitting in the reception area waiting to see the boss while he was there to sign Dave Mackay. He asked me my name and how long I had been at Spurs. I don't suppose he would remember now but I do, not because he possessed any great presence or charisma but because I was struck by his very unusual accent.

I have enormous respect for what he has achieved in the game but not necessarily for the way he has done it and, from what I know and have been told, I could not possibly work for that type of manager. He seems to talk down to players, just like certain referees, and he has double standards. I remember him going into the boot-room for a drink at Anfield but not letting his players go into our lounge for a drink after one game. I suppose it is because I have become used to being treated like an adult by the Anfield staff who put themselves on the same level to the extent that when they sit down to eat with you before a match, they will have exactly the same things to eat and drink. Still, if Clough can get players to perform for him then good luck, I just couldn't see myself part of that set-up and he probably wouldn't want me anyway.

In terms of success Clough is on a par with managers like Bobby Robson at Ipswich and Laurie McMenemy at Southampton, who have both won major honours at small town clubs with limited resources. I have terrific respect for McMenemy, and particularly for the way he scores at man management. Like Clough he manages to get the most out of players but whereas the former likes his players to touch their forelocks to him, McMenemy has managed to do it with the so-called bad boys and players who, by other people's standards, were finished. I have no doubt that I could have played for him. He is larger than life and would, I am sure, fit into a big club just as well as he has at Southampton. He has the same sort of image as Big Ron Atkinson, both relying heavily on personality.

Ron can always manage to laugh in any situation and he works on the principle that there is no such thing as bad publicity. Some time, perhaps, he should stop and take stock in the same way that Bobby Gould did at Coventry after they had beaten us by four goals and were being hailed as the next Champions. What a fool he would have looked if he had fallen for that one because, after that, they barely won a game. John Bond is another who speaks without thinking. I remember him having a go at Liverpool for some reason or another when Norwich were having a reasonable run under him. He became rather malicious and it stirred up the chaps so much that

Norwich took some fearful hammerings from us for a while. It was always instilled into us at Liverpool to play everything low key and to offer nothing to opponents which would set their adrenalin flowing. I know from my own experience that a rash comment, like Bond's, can really stir a team up.

Some of the so-called 'name managers' talk to the press for the sake of it and it would not hurt them to take a leaf out of the book of the most successful manager of them all, Bob Paisley, who consistently refused invitations to go on television, steering the cameras instead towards the players. It was only in his last year at the club that he relented but, even then, he conducted himself magnificently. Another manager who intrigues me is Terry Venables and I thought I had the opportunity to learn a little more about the man rather than the manager when I bumped into him while on holiday in Miami. I wanted to talk to him about his book and his television series *Hazell* but all Venners wanted to do was ask 20 questions about Liverpool. He struck me as a great Liverpool fan but I would much rather have put the ball away out of season and moved on to other topics.

Among the players in the game for whom I have a great respect are goalkeepers Pat Jennings and Peter Shilton. As for the outfield players, I really admired Paul Madeley. He played in a team of real old moaners but you never heard a word from Paul, he just got on with the game and how well he played it. The nearest I came to having an idol was Slim Jim Baxter. I loved the casual, easy way he stroked the ball around. This great player would have been around a lot longer if he had shown the same intelligence off the field as he did on it. Unfortunately we do not belong to a mutual admiration society judging by his criticisms of me in the media.

One of the most respected players in the game during

my time was undoubtedly Kevin Keegan. They still talk about him at Anfield in terms of great reverence and I can honestly say that I have never heard a bad word about him. Our paths have crossed only rarely and I am convinced that, on the last occasion, Liverpool prodded him into retirement. It was a televised FA Cup tie between Liverpool and Newcastle at Anfield. The game received a tremendous build-up because of the return of Keegan and Terry McDermott allied to the fact that Newcastle were bombing along in the Second Division.

The Newcastle players and management had talked about this being their big test and that through it they would be able to judge their First Division potential against the Champions. Well, to cut a long story short, we gave them a terrible roasting, scored four times and hardly gave the little man a kick of the ball. He was terribly depressed about it all and afterwards he talked about the difference between the two teams and especially about how he had had a yard on Mark Lawrenson and still lost out without even getting a touch on the ball. Kevin obviously took it to heart and, I guess, decided then and there that he was not going to expose himself to that type of a beating again.

However, he was wrong. We all have our off days and the number of goals he scored in his last season showed he still had that magic touch where it mattered most, in the penalty area. It is my opinion that he owed Newcastle and himself a season in the First Division and he may well regret it for the rest of his life. Too much stress is put on age in football and I believe that as footballers get older they compensate for a loss of pace and stamina with experience and knowledge. I hope, however, I know the right moment to quit.

17

The State of the Game

Football's gravy train has been derailed or, at least, shunted into siding. I have enjoyed my first-class ride and not only do I have no regrets but neither do I accept any blame for the sorry financial state of the game. I feel a certain sympathy for the old time greats like Stan Matthews and Tom Finney who missed out on the big money but it is no use them nor anyone else feeling sour about it and as in any walk of life it is all about being in the right place at the right time.

I was – and I enjoyed every minute of it. In what other profession could I have been so well rewarded for doing something I basically enjoy? However it is still a job and most of us in the game have family responsibilities as well as futures to consider and I know of more than one First Division footballer who plays simply for the money with no feeling at all for the professional game. Therefore it is hardly surprising that players accept when big money is offered. Not many people in other professions would turn down a huge salary and lucrative contract.

It is the increased demand for success that has torn the professional game of football apart over the past few years. And if you are looking for a direction in which to point the finger, then look beyond the players and even the managers to the businessmen who have come into the sport hoping to buy glory but without applying the principles which helped them reach the top in their own professions. The game went berserk as millions of pounds changed hands for sometimes quite ordinary players; and don't think that the stupidity was confined to Britain. It happened all over Europe and in South America as clubs bankrupted themselves in a bid to buy cups and titles. Amazingly it is still going on though fortunately to a lesser degree at home. It still happens in Italy but there it is the individual, millionaire presidents who invest their own money to bring in talent from all over the world, often on reputation alone. But then football is, of course, more than a business and it is the reflected glory, not the returns, which causes otherwise sane, adult men to do the most ridiculous things.

Unfortunately this madness almost led to the destruction of the game as we know it in Britain and, indeed, those silly years have brought about such dramatic change that football will never be the same again. The directors and chairman who authorized bids of a million pounds and more back in 1980 have a great deal to answer for. How, for example, could Wolverhampton Wanderers justify paying £1,175,000 for my fellow Scot Andy Gray, no matter how good a player he was? The fact that they had just received an even crazier million pounds from Manchester City for Steve Daley was no excuse. How can these men explain transactions like the one which took Clive Allen to Arsenal for £1,250,000 in June 1980 and then on to Crystal Palace for a reputed £800,000 in August of the same year? For goodness sake – that was the close season! Certainly some of the managers must take some of the responsibility as well. Brian Clough was always bigger than his club or, in those days, his committee, so he must be answerable for the million-pound deals he was involved in for players like Ian Wallace from Coventry, Justin Fashanu from Norwich and Trevor Francis from Birmingham City. One factor in Clough's defence is that he has worked hard at putting the club back on a sound financial footing while others left behind

them not always wiser but usually poorer chairmen and
near bankrupt clubs.

There was also the fad for buying foreign stars. After
Spurs had plunged in for Ossie Ardiles and Ricardo Villa
from Argentina, other clubs seemed to think it necessary
to follow their lead. There were: Drazen Muzinic from
Hadjuk Split; Claudio Maragoni from San Lorenzo; Ante
Mirocevic of Budocnost to name just three of the scores
who were granted work permits to play in our game.
Who? Where? These foreign mercenaries may or may
not have been beneficial for the game though I believe
that not many were good enough to help the overall
standards, but, far more important, was the fact that the
fees paid to those foreign clubs were totally lost to British
football. At least when one First Division club coughed
up a million pounds to another English side, the cash
remained in circulation – or should have done!

Throughout this period the players involved were little
more than horseflesh to be sold at auction and the fees
being bandied around were hardly of their making. But
when people in the game finally realized what idiots they
had been, players became an easy target. Greed, said
those pious chairmen, had ruined our game, the players
were holding them to ransom and demanding far too
much money. The players, of course, were only the
vehicle but some of them were bright enough to see that
if they were worth that sort of money to the clubs they
deserved a share of the spoils. Most of us leave school
early to go into the game and, consequently, do not fully
complete our educations. So it was a natural progression
that agents, solicitors and accountants became involved
to draw up the best possible deals with the clubs. In
some instances the players have not helped themselves,
particularly at a time of rife unemployment when the man
standing on the terraces has maybe paid his admission fee

out of his dole money. It made me squirm when the demands of Paul Mariner and John Wark were made public in the newspapers while they were in dispute with Ipswich Town. Whoever made those figures public did the game no good at all, in fact I would go further and say it brought football into even greater disrepute than did Sammy Nelson by dropping his shorts in that infamous and defiant gesture at Highbury.

It has been my policy to keep as low a profile as possible where cash is concerned, particularly at Liverpool where the slightest sign of affluence often makes you a legitimate target for the scallywags. It is also a trend at the club that the players do not talk about their wages to each other or to the media. The only time salaries become obvious is when the accounts are published at the end of the financial year and it was recently clear to everyone which two players earned over £80,000 after one successful season.

Such sums, of course, are peanuts compared with some of the wages revealed when players like Chippy Brady, Trevor Francis, Ray Wilkins, Falcao, Platini and the rest have moved into the multimillion lira world of Italian football. At the other end of the scale, many of the players outside the First Division are earning the sort of wages which would have other trades striking in protest at being too near the breadline in a job which promises you nothing once you pass the age of 30 or suffer a bad injury. Those players are suffering for what people like myself have creamed off at the top level but I feel I have earned the money I have taken from Liverpool. It seems to me that, compared with other clubs, Liverpool pay high basic wages but offer less than most for winning pots because they know they stand more than an even chance of taking one of the top prizes. A footballer's salary is complicated by such things as loyalty bonuses (that's a joke in modern football), so much a point in the League and, in some cases, a crowd bonus as well. Highly deserved in the case of a real crowd puller like Kevin Keegan at Newcastle.

The wage structure at Anfield has never, to my knowledge, led to any great upheavals which is more than can be said for some clubs where players are always comparing notes and becoming dissatisfied. More often than not this occurs at international squad gatherings when players from different clubs tap each other for a possible transfer and mention the sort of wages they are earning. However, there is a lot of storytelling for no one wants to be seen to be earning less than someone else. I understand that, in the lower divisions, some managers are developing wage structures with high and low grades which are not very far apart. Charlton Athletic are one such club and they should know more than most how paying a superstar vastly more than the rest of the staff can rebound. They have dabbled in the European market with former European Footballer of the Year, Allan Simonson, whom they bought for £324,000 from Barcelona in 1982. It was a brave but somewhat naïve gamble for the people of London were not prepared to flock to the Valley in their tens of thousands as the Geordies did for Keegan in the north east. In the same way, the Royal Shakespeare Company will quickly sell out all its performances on its tour of the north east because there is not the competition for people's leisure time in Newcastle that there is in London.

Charlton nearly went to the wall because of it and others have bankrupted themselves after buying two or three players for phenomenal fees and then having to pay them wages to match. It has been tragic to see big clubs like Manchester City, with their tremendous local support and great stadium, struggle because of their dealings in the transfer market. If these clubs had been businesses they would have gone into liquidation but, because of the mystique surrounding football and the strange reluctance of the banks to close them down, the dramatic consequences predicted have yet to happen. But things must change and change they will. I fear it is inevitable that some clubs will eventually go out of business and that the gravy train will get smaller and smaller with fewer first-class seats and a lot more steerage.

I am also afraid that it will be a case of 'the rich getting richer and the poor getting poorer'. I do not see any sudden restructuring of the First Division other than it being reduced in size, if only by two or four clubs. It is lower down the scale that the biggest effect will be felt, though that could be as high as the Second Division. The revolution in communications is one of the reasons. In the old days teams like Blackburn Rovers, Bury and Bolton Wanderers each had their own hardcore of local support and all the supporters knew of the big stars and sides was what they read about them. But now the stars are household names because of television, while modern transport and the road and rail systems have made it relatively simple to go and watch the top players and top teams every week.

If you talk to schoolkids these days, they will tell you that they support Manchester United, Liverpool or one of the other top teams, and that their local teams are their second favourites only. Teams like Liverpool and Manchester United get support at every home match from all over the country and most towns have branches of their supporters' clubs. It is so easy to share the cost of the petrol on the motorway, buy a day return on the train or even go across London on the underground that there seems to be no way to reverse the trend. Not only will the League, as a result, become considerably smaller through natural wastage, but the Third and Fourth Divisions are likely to become regional again to save on travel expenses in the face of falling gates. A great many clubs will also become largely part-time with just a handful of full-time professionals.

It may sound a grim picture but it need not be because losing the smaller clubs may strengthen the League. Also, by reducing the commitments of the clubs on the domestic scene, it may open the door to other possibilities, not least of all helping the Home International sides to improve their preparations and increase their world standing. Top clubs will still need the fixtures to ensure that their revenue is still high and this could bring about the European Super League which has been discussed for so many years. If the clubs and the ruling bodies could get it right it could prove to be a magnificent flagship for the game in general. Can you imagine Liverpool against the likes of Real Madrid; Manchester United facing Juventus; and Celtic meeting Bayern Munich! It sounds the ideal formula to me for natural progress in the game and for live television.

There will, I feel, also be some reorganization within the clubs with the form being closer to that on the Continent than the accepted norm in Britain where managers have virtually run clubs single-handed. In West Germany or Italy the coach selects the team and looks after the players while a Gunther Netzer type figure will handle the administrative side. There was considerable upheaval in North London not so long ago when, seemingly against the odds, Don Howe was appointed manager at Arsenal while Keith Burkinshaw quit Spurs despite leading them to their first European triumph for 12 years. From what I could glean and from my own insight, it seemed that Howe was perfectly willing to accept the modern concept of coaching and team selection while being perfectly content to accept a star name being handed to him on a plate by his directors and told to fit him into the team. Keith, on the other hand, had been used to running things his way and saw the change as board room interference. I wonder if he has since regretted his decision to leave a club where he was obviously happy and well respected.

Liverpool, typically, were way ahead of their time and have for many years split the running of the club into two distinct sections by appointing a playing manager or coach and a business manager, Peter Robinson. The two are kept so far apart at Anfield that there was some embarrassment when Anfield old boy, John Toshack, was on the point of signing Tommy Smith for Swansea, when he bumped into Bob Paisley who asked: 'What are you doing here, John?' The manager did not even know that Tosh had just purchased Smithy!

Liverpool were also quick to spot the possibilities with sponsorship and after a brief flirtation with the Japanese electronics firm Hitachi, they linked up very successfully with Crown Paints. It was very much a two-way relationship right from the start with Crown being more closely involved than their predecessors. Crown became a part of the club, opening their own lounge where they entertained not only the big names from their own and other companies but also the man who sold Crown paint in the corner shop, or the man who mixed the colours in one of their factories. Their lounge was like a five-star hotel's cocktail bar and they would always make sure that there were a few players on hand to say hello after games. We were only too happy to help them as they went out of their way to help us.

With gates falling, Liverpool and other clubs were quick to realize that the necessary income had to come from somewhere and the players were hardly selling their souls to the devil simply by wearing a respected company's name on their shirts. Even so there was a strong protest from the television companies, despite the accepted advertising in other sports like Grand Prix motor racing and tennis. I think we should be pleased that commercial enterprises still want to have their names associated with a sport which has such an awful reputation due to its so-called supporters who riot their way around Europe making life unpleasant for everyone involved. Companies have turned their backs on top tennis stars like Ilie Nastase and Billie Jean King because they did not like their image.

Football has done everything in its power to curb the violence which is destroying the game. I actively discourage my wife Danny from taking our children to games. Danny has a fortunate temperament in that she finds the abuse handed out to me funny and will even join in but others find it difficult to cope with hearing a husband or son being slated in the foulest terms. Apart from the verbal abuse, clubs seem to have sorted out the problem inside the stadiums and while I was at Liverpool there was never very much trouble at the ground. However, you had to be wary on some away trips. I was at Manchester City the day the young lad was led away with a dart sticking in his head. That really came home to all of us because it showed how vulnerable we were to the coward who, from the shelter of the crowd, would attack you. I have seen potatoes full of razor blades, fifty-pence pieces with filed edges and even ball bearings catapulted on to the pitch. I have had a few coins bounce off me and there are some grounds where you keep your head tucked well in when you take a corner or a throw-in.

These crimes are perpetrated by the mindless idiots who feel nothing for the game other than to use it as a means of releasing their aggression. They are spawned from a violent society and are society's problem rather than football's because if there were no football matches, the hooliganism wouldn't stop. The vast majority of them wouldn't have the courage to look a footballer in the eye if they met one face to face – but, then, that is usually true of people who fight in gangs.

I still love my football but, I must say, if it meant standing on the terraces I wouldn't go to a match. It could be pointed out that I and some of my fellow professionals have not helped the situation with our behaviour on the pitch: provoking a response when we foul; appealing for a decision which we know should go the other way; or making extravagant gestures. There is no real excuse other than the fact that we play for very high stakes these days and we are only human, playing in an emotional and physical game. One of the reasons that the British game attracts such huge television audiences in Scandinavia and in other areas of Europe is because it is fast and physical, a man's game with not too much acting, diving or posing. It was briefly the vogue for some players to hurl themselves theatrically to the ground but you don't see a lot of that now and when a player does try it on too often he tends to be ridiculed by players from both sides.

It is a pity that everyone involved does not see it the same way, particularly referees who, on a bad day, can incite more trouble in the crowd than any player. Jimmy Hill, having played and managed, should have known better when he singled out Kenny Dalglish on one programme and criticized him heavily. The power of the media, and television in particular, could be judged from that one incident as referees were so influenced that, for a year, Kenny was chopped and kicked and got nothing for it. The power of the press is an old cliché but it is still true and, sometimes, their lack of scruples disgusts me.

Constructive, justified criticism hurts no one but when newspapers start campaigns to have a manager sacked it frightens me. One example was when Bobby Robson, after a particularly unlucky spell at England with injured and unavailable players, was savagely attacked by one newspaper which even went so far as to offer free badges saying: 'Robson must go.'

The higher you go the more you seem to come in for vicious criticism and, season after season, people were always ready to write off Liverpool. That sort of thing we could stand and, in fact, it often used to help motivate us. You listen to television saying that the party is over and you read the next day that the empire is crumbling, so you roll up your sleeves and give it that bit more. I am not sure, however, that I could stomach the sort of attack that Daley Thompson and Neil Adams were subjected to just before the Los Angeles Olympics when one Sunday paper embarked on a private crusade to get those two athletes banned for allegedly taking a few quid on the way. Daley and Neil actually went on to win a gold and silver respectively. I bet the West Germans and Americans couldn't believe their luck as we tried to undermine our own chances. It wouldn't be so bad if the same papers weren't the first to ask why Britain did not win many gold medals. It is enough to make strong men weep. The press is only too keen to criticize the game that gives it such a good living and, goodness knows, football seems intent on furnishing the sensation seekers with a bottomless pit of garbage to sift through.

There are aspects of the game which sicken me and it is not confined only to the malicious section of the media or to the violence among the supporters; it is also the attitude of some of the people who run the game. Like the manager who urged his fans not to bother watching his team play at Anfield because they were going to defend and not entertain. He only said in public what many of his counterparts said in private: man-for-man marking, defence in depth and try to nick a point. At least the three-point system did something to help in that respect.

As I developed as a player I simply could not see myself remaining a part of the crazy world of football once my playing days were behind me but, in the past few years, I began to think that, after all, I would like to have a stab at management. I don't think it has anything to do with my success in recent years as a player because there is ample proof that being captain of a successful side in no way guarantees that you'll be a good manager.

When I made it known that I might be interested in a player-manager type of job I was flattered by the number of clubs who showed an interest. Some wanted me as a player and others to manage and play. It seemed fairly certain that I would be heading back to London until a Scottish-based journalist asked me if I would be interested in Glasgow Rangers. It was a bolt out of the blue and, I must admit, a secret dream of mine to return to the club I had watched as a youngster.

The initial obstacles looked to be enormous. After all, what did I know about Scottish football? The nearest I had been since leaving Edinburgh for Spurs as a kid was to play for my country at Hampden Park. Then there was the sectarian business, for I was married into a Catholic family and, anyway, I couldn't see myself asking a player his religion before signing him. But all of these arguments were brushed to one side and gradually the impossibility became a reality.

In the end I could not resist the challenge. I have signed a five-year contract at Ibrox but if I fail I will not be around long enough to see it through. Football is about winners, not losers.

18

All Roads Lead to Rome

I heard all sorts of reasons why I finally quit the most successful club in Europe to join the exodus to Italy. But most of them bore little or no relationship to the truth. I would be lying if I did not admit that a big part of it was the offer of financial security for my wife Danielle, daughter Chantelle and son Fraser. For a 31-year-old footballer the money is tremendous and a three-year contract takes away the worry and the pressure. But there is something else as well. Footballers, by nature, are showmen – at least they should be – and to be given a chance to play in the Italian League has to be the equivalent of an entertainer being asked to top the bill at the London Palladium on a show which is to be televised live coast to coast in the United States.

I have to own up to being a great admirer of Italian football, not just because they have managed to create an International Super League of their own but because they have grown up and learned to give their supporters the sort of football that made Pelé call our sport 'the beautiful game'. While the Spaniards are still kicking lumps out of each other and putting defence above attack, the Italians have cast away their inhibitions to blend the best of the European game with the best of South American football.

Just look at the people Sampdoria asked me to play against. It is like the World Cup every week. Apart from their own highly-talented players, good enough to win the World Cup, there are: the brilliant Brazilians Zico, Socrates, Batista, Falcao, Cerezo, Edinho, Dirceu and

Junior; there are Maradona, Diaz, Hernandez and Passarella from Argentina; Platini from France; Rummenigge and Briegel from West Germany; Boniek of Poland; Schachner of Austria; Laudrup and Elkjaer of Denmark; Barbadillo from Spain; Coeck of Belgium; Stromberg and Larsson of Sweden; not to mention my own fellow Brits Trevor Francis, Liam Brady, Mark Hately, and Ray Wilkins. It reads like a *Who's Who* of international football and when you also remember that the demands on a player in Italy are considerably less than in Britain, it is easy to see why it took only minutes for me to agree my move from Liverpool to Genoa.

Of course it was a wrench to leave Liverpool but the time was right not only for me but also for the club as well. They doubled their original outlay on me at a time when, in England at least, the value of top players had dropped quite alarmingly. As for me, how could I follow what had gone before: League, League Cup and European Cup all in the same season? There are top-quality players in Britain who have never won one of those in their entire career. Until the European Cup Final in Rome the prospect of my playing in Italy was just talk and mainly talk in the press into the bargain. I was always aware of what was happening in Italy because it was reported almost daily after the World Cup which foreigner was going to be signed and who was going to manage which club.

The nearest I had come to thinking about playing over there was after a pal of mine had returned from visiting Trevor and Helen Francis at their seaside home in Nervi, just outside Genoa, and raved about the lifestyle and how well Trevor and Liam Brady were being treated by the club and their supporters. Little did any of us realize then that the first seeds were being sown, almost a year before anything tangible began to happen. I was told how well suited my game would be to the Italian style of play while Trevor, unknown to me and without any ulterior motive, mentioned my name at his club and to journalists when potential British signings were being discussed. That, presumably, was how it became common knowledge that Souness would play his last game for Liverpool against AC Roma in the European Cup Final and would line up in the star-studded Italian League for the first game of the new season. Everyone who spoke to me seemed to be involved in the deal one way or another but, quite honestly, when Sampdoria began to show a genuine interest it was all done above board and in the open just as you would expect from two such gentlemanly chairmen as John Smith of Liverpool and Paolo Mantovani of Genoa. The whole affair was conducted in the most professional manner. I would have hated to have been subjected to the protracted rumours which dogged both Bryan Robson and Ray Wilkins at Manchester United. It must have been incredibly unsettling for everyone involved and you wonder how much it affected their chase for the League Championship.

Ian Rush and I suddenly became targets for the head-hunters just before the European Cup Final in Rome. Agents began to appear out of the woodwork and I began to wonder if it was all a wind-up to unsettle us before the final especially when one of the Roma vice-presidents began to ask highly personal questions about me, my family and my lifestyle at the Holiday Inn in Liverpool. As it turned out, it did not bother me at all for I knew that I would be told the moment anything began to happen and I would believe it only when Liverpool secretary PBR Robinson told me himself. Even when we went to Israel to prepare for the European Final a couple of Italian journalists followed us out there and told me that Sampdoria had already confirmed that I would be signing for them. By then Peter Robinson had kept his word and told me that there had been an inquiry but, in view of what was coming up, they played it down.

It was a good job we went on to win that European Cup otherwise those Italian journalists would have been running home with tales of how we threw it away. While Roma were living up in the hills outside Rome and travelling down to train in the Olympic Stadium every night at kick-off time, we were relaxing in the sun and sipping a few beers. That is the Liverpool style and how well it worked after a long, hard season. Joe Fagan and his backroom boys treated us like adults and we responded, even to the degree of whipping the Israel National team 4-1.

There were no thoughts of playing in Italy when we went out to Rome and no question of trying to impress potential buyers in the European Cup Final. All that mattered when we ran out into the Olympic Stadium was the result. Afterwards was a different matter. I felt I had done pretty well against the much praised Brazilians Falcao and Cerezo and this seemed to be confirmed by the number of so-called agents who sidled up to me after the game telling me I was fixed up with all sorts of interesting clubs for all sorts of money.

One of these guys even came up to my wife Danny and me saying how crazy it would be to sign for Sampdoria, that it would be much too hot and he would arrange for me to join a club in a country with a climate more like that of England. He obviously hadn't done his homework. If he had he would have discovered that both Danny and I are sun-worshippers.

Even then nothing happened and, quite happily, I set off for a club tour in Swaziland. Not that you could convince the Liverpool players of that, especially when I missed the first game against Spurs. It was all nudge,

nudge, wink, wink and no matter how I tried to convince them they would not believe that I was ill and suffering, in fact, from a combination of jet lag, the strain at the end of a long, successful season – and a very long, boozy session with Spurs defender Paul Miller the night before the game when we somewhat over-toasted our respective European triumphs! They thought their suspicions were confirmed when, after the game, a few of us hired a small aircraft to further our sunbathing in Durban. I was up and down from the side of that pool like a ballboy on the Centre Court at Wimbledon. The hotel must have paged me 25 times with calls from journalists and the club. I knew it was all genuine when PBR told me that Sampdoria's offer had been accepted by Liverpool and that I would be silly not to talk to them. He said that the club did not want me to go but that they thought I would be interested. I jetted straight back home after speaking to Ron Teeman, the Leeds solicitor who had handled the smooth transfers of both Trevor Francis and Liam Brady to Sampdoria, and he confirmed that agreement had been reached and promised me that I would be impressed by the personal terms.

Within 48 hours I was on my way to the Italian port of Genoa, accompanied by Peter Robinson, Liverpool's solicitor Tony Ensor, my wife Danny and, as always, my father-in-law Austin Wilson. I am very fortunate in having such a father-in-law. While other footballers have to rely on outsiders for their financial advice I have a person I can trust totally in Austin, as shrewd a businessman as you would ever meet. He happily took time off from his home in Majorca to assist me, but even he was surprised by what happened when we arrived at Genoa airport.

Goodness knows what the other people on the aeroplane must have thought when we touched down for it was like carnival time with what seemed to be thousands of people on the tarmac. There were flowers for my wife, kisses and hugs from old ladies and a Sampdoria shirt with a number eleven on the back was thrust into my hands. The President of the club was there to meet me himself with his car on the runway ready to escort our party through customs. I was also pleased to see the familiar face of Trevor Francis. To say I was impressed with the welcome would be a gross understatement and it flashed through my mind that, after this, it would be difficult for the club and me not to reach agreement. But it did not end there. We had a police escort from the airport to the club offices in Genoa and all the way there people were chanting my name, cars were hooting and motorcyclists were riding up and waving at me through the window and when we arrived there were another thousand or so waiting outside.

Throughout the discussions – you could hardly call the friendly meeting negotiations – we had to keep breaking off to go and give the crowd a wave. It was clear that they held Signor Mantovani with what amounted to reverence. It took me about three minutes to accept the offer and the only delay was a telephone call back to Liverpool to confirm final arrangements and then it was out on to the balcony where the President and I shook hands to show the crowd that the deal was done. The press conference was just as chaotic and out of the corner of my eye I saw Trevor Francis at the back of the room laughing at my bewilderment because he knew the sort of treatment I would receive. He had been a big help and Trevor and I were delighted when we found out that we would be living next door to each other.

One of the most important factors in the move was that Trevor had told me that I could trust Paolo Mantovani completely just as I was able to with the Liverpool hierarchy. He is a charming man and very popular. There was no haggling or arguing. He made an offer and I accepted. When I asked for three years rather than two, he understood immediately that I wanted security for my family. There were no outside influences, only Teeman and my father-in-law, despite the many and varied claims including a bill from one man for £5500, someone I had never even heard of let alone done business with. There were also a couple of journalists who claimed to have arranged the whole thing. I didn't mind. If it massaged their ego, then that was fine. There was only the mutual friend of Trevor Francis and me who was involved and when I signed he was away in South America! I knew from the moment I agreed to sign that I had made the right decision as we looked at the resort where we were going to stay and then were taken out to a Gentleman's Club for dinner. With the police escorts and all I felt like James Bond and not even Liverpool's fabulous welcome home after winning the European Cup could match the reception I was given in Italy.

When I related that to one of the newspapers back in England I was rebuked in Liverpool but it was not meant as criticism. Someone kept the cuttings for me and one of the local papers gave me a six-inch farewell column for my seven years at the club. It seemed a little meagre but it didn't upset me. I know only too well that in football you are hero one day and nothing the next. Long live the king and all that nonsense. For all the problems of that second season in Italy I enjoyed the experience enormously and do not regret my decision at all. What I learned in Genoa improved my football education and, hopefully, I can put something of that back into the British game.

Postscript

My two years under the sun in Italy was an experience I shall never forget and would not have missed for the world. I enjoyed every single minute and would recommend it to any footballer.

I will admit I was fortunate in that Sampdoria proved to be the most honourable of clubs thanks to their gentleman president Signori Mantovani. They not only treated me and my family with great courtesy and respect, but fulfilled every promise, financial and otherwise.

My only regret is that I did not have the opportunity to take the plunge earlier, like Liam Brady who built himself a wonderful career and lifestyle after leaving Arsenal. For midfield players like Chippy and me it was a dream, definitely the place to play. The difference between English and Italian football was huge, with little or no hurly-burly, just getting the ball, giving it and with time to spare. The opposition would stand off and let you play until the final third of the pitch – then it became serious. But the dire warnings I received from well-meaning friends about cynical fouls and the trouble I would get into with referees proved to lack any sort of foundation. In two seasons I was sent off twice – both times by the same official, the second time for threatening to retaliate after I had been kicked. I'll ask for no sympathy nor do I expect to get any! But, on the whole, the Italian referees were very good and very strict, perhaps better than their British counterparts. They let little go and, as a consequence, there were few who tried to take advantage of the situation.

Football is so big in Italy that everyone connected with the game takes a slice of the action. Whereas referees are encouraged to preserve their anonymity in Britain, even to the extent of stopping details of town of residence, jobs and hobbies being printed in English League programmes, in Italy the referees are as easily picked out as the players and many of them enjoy the fame. They are feted and only now and again has it been known to go to their head; largely they have responded well to the pressures they are under.

For me it was just a joy to play every week against some of the world's top footballers: Maradona of Argentina; Platini of France; Boniek of Poland; Brady of Eire; Wilkins of England; Rummenigge of West Germany; Elkjaer of Denmark; and, of course, the majestic Brazilians, especially the great Zico. It was like a United Nations of football.

My first season at Sampdoria was an unqualified success as we won the Italian Cup for the first time in the club's history, having already clinched a place in Europe by finishing fourth in the League, the highest placing ever achieved by the Genoa club. It must have gone quite well for me because I was selected to play for the pick of the League against Champions Verona, and that gave me the opportunity of playing alongside some of these genuine greats. It was only as we won 6-1 that I appreciated just how good Zico was, better even than Maradona or Platini.

I fully appreciated him as an opponent, for I not only came face to face with him during the course of the Italian season, when Sampdoria played his club Udine, but I had also met him playing for Scotland against Brazil and for Liverpool when we played South American Champions Flamenco in Tokyo. But it is when you play alongside him that you realize his true qualities – all you have to do is give him the ball, stand back and watch him play.

The second season was not so good, either for me or the club. We all felt that we had built a platform strong enough to go on and win the League, especially when the President made more money available to strengthen the team. But the manager made some strange decisions, not only in the transfer market but also in team selection and tactics. Instead of chasing the leaders in the early part of the season, we were trying to lift ourselves out of the basement and possible relegation trouble.

It was helpful that, during these problems, my next-door neighbour, a step across the hallway, was English international striker Trevor Francis. Our wives and families got on well, while we always had someone on tap with whom to chew over our own individual difficulties. Trevor had a few more than me, for not only was he beset by injuries, including a depressed fracture of the cheekbone, but he fell out of favour with the manager and spent more time on the bench than on the pitch.

There was some talk of Trevor going at the end of the season to make way for another 'stranger', as the foreigners were called, but it soon became obvious that it would be the manager who went first. I had a year of my contract to run and I was happy with the prospect of extending my tenure at my seaside apartment in attractive Nervi, even though there were indications that there were a number of clubs in England who were prepared to bring me back, including several in London.

I had now decided that I would eventually like a crack at football management and that I would only return to England if I was offered a player-manager or player-coach job that promised something for the future. Going home to Scotland had not even been a consideration. It had not crossed my mind until a Scottish journalist telephoned to tell me that my name had been brought up in discussions by Glasgow Rangers.

Now there was a turn up – the team I had supported as a kid wanting me to go back and manage them! I was instantly very interested but at the same time aware that many a bear trap lay ahead before the idea became a reality.

Of course, I knew that Rangers were a big, big club, one of the biggest in the world, but I did not realize how big until I stepped into Ibrox Park once the clubs had agreed terms and the first tentative discussions had taken place. Fortunately, the Board wanted the same thing as me – in a word, SUCCESS! If it meant signing a Catholic, an Englishman or a black American Jew they were happy to go along. They wanted the mould broken and trophies back in the cabinet, and they were prepared to back up their wishes with the necessary cash to buy those vital players.

My biggest problem, once I had made up my mind that this was the right move for both my family and me, was that I knew absolutely nothing about the domestic scene in Scotland, never having kicked a ball in anger in the Scottish League. That was solved by the appointment of Walter Smith as my number two. As assistant manager of Dundee United, and having been deeply involved with all levels of Scottish international football, he was a godsend, and I was well and truly on my way to building the sort of staff I knew I would need if we were to honour our promises to the fans.

There was plenty to do as Rangers had just squeezed into the UEFA Cup in their last game of the season, finishing fifth in a ten-team table, ahead of Dundee on goal difference. But the passion surrounding the club gave us a head start. When I agreed to a five-year contract I thought that I was going to a club bigger than Liverpool,

Spurs, and Arsenal – in fact every club apart from Manchester United. Now I am not even sure that the team from Old Trafford stand ahead.

To be honest I could have done without the World Cup coming at that precise moment in my career. After the joy of beating Celtic in my first match as manager in the Glasgow Cup, I found myself trying to run the team by long-distance telephone, first from America and then from Mexico.

I knew straight away what my priorities were and what I had to work on first – the defence. Get it right at the back and you have a chance. That seemed to have been Rangers' problem in their recent past, with the players being nervous in front of their own passionate, demanding fans. A few clean sheets would give everyone confidence.

I made up my shopping list, with a goalkeeper and a centre-half right at the top. I knew from personal experience that Bruce Grobbelaar at Liverpool would fit the bill and be enormously popular if I could persuade my old room-mate Kenny Dalglish to let me have him. The alternative was to try for England's number one Peter Shilton or his deputy Chris Woods. Dalglish said no; Southampton wanted £750,000 for someone older than me; but Norwich City surprised me by accepting my offer for England's next goalkeeper, Chris Woods. He was ours before the World Cup, but we agreed with Norwich manager Ken Brown to keep it quiet.

Next in line was a centre-back. Having been knocked down by Kenny Dalglish over Bruce I didn't much fancy my chances of being able to sign Mark Lawrenson. I was right. If I couldn't get him what chance had I got with the one I really wanted, Terry Butcher? I knew that he was up for grabs with Ipswich Town having been relegated, but how was I going to be able to persuade him to see what we had on offer when Spurs and Manchester United were offering a more orthodox move within the accepted boundaries.

The task was made more difficult by the fact that we were both in different parts of America preparing for the World Cup. Fortunately, I had a friend who was close to England and the players. He had already helped me with Woods and when I mentioned Butcher he promised that he would bring up the subject around the pool that day. It scarcely amounted to an illegal tap, but the response was enough to encourage me to pursue the matter officially.

In the meantime I had a World Cup to concentrate on as Scotland, under the management of Alex Ferguson, took on not one but three of the pre-tournament favourites, Denmark, Uruguay and West Germany. Hard as Group E looked I still thought we had the players to throw a spanner in the works and take one of the three possible places in the next round. In the event I was disappointed, not only in us as a team, but in my own part in the proceedings.

We were never going to outplay any of our rivals, so the only way we could progress was by keeping it tight and trying to nick a goal or two on the break. We started well against the talented Danes in Neza and we were distinctly unlucky not to take something out of the game as we lost to an Elkjaer goal in the 57th minute.

That same day the West Germans had drawn with Uruguay, so there was still plenty to play for when we faced Franz Beckenbauer's team in the heat of Queretaro four days later. Our hopes were high when Gordon Strachan gave us the lead after only 17 minutes, but Völler put them back on terms within five minutes and Allofs scored what proved to be the winner four minutes after the interval.

The mutterings and murmurings began after that defeat, and I knew then that I was for the chop. That is the way it goes in World Cup competitions, with the senior players shouldering not only the responsibility but also the blame when things go wrong. I half expected to be left out for the final game against Uruguay, even though I had played no worse or better than anyone else in the team. My fears began to be confirmed when I heard that I was tired; feeling the heat; struggling for breath; and weary from my pre-World Cup work as player-manager of Glasgow Rangers. No one asked me.

Sure enough when the team was posted both Alex McLeish and I were left out. Although I had anticipated the worst it was still a huge let-down, and the fact that they were saying I was tired made it worse, for I pride myself on having learned in Italy how to keep myself fit and rested in order to give my best during a game.

I should have been able to prove it later in the competition, for Scotland were given great encouragement when Uruguay were hammered 6-1 by the Danes and warned as to their future conduct in the competition by FIFA. If that did not destroy the South Americans' preparation for us then, within 55 seconds of the start of the game in Neza, they should have been dead and buried when defender Batista was sent off by the French referee Quiniou after a violent tackle on Strachan. Instead of taking advantage we froze, and I could only watch in frustration as we slipped out of the World Cup with a feeble goalless draw that left us bottom of the table with one point.

The rest is history. We would have played the eventual winners Argentina had we won that last game, while our group leaders Denmark sensationally lost 5-1 to Spain. Those solid West Germans went on to squeeze past

Morocco (1-0), Mexico (on penalties), and France (2-0), before losing 3-2 to Argentina in the final. But, by then, my interest had turned to the future. I felt let-down by Scotland and could not wait to get myself involved with Rangers.

I knew that if I could persuade Terry Butcher to come and have a look at Ibrox it would increase my chances of signing him. While everyone waited for him to reach agreement with Spurs I got in touch with him in America, where he was starring in a UNICEF Charity Game in Los Angeles, and arranged to meet him at the airport on his return. It worked. Terry loved it and when his wife Rita came up she did too. I had my man.

However, I was misled. Terry Butcher is not the best centre-half in Britain – he is the best in the world. Technically he would waltz through any European League and he has a left foot that I would put up against the best. Add to that his aggression and this man is some player. The fans of Glasgow Rangers know it too.

Chris Woods, the next England goalkeeper, is also everything I hoped for, and I captured a third Englishman when I signed Colin West from Watford – the big striker I needed to lead the line.

We were on our way – or were we? Football has a funny habit of kicking you in the teeth when you are smiling most. My first League game as a manager was against Hibs in Edinburgh, the club my Dad had always supported. He was in the front row of the directors' box as proud as punch. I was sent off, 21 players were booked and we lost. I have been a target in Europe, set-up in the First Division and needled in Italy, but here I was reacting in my first game in Scotland.

My Dad shook his head and said, 'Son, you should have known better.' He was right. After 18 years I was too old to be fighting other people's battles for them, and

I regret what I did tremendously. But, like everything else that has happened to me throughout life, I learned from it and, it is to be hoped, it will make me a better manager. At least it allowed me to take a step back during my four-game suspension and look at what I had. I liked what I saw. Rangers are on their way and me with them.

Appendix: Career Record

FOOTBALL LEAGUE RECORD

Club	Date signed	Appearances	Goals
Tottenham Hotspur	May 1970	0	0
Middlesbrough	January 1973	176	22
Liverpool	January 1978	247	38

ITALIAN LEAGUE RECORD

Club	Date signed	Appearances	Goals
Sampdoria	July 1984	56	8

SCOTTISH LEAGUE RECORD (to 3.2.87)

Club	Date signed	Appearances	Goals
Rangers	May 1986	13	1

FA CUP RECORD

Season	Club	Round	Opponents (Venue)	Result	Goals
1972–73	Middlesbrough	3	Plymouth Arg. (A)	L 0–1	0
1973–74	Middlesbrough	3	Grantham (A)	W2–0	0
		4	Wrexham (A)	L 0–1	0
1974–75	Middlesbrough	3	Wycombe W. (A)	D 0–0	0
		R	Wycombe W. (H)	W1–0	0
		4	Sunderland (H)	W3–1	0
		5R	Peterborough U. (H)	W2–0	0
		6	Birmingham C. (A)	L 0–1	0

FA CUP RECORD (*continued*)

Season	Club	Round	Opponents (Venue)	Result	Goals
1976–77	Middlesbrough	3	Wimbledon (A)	D 0–0	0
		R	Wimbledon (H)	W 1–0	0
		4	Hereford U. (H)	W 4–0	1
		5	Arsenal (H)	W 4–1	0
		6	Liverpool (A)	L 0–2	0
1978–79	Liverpool	3	Southend (A)	D 0–0	0
		R	Southend (H)	W 3–0	0
		4	Blackburn R. (H)	W 1–0	0
		5	Burnley (H)	W 3–0	1
		6	Ipswich T. (A)	W 1–0	0
		SF	Manchester U. (At Maine Road)	D 2–2	0
		SFR	Manchester U. (At Goodison Park)	L 0–1	0
1979–80	Liverpool	3	Grimsby T. (H)	W 5–0	1
		4	Nottingham F. (A)	W 2–0	0
		5	Bury (H)	W 2–0	0
		6	Tottenham H. (A)	W 1–0	0
		SF	Arsenal (At Hillsborough)	D 0–0	0
		SFR	Arsenal (At Villa Park)	D 1–1	0
		SFR	Arsenal (At Villa Park)	D 1–1	0
		SFR	Arsenal (At Coventry)	L 0–1	0
1980–81	Liverpool	4	Everton (A)	L 1–2	0
1981–82	Liverpool	3	Swansea C. (A)	W 4–0	0
		4	Sunderland (A)	W 3–0	0
		5	Chelsea (A)	L 0–2	0
1982–83	Liverpool	3	Blackburn R. (A)	W 2–1	0
		4	Stoke C. (H)	W 2–0	0
		5	Brighton & H. A. (H)	L 1–2	0
1983–84	Liverpool	3	Newcastle U. (H)	W 4–0	0
		4	Brighton & H. A. (A)	L 0–2	0

ITALIAN CUP RECORD

Season	Club	Round	Opponents (Venue)	Result	Goals
1984–85	Sampdoria	Q*	Catanzaro (A)	D 1–1	0
		Q	Lecce (A)	W 3–0	0
		Q	Cavese (H)	W 8–1	0
		Q	Bari (H)	W 2–1	0
		Q	Udinese (A)	D 3–3	0
		O**	Pisa (A)	W 2–1	0
		QF1	Torino (A)	D 0–0	0
		QF2	Torino (H)	W 4–2	0
		SF1	Fiorentina (A)	D 0–0	0
		SF2	Fiorentina (H)	W 3–1	0
		F1	Milan AC (A)	W 1–0	1
		F2	Milan AC (H)	W 2–1	0
1985–86	Sampdoria	Q	Taranto (A)	W 4–1	2
		Q	Catania (A)	D 0–0	0
		Q	Monopoli (H)	W 1–0	0
		Q	Lazio (A)	D 0–0	0
		Q	Atalanta (H)	D 2–2	0

*Q = Qualifying Round   **O = Eighth Finals

SCOTTISH CUP RECORD

Season	Club	Round	Opponents (Venue)	Result	Goals
1986–87	Rangers	3	Hamilton A (H)	L 0–1	0

LEAGUE CUP RECORD

Season	Club	Round	Opponents (Venue)	Result	Goals
1973–74	Middlesbrough	2	Manchester U. (A)	W 1–0	0
		3	Stoke C. (A)	D 1–1	0
1974–75	Middlesbrough	3	Leicester C. (H)	W 1–0	0
		4	Liverpool (A)	W 1–0	0
		5	Manchester U. (H)	D 0–0	0
		R	Manchester U. (A)	L 0–3	0

LEAGUE CUP RECORD (*continued*)

Season	Club	Round	Opponents (Venue)	Result	Goals
1975–76	Middlesbrough	2	Bury (A)	W2–1	0
		3	Derby Co. (H)	W1–0	0
		4	Peterborough U. (H)	W3–0	0
		SF1	Manchester C. (H)	W1–0	0
		SF2	Manchester C. (A)	L 0–4	0
1976–77	Middlesbrough	2	Tottenham H. (H)	L 1–2	0
1977–78	Middlesbrough	2R	Sunderland (H)	W1–0	0
		3	Everton (A)	D 2–2	0
		3R	Everton (H)	L 1–2	0
1978–79	Liverpool	2	Sheffield U. (A)	L 0–1	0
1979–80	Liverpool	2.1	Tranmere R. (A)	D 0–0	0
		2.2	Tranmere R. (H)	W4–0	0
		3	Chesterfield (H)	W3–1	0
		4	Exeter C. (H)	W2–0	0
		5	Norwich C. (A)	W3–1	0
		SF1	Nottingham F. (A)	L 0–1	0
		SF2	Nottingham F. (H)	D 1–1	0
1980–81	Liverpool	2.1	Bradford C. (A)	L 0–1	0
		2.2	Bradford C. (H)	W4–0	0
		3	Swindon T. (H)	W5–0	0
		4	Portsmouth (H)	W4–1	1
		5	Birmingham C. (H)	W3–1	0
		SF1	Manchester C. (A)	W1–0	0
		SF2	Manchester C. (H)	D 1–1	0
		F	West Ham U. (At Wembley)	D 1–1	0
1981–82	Liverpool	2.1	Exeter C. (H)	W5–0	0
		3	Middlesbrough (H)	W4–0	0
		4	Arsenal (A)	D 0–0	0
		R	Arsenal (H)	W3–0	0
		5	Barnsley (H)	D 0–0	0
		R	Barnsley (A)	W3–1	1
		SF1	Ipswich T. (A)	W2–0	0
		SF2	Ipswich T. (H)	D 2–2	0
		F	Tottenham H. (At Wembley)	W3–1	0

LEAGUE CUP RECORD (*continued*)

Season	Club	Round	Opponents (Venue)	Result	Goals
1982–83	Liverpool	2.1	Ipswich T. (A)	W2–1	0
		2.2	Ipswich T. (H)	W2–0	0
		3	Rotherham U. (H)	W1–0	0
		4	Norwich C. (H)	W2–0	0
		5	West Ham U. (H)	W2–1	1
		SF1	Burnley (H)	W3–0	1
		SF2	Burnley (A)	L 0–1	0
		F	Manchester U. (At Wembley)	W2–1	0
1983–84	Liverpool	2.1	Brentford (A)	W4–0	1
		2.2	Brentford (H)	W4–0	1
		3	Fulham (A)	D 1–1	0
		R	Fulham (H)	D 1–1	0
		R	Fulham (A)	W1–0	1
		4	Birmingham C. (A)	D 1–1	1
		R	Birmingham C. (H)	W3–0	0
		5	Sheffield W. (A)	D 2–2	0
		R	Sheffield W. (H)	W3–0	0
		SF2	Walsall (A)	W2–0	0
		F	Everton (At Wembley)	D 0–0	0
		FR	Everton (At Maine Road)	W1–0	1

SCOTTISH LEAGUE CUP RECORD

Season	Club	Round	Opponents (Venue)	Result	Goals
1986–87	Rangers	2	Stenhousemuir (A)	W4–1	1
		3	East Fife (A)	D 0–0	0
			(*Rangers won 5–4 on penalties*)		
		QF	Dundee (H)	W3–1	1
		SF	Dundee U (At Hampden Park)	W2–1	0
		F	Celtic (At Hampden Park)	W2–1	0

EUROPEAN CUP RECORD
(All matches with Liverpool)

Season	Round	Opponents (Venue)	Result	Goals
1977–78	SF1	Borussia Moenchengladbach (A)	L 1–3	0
	SF2	Borussia Moenchengladbach (H)	W3–0	0
	F	FC Bruges (At Wembley)	W1–0	0
1978–79	1.1	Nottingham F. (A)	L 0–2	0
	1.2	Nottingham F. (H)	D0–0	0
1979–80	1.1	Dynamo Tblisi (H)	W2–1	0
	1.2	Dynamo Tblisi (A)	L 0–3	0
1980–81	1.1	OPS Oulu (A)	D1–1	0
	1.2	OPS Oulu (H)	W10–1	3
	2.1	Aberdeen (A)	W1–0	0
	2.2	Aberdeen (H)	W4–0	0
	QF1	CSKA Sofia (H)	W5–1	3
	QF2	CSKA Sofia (A)	W1–0	0
	SF2	Bayern Munich (A)	D1–1	0
	F	Real Madrid (In Paris)	W1–0	0
1981–82	1.1	OPS Oulu (A)	W1–0	0
	1.2	OPS Oulu (H)	W7–0	0
	2.1	AZ 67 Alkmaar (A)	D2–2	0
	2.2	AZ 67 Alkmaar (H)	W3–2	0
	QF1	CSKA Sofia (H)	W1–0	0
	QF2	CSKA Sofia (A)	L 0–2	0
1982–83	1.1	Dundalk (A)	W4–1	0
	1.2	Dundalk (H)	W1–0	0
	2.1	HJK Helsinki (A)	L 0–1	0
	2.2	HJK Helsinki (H)	W5–0	0
	QF1	Widzew Lodz (A)	L 0–2	0
	QF2	Widzew Lodz (H)	W3–2	0
1983–84	1.1	Odense BK (A)	W1–0	0
	1.2	Odense BK (H)	W5–0	0
	2.1	Athletic Bilbao (H)	D0–0	0
	2.2	Athletic Bilbao (A)	W1–0	0
	QF1	Benfica (H)	W1–0	0
	QF2	Benfica (A)	W4–1	0

EUROPEAN CUP RECORD (*continued*)
(All matches with Sampdoria)

Season	Round	Opponents (Venue)	Result	Goals
1983–84	SF1	Dinamo Bucharest (H)	W1–0	0
(*cont.*)	SF2	Dinamo Bucharest (A)	W2–1	0
	F	Roma	D 1–1	0
		(In Rome, Liverpool won 4–2 on penalties)		

EUROPEAN CUP-WINNERS' CUP RECORD
(All matches with Sampdoria)

Season	Round	Opponents (Venue)	Result	Goals
1985–86	1.1	Larissa (A)	D 1–1	0
	1.2	Larissa (H)	W1–0	0
	2.1	Benfica (A)	L 0–2	0
	2.2	Benfica (H)	W1–0	0

INTERNATIONAL RECORD
Scotland Full Caps

Date	Opponents	Venue	Result	Goals
(With Middlesbrough)				
30.10.74	East Germany	Glasgow	W 3–0	0
20.11.74	Spain	Glasgow	L 1–2	0
16.4.75	Sweden	Gothenburg	D 1–1	0
(With Liverpool)				
22.2.78	Bulgaria	Glasgow	W 2–1	0
17.5.78	Wales	Glasgow	D 1–1	0
20.5.78	England*	Glasgow	L 0–1	0
11.6.78	Netherlands†	Mendoza	W 3–2	0
20.9.78	Austria	Vienna	L 2–3	0
25.10.78	Norway	Glasgow	W 3–2	0
19.5.79	Wales	Cardiff	L 0–3	0
22.5.79	N. Ireland	Glasgow	W 1–0	0

INTERNATIONAL RECORD (*continued*)

Scotland Full Caps

Date	Opponents	Venue	Result	Goals
(With Liverpool)				
26.5.79	England	Wembley	L 1–3	0
12.9.79	Peru	Glasgow	D 1–1	0
17.10.79	Austria	Glasgow	D 1–1	0
21.11.79	Belgium	Brussels	L 0–2	0
26.3.80	Portugal	Glasgow	W 4–1	0
16.5.80	N. Ireland	Belfast	L 0–1	0
15.10.80	Portugal	Glasgow	D 0–0	0
25.2.81	Israel	Tel Aviv	W 1–0	0
28.4.81	Israel	Glasgow	W 3–1	0
14.10.81	N. Ireland	Belfast	D 0–0	0
18.11.81	Portugal	Lisbon	L 1–2	0
24.2.82	Spain	Valencia	L 0–3	0
24.5.82	Wales	Glasgow	W 1–0	0
29.5.82	England	Glasgow	L 0–1	0
15.6.82	New Zealand†	Malaga	W 5–2	0
18.6.82	Brazil†	Seville	L 1–4	0
22.6.82	USSR†	Malaga	D 2–2	1
13.10.82	East Germany	Glasgow	W 2–0	0
17.11.82	Switzerland	Berne	L 0–2	0
15.12.82	Belgium	Brussels	L 2–3	0
30.3.83	Switzerland	Glasgow	D 2–2	0
28.5.83	Wales	Cardiff	W 2–0	0
1.6.83	England	Wembley	L 0–2	0
12.6.83	Canada*	Vancouver	W 2–0	0
16.6.83	Canada	Edmonton	W 3–0	0
20.6.83	Canada	Toronto	W 2–0	0
21.9.83	Uruguay	Glasgow	W 2–0	0
13.12.83	N. Ireland	Belfast	L 0–2	0
28.2.84	Wales	Glasgow	W 2–1	0
(With Sampdoria)				
12.9.84	Yugoslavia	Glasgow	W 6–1	1
18.10.84	Iceland	Glasgow	W 3–0	0
17.11.84	Spain	Glasgow	W 3–1	

INTERNATIONAL RECORD (*continued*)

Scotland Full Caps

Date	Opponents	Venue	Result		Goals
(With Sampdoria)					
27.2.85	Spain	Seville	L	0–1	0
27.3.85	Wales	Glasgow	L	0–1	0
25.5.85	England	Glasgow	W	1–0	0
28.5.85	Iceland	Reykjavik	W	1–0	0
16.10.85	East Germany	Glasgow	D	0–0	0
20.11.85	Australia	Glasgow	W	2–0	0
4.12.85	Australia	Melbourne	D	0–0	0
26.3.86	Rumania	Glasgow	W	3–0	0
23.4.86	England	Wembley	L	1–2	1
4.6.86†	Denmark	Nezahualcoyotl	L	0–1	0
8.6.86†	West Germany	Queretaro	L	1–2	0

KEY

* *Substitute appearance*

† *World Cup Final Tournament*